SEEDS OF WEALTH

*A step-by-step program to help
your children begin to build wealth
and sound money habits from an early age.*

JUSTIN FORD

AGORA
FINANCIAL

ISBN: 1-891434-24-1

Published by:

Seeds of Wealth, LLC
Agora Financial
808 St. Paul Street
Baltimore, MD 21202

Table of Contents

PART III: Cultivating Good Habits and Nipping Bad Habits "In the Bud"

PART IV: Tilling the Earth (or they've got to rake it before they can sock it away)

PART V: How to Make the Seeds Grow

APPENDIX: Smart Money Tips for Young Grownups

A Very Short Preface:

How to Use This Guidebook to Help
Your Children Develop Good Money Habits
and Achieve Lifelong Financial Security

This program is for your children. Its purpose is to help them develop good money habits that will serve them well their entire lives. They will begin immediately by taking small steps every day that can help them build a nest egg that will be worth hundreds of thousands of dollars — even millions — a generation from now.

The program guidebook you have in your hands is for you, the adult guiding the child in this process. It doesn't assume an advanced level of financial knowledge, but it is written at an adult level.

Although the program covers such "grownup" topics as investing in the stock market and financing college, they are all discussed in the context of your child's growth and development.

Also, in various clearly marked sections throughout this guidebook that are in this kind of text, we break away from adult discussion to translate the main ideas into children's terms. You can read these sections to, or with, your children.

So when can you begin? Immediately!

If some of the children in your life are younger than five, you're going to plant the initial *Seeds of Wealth* for them. From the age of five and up, they will be the primary creators of their own wealth. You will be guiding them.

A final note: for the sake of simplicity, we refer to "your children" throughout the guidebook. However, with these same techniques, you can of course help your grandchildren, nephews, nieces, or other children in your life build good money habits, a financially secure future, and even a fortune of a quarter-million, half-million, or more dollars by the time they begin to raise families of their own.

Introduction

Dear Parent:

Congratulations. You're about to start your children on the path to lifelong financial security.

This program will help your children develop good money habits that will last their entire lives. And it will do something else too.

By following this program, starting today, your children can achieve a substantial six-figure nest egg by the time they're ready to start families of their own.

Exactly how much wealth they accumulate depends on how much they put in and the investment returns they get. But in this course you're going to learn uncomplicated investment methods that have produced returns ranging from 13.2% to 18.8% over a period of 44 to 50 years.

The first seed for creating these habits and wealth will be a simple yet highly effective savings program your children will use to create "investment capital" out of just a few dollars a week.

Combining the two, the results can be very powerful.

Even if your children average just over $1 a day in savings through the pre-teen years and a little more than $2 a day through the age of 21, they can still end up with anywhere from $335,854 (at 13.2% return) to $855,279 (at 18.8% return) a generation from now.

What's more, as they continue practicing the lifelong good money habits they'll learn here, it's very possible they can achieve a fortune in the *millions of dollars* during their 30s or 40s — *even if they never make a great deal of money in their chosen careers!*

Specifically, you'll help your children build good money habits and financial security through little-known wealth-building techniques that are ideal for children, including...

✓ The simple yet highly effective two-box wealth-creation system,

✓ Methods to make the best use of their Four Great Advantages as young investors,

✓ The best mutual funds and other diversified investments that have low investment minimums and allow you to help your children begin to build wealth immediately,

✓ Ways to help your children take advantage of the incredible wealth-building power of real estate from a very early age,

✓ Ways to help your children maximize their investment returns by keeping expenses and taxes low,

✓ Ways to help your children create six- and even seven-figure fortunes by the time they're your age — even if they never make an above-average income,

✓ Ways to get your children to adopt six smart savings ratios, each for a different stage in their lives, that will create lives of plenty for them,

✓ Ways to protect your children from developing bad money habits,

✓ Ways to help your children lock in a future multimillion dollar retirement nest egg — even if they never contribute to an IRA or other tax-deferred plan past the age of 20,

✓ Ways to help your teenage child save for his or her first car — and buy it for 17% less than book value,

✓ 14 kids' businesses that can help your children learn and earn at the same time,

✓ Ways to save $22,500 or more on a first-rate college education,

✓ Ways to help your children build wealth and develop habits of financial responsibility and generosity at the same time.

I'll show you how it all works in just a minute. But before I do, let me ask you to imagine two young people of similar backgrounds for a moment.

A Tale of Two 30-year-olds

Picture two young friends — each about 30 years old. They went to the same schools, entered the same careers, and are making the same salary.

Yet one is struggling to qualify for his first mortgage. He has high credit card and personal debt, so he can't quite get the financing for the home he'd like. He also realizes he's going to have to put off funding that 401(k) for a while, until his next raise...

The other young man, however, not only already owns his own home, but two other investment properties and has a mutual fund portfolio worth well into six figures. Plus, he has no credit card debt and continues to fund his 401(k) and create future wealth without a problem...

Are these two scenarios strictly imaginary?

Unfortunately not. The first scenario is common today.

As you'll see in the next section, national income statistics show that the personal savings rate has declined to the lowest level since the Great Depression, consumption is growing faster than income, and the number of personal bankruptcies filed each year are up *over 300%* from just 15 years ago!

The second scenario, however, is indeed rare...

Yet it's exactly the kind of financial future you can give your children the power to create.

They can create futures of prosperity instead of debt simply by beginning to plant the seeds of their own wealth starting today.

And, ultimately, the result will not only be wealth, but a number of other important benefits as well...

Your Children Will Gain Much More than Future Wealth

As your children follow this program throughout their young years and into adulthood, they'll develop financial responsibility. They'll recognize credit come-ons like "no-money-down," "pre-approved credit," and "no-interest payments for a full year" for what they are — debt traps.

Living within their means will be second-nature to them. They won't constantly find themselves broke a week before payday, or have to decide which bill _not_ to pay this month...

At the same time, they'll also develop the ability to consistently _expand_ their means. They'll understand how to invest wisely because they'll have been doing it most of their lives. And they'll know from experience _that even at average market returns_, each dollar they invest has the potential to multiply dozens, even _hundreds_ of times in their lifetimes.

They will likely also become more entrepreneurial — because this program will teach them the value of money. Not in theory, but in practice. After all, it's _your children_ who will be creating their own wealth out of their own money. You'll simply guide them along the way.

They will have greater confidence in business and financial dealings when they become adults. By the time they go on their first job interview, negotiate for their first raise or close their first business deal, they'll already have been saving and investing their entire lives — not just learning about money as a "subject" in a college course.

They'll make better financial decisions when buying a car or home or starting a business. Instead of trying to scrape together the down-payment for a "starter home" soon after your children get married, they could already own their own homes (bought at very good prices!) plus two or three investment properties...

They'll be less susceptible to financial scams and get-rich-quick schemes. By the time your children celebrate their 30th birthdays they'll already be well on their way to lifelong financial security, having achieved net worths that could reach a quarter-million to a half-million dollars or more...

They'll know beyond a shadow of a doubt that those who can postpone gratification tend to achieve their long-term goals. Those who don't tend to end up with debts and regrets.

In short, they'll understand just a little bit better the necessity for discipline and balance in their lives. And they'll gain a first-hand knowledge of the remarkable things that can be achieved with applied effort over time.

If your children are budding entrepreneurs or businessmen, this program will give them a tremendous head start in their careers. But if you have children who aren't interested at all in business — if they are budding artists, teachers, or social activists — this program is even more important for them. They will be able to pursue their own paths without worrying about becoming financially dependent later on in life.

By beginning the *Seeds of Wealth* program today, you've helped assure that when your children are your age, money will be *the least* of their concerns... and the things they can accomplish are limited only by their imaginations.

Sincerely,

Justin Ford
Founder
Seeds of Wealth

Addison Wiggin
Publisher
Seeds of Wealth

PART I

Clearing Away The Brush

Putting Money in Its Proper Place

Before we address the mechanics of helping your children create substantial wealth over time, we should first address the psychology of money. The reason for this is you cannot commit to something — especially over the long term — unless you fully believe in the rightness of what you are doing.

This is true in all aspects of life. But money is a particularly thorny area. It's an area in which most people are greatly conflicted.

The True Value of Money

Most people want money. But they also fear it.

On the fear side, many of us vaguely remember the often misquoted Biblical passage "money is the root of all evil." The actual quote, however, is "the _love_ of

1

money is the root of all evil" (I Timothy, 4.10).

If we take this to mean an _excess_ devotion to your own well-being is the root of all evil (to the exclusion of concern and responsibility toward others), then money itself isn't the problem. The failure to put money in its proper place is the problem.

At the other extreme is the modern message, "money talks," implying that money is all that matters. This view is usually held by people who hope that by building up their net worth they can increase their personal worth. But this effort has to end in disappointment. First, because there's more to life than money (If you doubt it, just ask anyone who's seriously ill.). Second, because there is always someone else with "more."

The point is, money in itself is neither good nor bad. It all depends on what you do to get it... and what you do with it.

If you think you need to cheat people to make a lot of money, you're going to create a life where _you_ can't trust anyone and where you will probably never feel truly good about what you do. On the other hand, if you earn your money honestly, but then use it to finance a nonstop party lifestyle — your "financial success" will have a negative effect on your life.

That's why the _experience_ of building wealth will prove to be so valuable for your children.

In order to achieve wealth by the time they have families of their own, they'll have to practice discipline, patience, perseverance, and foresight. By the time they turn their modest regular contributions into a six- or even seven-figure fortune, they will understand from experience what it requires to build significant wealth.

At the same time, because building that wealth will not have been quick nor an "easy come" proposition, they are very unlikely to have an "easy go" attitude about spending it.

"Wealth quickly gotten dwindles away, but amassed little by little, it grows."
— Proverbs, 13. 11

An Important Part of Life — But Only One Part

Through this course your children will create wealth, and they'll learn to deal with money effectively. But that doesn't mean money will or should become the primary goal in their lives.

By planting and nurturing the seeds of their own future wealth, your children will come to understand that having good money habits is an important *part* of life. But it's only one part of life.

More important are the personal values that you pass on to them, which no one but you can best teach your children.

Also more important than money are good health and a sound state of mind (or "spiritual well-being," if you prefer). After all, if you don't have these, all the money in the world won't do you much good.

Then, of course, you need good friends and a strong relationship with your family because if you don't have

3

someone to share your good fortune with, it's a very lonely accomplishment.

A Practical Matter

Money, above all then, is a practical matter. But it's an area where many of us leave our children completely unprepared — just because we haven't been able to come to terms with money.

A survey of 2,500 adults of all ages conducted on behalf of *Modern Maturity* magazine bears this out.

On the one hand, the survey shows that many people give far too much importance to money, as 27% said making a lot of money was "absolutely necessary" for them to consider their lives a success.

On the other hand, the survey shows an even greater number of people fear money. Why else would a third of respondents answer "no" when asked whether they, themselves, would like to be wealthy?

After all, if these people are idealistic and altruistic in nature, wouldn't they want to have money to be able to help others in need? Theoretically, if they came into, or built up, a great deal of wealth, they could give most or all of it away.

Yet 33% say they'd rather not be rich...

I think it can be only because they're afraid of what money will do to their own characters — and how it might affect their children and other people in their lives. They suspect, in other words, that they themselves will not have the discipline to use their wealth as they think they should.

Answers to other questions in the survey also show a widespread ambivalence about money.

More than four out of five respondents said that having a lot of money makes people be too greedy and feel too superior, and three quarters think the rich are insensitive to others. At the same time, however, 71% recognized that money can buy the freedom to live as you choose, while 68% said it can help bring excitement to life, and 56% said it can help you lead a less stressful life.

Overall, the survey shows that most people realize money's limitations:

Just over half said money can't buy peace of mind, while 2/3 realized it can't buy good health or self-fulfillment, and 76% said it can't buy self-esteem or family togetherness. Sixty-five percent said they would like to give wealth a shot, even though they're not particularly interested in imitating the rich and famous, and 92% agreed with the Beatles that money can't buy you love.

The overwhelming majority also had the good sense to put strong family relationships first in their life priorities (94%), followed by friendship (87%), helping people in need (87%), and becoming well-educated (82%).

Most people also profess to not being very greedy. And they believe they *could* handle wealth.

Over half said they'd feel wealthy even if they had less than $500,000 in total assets, while only 8% said it takes more than $1 million to qualify as rich.

And if they were to come into a million-dollar wind-fall?   Only 3% said they would use the newfound money primarily to "buy things," and 14% would give to charity.

That would seem to show a certain level-headedness about wealth. But not really, because only 20% said that if they suddenly came into a million dollars, they would save or invest for the future, while only 13% would pay off debt!

In between the two extremes of loving and fearing money, then, it would seem there's a great deal of uncertainty about how to value money.

And that's exactly what the national income statistics show!

They show that most people place far too little importance on learning to handle money responsibly! They don't learn how to spend it wisely or how to use a portion of it to create wealth instead of debt.

The numbers tell the ugly truth...

Don't Let Your Children Join the "Earn-it and Burn-it" Crowd

Nationwide, the personal savings rate has fallen to lows not seen since the Great Depression. Personal debt is at record levels, and spending has been growing faster than income since 1997!

This combination of out-of-control borrowing and spending and low savings is a recipe for disaster.

And it's also a sign that while most people may profess to be levelheaded about money, they are actually — at best — *naïve* about it.

But America is not only overspending and neglecting to save, we live in the most sophisticated marketing

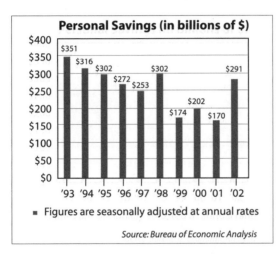

Personal Savings (in billions of $)

■ Figures are seasonally adjusted at annual rates

Source: Bureau of Economic Analysis

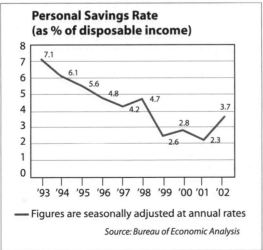

Personal Savings Rate (as % of disposable income)

— Figures are seasonally adjusted at annual rates

Source: Bureau of Economic Analysis

culture in the world. The result is that even people who make enough money in a single year to last a lifetime go broke.

Toni Braxton is a Grammy Award-winning, multimillionaire pop star who recently went bankrupt, thanks to her out-of-control appetite for jewelry and furs.

Burt Reynolds was a very successful movie actor in the '70s and '80s. Today he's making a comeback not only in his acting career, but financially, having gone bankrupt in the mid-'90s.

Willie Nelson is a best-selling country music star who is well known for having put on benefit concerts for farmers under the name of "Farm Aid." A few years ago, lawyers had to come to Willie's aid, as he declared bankruptcy.

Joe Louis was one of the great heavyweights of all time and made the equivalent of many millions of dollars in today's terms. He died nearly broke.

But it's not just actors and athletes who don't know how to manage their good fortune. Even highly educated, financially successful people can fail to develop the habits that help them protect and continue to grow their wealth.

Irving Fisher, for instance, was a renowned Yale economics professor and entrepreneur in the 1920s and 1930s who built a multimillion-dollar fortune over 70 years ago! Yet he neglected fundamental lessons about protecting wealth once it's been acquired.

He ended up broke, and Yale University bought the house he used to own and let him live out the rest of his days there.

It's not a new phenomenon, in other words. And it happens to people in all walks of life. But the problem has become worse than ever.

So many people today don't have the slightest idea about the difference between income and wealth. Income is money you receive. Wealth is money you keep and use to create greater wealth. Great wealth, in other words, comes only from having the right money habits.

But because so many people are making good incomes in today's booming economy, they think they're "wealthy," and they spend as if there were no tomorrow. The charts on page 7 are simply graphic proof of that fact.

And that's why, to make sure your children don't get swept up in the "earn-it-and-burn-it" culture, you have to teach them good money habits — just as you would teach them any other important, practical skill.

The Value of Good Habits

You teach your children to brush their teeth three times a day. You teach them good manners so they can get along with people. You teach them to study hard so they can get into good schools and, from there, good careers. And perhaps you teach them other valuable, practical things as well...

You may teach them to exercise and eat well so they don't become overweight and more susceptible to disease. You may teach them to read on their own so they learn how to find answers for themselves. You may teach them some form of self-defense so they can protect themselves a bit better and have a little more confidence. You may teach them music — for the benefit of their souls or for the sheer enjoyment of it.

These things are all good. And money can't replace any of them. But at the same time, none of these things can replace the need to teach your children good money habits.

Whether we like it or not, money _is_ a necessity in life, and that's why it's necessary we accept the responsibility to teach our children about money.

After all, can you imagine a hunter-gatherer a few thousand years ago reaching the age of manhood and never having been on a hunt? Or what if you were a farmer 300 years ago? Would you be doing your son a service by letting him reach the age of 18, 19, or 20 without learning anything about planting and caring for crops?

These acts would be inconceivable. Yet today the great majority of parents simply send their kids off to school, believing that's all they need to do to help their children learn to provide for themselves in life.

But at school, children don't learn about money. They (hopefully) learn to read, write, add, and subtract. And a lot of energy is spent trying to get them to obey orders and show up on time. But as far as economics goes, they learn to be "workers," not to gain more control over their own lives.

Make Sure Your Children Don't Learn
the Wrong Money Lessons

The _number one reason_ it's important to teach your children good money habits from a very early age is that if you don't, you can bet your children _will_ learn about money anyhow. But their first teacher is going to be Madison Avenue.

The lesson they'll learn from the advertising industry is to be "consumers," not stewards of their own wealth.

From the very earliest ages, children are bombarded with commercials for toys, cereals, sneakers, movies, junk food, and games. And when they become young adults, their mailboxes are stuffed with credit card offers.

At the same time, most children's experience with money is confined to spending, not earning, and certainly not investing. Their early money experiences, in other words, usually aren't very realistic.

On the one hand, most of the money they get is free in the form of allowance and gifts. The money they see their parents spend, meanwhile, also can seem like "free money."

They see the purchases parents make, but they don't necessarily see the work required to make the money. Nor do they see the choices we have to make for every purchase.

As a result, many children become adults who don't understand the trade-offs that are involved with every purchase. For instance, if you have $20,000 and spend it

11

all on a new car, that car will likely be worth about $7,000 in six years. Yet if the money were invested at 13.2% (the average market returns from 1950 to 2000), that $20,000 would now be worth $42,083.

How many adults understand that the new car costs more than the initial $20,000... that it can cost them somewhere in the neighborhood $35,083 in future wealth ($42,083 -$7,000)?

The point is, if you don't teach your children about money, others will. And they will very likely be the wrong lessons — developing habits of out-of-control spending and debt that can cost them years of hardship to undo.

By contrast, with this program you'll help your children learn about building wealth in the most effective and natural way possible — by _doing it_. Starting immediately, they'll begin to practice the habits of consistent saving and investing. As they grow older, not only will their wealth grow — but so will their understanding of the process of creating wealth.

The Payoff

Ultimately, your children will have more choices as young adults.

They can continue studying if they like. They can travel a bit more. They can pursue the careers they really want rather than settle for jobs they "have to" take just to pay the bills. They can buy a good home for their families. They can continue to grow their wealth much more rapidly than their peers, who will likely only begin to save and invest at a time when your children will have already built up six-figure nest eggs.

And not only will they achieve financial security from a very young age — they'll be better prepared to succeed in the practical world and perhaps even in their social lives.

After all, for persons of ordinary means to create wealth, they must develop characteristics that can also serve them well in their personal lives. These include restraint, knowledge, discipline, patience, experience, and foresight.

Through this program, your children will gain a little more of these characteristics with each passing year. As a result, their wealth will compound over time, as will their competence and confidence — assets that truly make a person wealthy in the best sense.

And they'll have you to thank for it.

So in this one important aspect of your children's lives, let's begin to help them build the best possible future they can. Shall we?

What You Need to Help Your Children Succeed

It's incredibly easy, and it doesn't have to cost you a _single dime of your own_ to help your children develop excellent money habits and build substantial wealth over time. All you need are the following:

Two cardboard boxes,

A custodial investment account for each child,

Fifteen minutes to explain to your child what he/she will be doing from now on with every dollar and dime he/she gets and why,

Fifteen minutes a month to guide them along,

Three or four hours every four to six months to invest new money, and

A personal commitment from you to stay with this program for good — for the immense benefit of your children.

All these things don't have to cost you any money at all — unless you want to replace the cardboard boxes with little desk safes or piggy banks. And it won't cost you a lot of time, either.

The only thing it will cost you is your personal commitment to see to it your children stay with the program every day. But this point is extremely important. I cannot emphasize it enough. You need commitment.

Even though it's not a lot of time, you have to make sure you do invest the little time that it does require. You'll be checking on the progress of their savings and reinforcing for them the benefits their good money habits will bring. And every few months when they gather a hundred dollars or so, you'll invest it *for* them if they're under 12, or *with* them if they're over 12.

You need to continue to do these quick, simple, easy actions every month until they leave the house at 17 or

18. And by the time they leave for college or work, you'll also have shown them how to follow a modified version of the program on their own.

Once they're living on their own, they won't save and invest so large a percentage of their income as they did when they were children because now they'll have bills to pay. But they will have a fixed percentage they'll know to put aside regularly and without exception for wealth creation.

And that's where the benefits really start to build up.

In fact, I've told you how starting with less than $1 a day can easily lead to a fortune of between a quarter-million and well over a half-million dollars. But you should know that it's also quite possible (in fact, even *probable*) that, as they continue these habits as adults, they could end up millionaires or even multimillionaires in their mid-thirties or early forties.

And, again, that's even if they never make a great deal of money in their careers!

But to make this happen, you must commit to following this simple yet extremely effective program. If you start it and then fail to follow up, you'll be wasting your children's single greatest asset as young investors — time. And they won't have the experience of building wealth themselves. So, at best, good money habits will exist for them only in theory, not practice.

But this program is not about theory. It's about doing, and helping your children build great wealth steadily and inevitably over time. And in order to assure success, there's just one more thing you need...

You have to make sure your children put aside the savings. You can't do it for them.

This is extremely important. You monitor the process, but you cannot put the savings aside for them! They have to do it for themselves with every single dollar they receive, whether it is from allowance, birthday or holiday checks, chore money, or part-time jobs when they're older.

Your children are going to consistently practice good money habits. And they are going to reap the rewards. You are going to coach them and guide them along.

But they'll learn about building wealth in the best way possible, by actually doing it. *So you've got to let them do it!*

What You <u>Don't</u> Need to Help Your Children Succeed

In order to help your children turn modest savings into a massive fortune, you don't need to be a financial expert. You don't even have to be good at math. And you don't have to try to explain complicated ideas to your children before they're ready for them.

All the information you need to know to successfully invest your children's funds is spelled out in the investment section (in Part V of this guide book) in plain English.

In fact, when you get to the investment section, you'll see the highly effective long-term investment systems you can choose from are incredibly simple. And that's done on purpose.

You see, learning complicated financial ideas doesn't mean you know how to truly build wealth. There are many stockbrokers who have gone broke from out-of-control spending habits. There are also many accountants who have been working for years but are still only just eking out a living because they haven't acquired the actual _habits_ of saving and investing.

In other words, the secrets to financial success are actually simple. But unless you learn how to incorporate them into your life from an early age, they become more difficult to adopt with each passing year. They require discipline and consistency, and those are traits your children will begin to master starting today.

And here's another reason the long-run investment systems you'll learn are simple and low maintenance: the last thing you want to do is try to turn your children's savings into a fortune by trading feverishly in and out of the market, playing every hot stock and inside tip.

Do NOT try to be a hotshot speculator with your children's savings!

You must not gamble with your children's money. And you're not trying to create a day trader in diapers or a mini Michael Milken.

Through this program, your children will learn about successful investing over the years. But the purpose isn't to make your children financially "sophisticated." It's to make them financially independent.

With *Seeds of Wealth*, you'll do more than teach them a subject. You'll start them on a lifelong <u>*course of action*</u> that will yield benefits for them their entire lives.

The emphasis, again, is on <u>*doing*</u>; it is more than mastering any complicated knowledge before they acquire actual experience. There's a very good reason for that. Let me explain…

How to Swim

You can't teach someone to swim just by lectures and demonstrations. At some point, they've got to get in the water. They've got to get wet.

In fact, infants can learn to swim at less than a year old simply by being introduced to the water early on. They can master this practice, in other words, long before their "cognitive" abilities develop.

What we absolutely <u>*don't*</u> want, is for the ideas and theory of wealth creation to <u>*get in the way*</u> of the development of the right money habits and the actual steady <u>*building*</u> of wealth.

To make it absolutely clear why I say that, let me give you one more example.

How to Speak a Second Language

In high school I spent a year in Chile as an exchange student. When I first arrived in the country, I spoke only a handful of words of Spanish — stuff I picked up from two years of high-school Spanish. Still, by the end of the year, I was speaking pretty fluently — basically because I was "immersed" in the language on a daily basis.

A few years after that, I began to teach English as a second language. I soon realized that for most people the best way to learn a language is actually to *skip* the grammar initially. Later, you can come back to it if and when the student is ready for it.

You see, when communication is the reason for learning a language, grammar can be a hurdle rather than a help.

Why? Because grammar is a separate discipline (and one that most people have no desire to learn). And that means if people have to learn grammar <u>before</u> they learn a foreign language, most will give up. Due to the hurdle of acquiring formal knowledge, they'll never acquire the practical knowledge they would otherwise naturally acquire.

So the best way to teach a language is usually to let the students immediately begin to use words and phrases that are relevant to their everyday lives. They can learn parts of the grammar as their experience requires it. For instance, when they begin to understand "he *says*" and "I *say*" are different uses of the same verb, you can then explain the concept of conjugation.

In similar fashion, the purpose here is to teach children to save and invest and to get them to begin to actually *build* wealth. And that means we don't want a premature focus on complicated terms and ideas that could get in the way of that primary goal.

That's why this program *intentionally* bypasses explanations of complicated financial issues — especially at the beginning.

Remember, there are a lot of MBAs out there who live from paycheck to paycheck and a lot of accountants who are struggling with their own personal debts. They've got the financial terms down, but they haven't mastered the simple habits.

At the same time, there are schoolteachers who are not financial experts, but who have acquired millions of dollars over the years through steady, diversified, long-term investments.

Throughout this course, we will break from the adult-level conversation from time to time and we'll provide bite-sized introductions into ideas about money and investing that children can understand. But you don't want to put too strong an emphasis on *teaching* them first; you want to get them *doing* first.

As they continue to practice these habits, questions will come up over the years. And that means they'll be ready to learn more about money at those points. And they'll be prepared to *use* that new knowledge because they won't just be getting information. They'll be getting information they themselves are seeking because of their own *experience*. And it will be information that will complement their good money habits.

For Kids of All Ages

Another reason we begin by doing, rather than teaching: The sooner your children begin to actually invest,

Continued on pg.22...

Dumb and Dumber

The non-profit Investor Protection Trust did a survey of adult _investors_ in 1996 and found that fewer than 20% are financially literate. The following year, the National Association of Securities Dealers got similar results. The NASD found that 78 percent of Americans can name a character on a sitcom, but only 12 percent know the difference between a "load" and "no-load" mutual fund.

With adult investors showing such a poor grasp of the fundamentals, then, it's not surprising that most American students are also financially illiterate. The Jump$tart Coalition for Personal Financial Literacy, for instance, recently administered a financial literacy test of sorts to high school students nationwide. The average score was 57 percent; only 5% of the students scored higher than a 70, and 59% of the students failed! In 2002, they repeated the test with 4,024 students nationwide. This time, 68 percent failed!

Even worse than financial ignorance, however, is financial negligence. It's one thing for an adult not to know what a "no-load fund" is, but running up record debts and posting a negative savings rate are far worse. And that's just what American adults are doing — and it's exactly what the next generation will learn to do, unless we teach them otherwise and get them to begin to _practice_ good money habits from a very early age.

the better. In fact, even if you have a child just a month old — or even a day old — you should immediately begin this program for him.

By the time, he/she begins to do the saving, at age 5, already some capital will have been built up. And by the time he or she begins to ask questions about money, say between the ages of 7 and 10, money experience and all the answers will have more *relevance* for him or her.

If your child is now between the ages of 10 and 17, he/she can begin to learn about finance and build on that knowledge. But it's not a must to learn the terms or theory first. It's enough to impress upon your child that by saving according to the program, and investing for the long term, he or she will have substantial wealth in a generation.

By getting your children to begin not only to learn and develop good habits, but also actually begin creating wealth right away, you will help them take advantage of their Four Great Advantages as Young Investors...

The Four Advantages Your Children Have Over the World's Greatest Investors

1) Your children have time ahead of them (and that means maximum compounding for their investments). In fact, when Albert Einstein was asked what the greatest force in the universe was, he answered, "compound interest!" He was half joking, of course. People expected him to say something like nuclear fission or gravity. But when it comes to investing, he was right.

Nothing creates wealth like the effects of long-term compounding.

2) Your children have an ability to learn new habits quickly. (This, by the way, is why it's easier for children to learn a new language when they're young. And it's why so many people who smoke picked up the habit as kids and then have spent a lifetime trying to kick the habit — if they're able to kick it at all. But the habits your children will pick up here will be the right money habits — habits that will serve them well their whole lives long.)

3) Your children have no bills to pay. They have, in other words, 100% disposable income. And that's a unique opportunity to build wealth. But if you do as most parents do and let them spend it all, they'll do just that, and they'll have nothing to show for it down the road.

4) Your children are naturally tax-efficient investors. (While living at home, most of the money your children receive is tax-free. Even when they begin to earn money from part-time jobs, much of that will be tax-free, since the tax rate on the first $4,700 of income is zero. Also, your children are naturally suited toward growth-oriented investments that do not pay dividends and so are more tax-efficient. Finally, you'll learn an exclusive *Seeds of Wealth* Strategy in this guidebook with which your children can earn money tax-free, have it grow by hundreds of thousands of dollars tax-free, and even withdraw the gains tax-free!)

So let's begin to help your children make the most of these important wealth-building advantages right away.

We'll get them to immediately take their first steps toward building wealth (even if it's beginning with just a couple of dollars). We'll introduce them to some important fundamental concepts (namely interest and compound interest). And we'll let their knowledge of money and wealth creation steadily *compound* over time, just as their wealth will compound.

PART II

Planting The Seeds

Four Basic Steps to Wealth Creation

There are four basic components to creating wealth:

• Establishing clear goals,

• Earning income,

• Saving a fixed portion of that income, depending on the child's age, and

• Investing those savings for high returns over the long run.

Establishing clear goals is like clearing the brush away. Earning the income is like tilling the earth. Saving is like planting the seeds. And investing is like watering, weeding, and caring for the plants as they grow.

We've already looked at the first of these components as they concern children. We've talked about clearing away the debris of conflicting thoughts about money and helping your children begin to build wealth so that, when they're adults, they can focus on things that are more important than money.

For the next three sections, however, we're going to change the order a little bit. Instead of talking about income right now, we're going to begin with savings. That's because your children already have income, and so they should *immediately* learn to save a fixed portion of that income.

In fact, even if your children are still in the cradle, it's likely they have income in the form of savings bonds or gift checks they receive on birthdays, holidays, and special occasions — perhaps from you and your spouse, other family members, and friends.

If they're a bit older, they may also receive an allowance. No matter how modest it is, for the purposes of saving and creating investment capital, that too is "income" for your children.

And, of course, if they're teenagers or approaching adolescence, they may have already begun (or may soon begin) to do extra chores around the house for a few extra dollars such as mow the lawn on weekends or wash the cars. They may also be starting to make a little money outside of the house, delivering newspapers, caddying, baby-sitting, or working at a part-time job.

Now allowances, chore money, and holiday checks you give your children are not "earned income" in the legal sense of the word. That's because you don't deduct it as an expense, and you've already paid taxes on it from your own income. Instead, this money (as we'll explain a bit more in Part V) falls under the $11,000 annual gift exclusion and the IRS rightly doesn't expect your children to pay taxes on it.

And even when your children become teenagers or so and begin to make "earned income" from outside sources (or even from you if you employ them in your business), they can earn up to $4,700 income-tax-free (the standard deduction for dependents) without having to file an income tax return.

But for the purposes of creating *Seeds of Wealth*, every dollar your children receive is to be considered "income." That applies to money they receive from any source — whether it's from allowance, household chore money, gifts, or formal earnings later on.

So let's take a look at how your children can begin to plant a portion of their income to create considerable wealth over time. And let's begin with some very simple numbers....

A Combination for Success

Here is a combination that can have a huge positive impact on your children's future:

100
50
10
15
15
10

These are the *Seeds of Wealth* savings ratios. They can turn your children's modest incomes into six- and even seven-figure wealth by the time they're your age.

Let me explain...

Stage 1 — Ages One-Day to Four Years Old (Tycoon Tots), Save 100%.

From the ages of one-day to four years, you'll save 100% of your children's "income" for them. This is the only stage during which you'll actually put the money away for your children. From the age of 5 onward, they'll do it themselves, with your supervision.

This first stage of life is usually the _only_ time the great majority of parents actually do implement some kind of savings program for their children. The only problems are, it usually doesn't last far beyond this stage, the children are completely unaware of it, and they are too young to learn from it.

By the time the children're five, then, most parents let them spend all (or almost all) the income they receive. So the only conscious economic experience children remember is of spending, never of saving or investing.

Also, during this period most parents leave their children's savings in investments that yield far too little. They either hold the children's wealth in the form of the original savings bonds — paying in the neighborhood of 4% a year — or they deposit gift checks for the child in a savings account paying even less, currently about 1%.

The net result is that even if the child doesn't touch that small bit of money for thirty years, it grows only at an average of perhaps 4% a year. And that means it doubles in value about once every 16 years.

In the investment section of this course, you'll learn how to put the money in long-term, high-growth investments instead. And that includes _immediately_ turning those 4% savings bonds into investments yielding two or three times that much, and doubling in value as soon as every 5 to 6 years.

In fact, your children's total wealth could well double even faster — every four to five years — since they'll also be adding new savings to their investment account on a regular basis.

From Tots to Tycoons

Warren Buffet, Mario Gabelli, and Peter Lynch have quite a few things in common. They're very well known professional investors, and their personal fortunes run in the billions of dollars. But there's something else they also have in common...

They all started investing as children.

That's not just a coincidence. Nothing helps you succeed financially like developing good money habits from a very early age.

But the best part is, you don't have to be focused on becoming a Wall Street tycoon to benefit from the same early education in matters of money. You can pursue the kind of job you want (whether it pays a lot or not) and still benefit from the extremely powerful effects of long-term compounding.

Second Stage — Ages 5 to 17 (The Wonder Years), Save 50%.

This is the point where your children begin to do it for themselves.

At five, children begin kindergarten, learn the alphabet, write their names, and do some counting and simple math. And one of the simplest of all math concepts they can begin to grasp at this age is "half." And you're going to tell them, beginning at the age of five, that they're going to save _half_ of every dollar they get.

(A little later, on page 61, I'll talk about how you can introduce the subject to your children and how to get them actually excited about it. For right now, though, we're going to cover the savings ratios for the different age groups and the logic behind them.)

Now, 50% may seem like a very high savings rate to ask of someone. But let me ask you this — when was the last time you were able to spend 50% of your income exactly as you pleased?

The answer is likely to be either 1) never, or 2) _not since you were a kid!_

Imagine if your mortgage was paid, your grocery bills taken care of, the utilities were free, your car ran on air, and you never had to pay any medical or emergency bills of any sort. And you made the same income you do now...

Would you be depriving yourself if you saved 50% of your income and only spent 50% on whatever you _wanted_ (since all your necessities are taken care of in this scenario)?

I think you'd have to agree... you'd be like a kid in a candy store. Some months you probably couldn't even come up with ways to spend half your income!

Well, our children live this kind of fantasy. All their material needs are taken care of. They have a roof over their heads, food, clothing — all paid for. They have, in other words...

100% disposable income!

And that means, even though their income may only be a few dollars a week, they'll never again have a time in their lives when saving — even 50% of income — will be so incredibly easy. (Except perhaps if they become multimillionaires later on in life, a real possibility with this program, and the income from their investments is more than twice what they need to live well.)

Because your children are beginning to save and invest so early in their lives, even those few dollars (when combined with more modest savings rates of higher income levels later on) should compound into wealth in the hundreds of thousands, possibly even millions of dollars, by the time your children are ready to have children of their own.

But in order for this to work, they have to take maximum advantage of their young years at home. By letting them make the most of The Four Great Advantages they have as young investors (see page 22), you'll be giving them a tremendous head-start.

This stage, from the ages of 5 to 17, is really the most important. Before the age of 5 you handle it for them. And after the age of 17, they'll have mastered good money habits to be able to follow the path to wealth on their own.

**How the Young Ben Franklin Planted the Seeds
for a Brilliant Future**

Benjamin Franklin was a truly remarkable man who led
a highly accomplished life. Franklin was a printer, states-
man, scientist, and writer. He was extremely successful in
his business and his business provided a great service, printing books at a time when books were relatively rare in the
America.

As a self-taught scientist, he invented bifocals and a more
fuel-efficient pot-belly stove, among other things. And, of
course, he conducted a famous experiment involving a kite
in a storm that proved the presence of electricity in light-
ning.

As an author, he wrote a book of sayings and common-
sense philosophy, Poor Richard's Almanac, that became a
best-seller. His autobiography is also well-known.

As a lover of learning and generous member of his community, he founded an academy that later became the
University of Pennsylvania. He also helped expand his
community considerably, fathering and raising 13 children
with his wife.

In 1775, he helped organize the American colonies in
opposition to certain British policies. He helped draft
theDeclaration of Independence in 1776. He was an
American delegate in Paris at the signing of the peace with
Britain at the end of the Revolutionary War in 1781. And
he contributed to the drafting of the U.S. Constitution in
1787.

Any one of these achievements would be enough to distinguish any normal person's life. Yet Franklin did all this and more.

And one of the facets of Franklin's character that made him so successful was his willingness to invest in his future! Literally and figuratively.

When Franklin was a teenager, he was an apprentice at his brother's printing shop. Franklin's brother provided him room and board and a small amount of pay, but mostly what he gave Franklin was the opportunity to learn a very valuable trade. That was the key idea behind apprenticeship a couple of hundred years ago.

Franklin soon got his brother to give him food-money instead of actually providing him with meals. Franklin saved half his food allowance and began to buy books. In this way, he built up his knowledge not only of his profession, but also of science and philosophy (which would later play a big part in his political decisions and activities).

A few years later, as Franklin became an independent printer in his own right, he continued to save. Eventually he became the owner of a number of printing shops and his wealth afforded him the leisure to pursue other interests — like science and writing.

His education and practical success also made him his wealth afforded him the leisure to pursue other interests — like science and writing.

His education and practical success also made him a person other people listened to when he was arguing for American independence from British rule. His crucial role in helping to bring about the birth of the United States, in other words, was largely possible because he invested in himself from a very early age.

As Ben himself said in Poor Richard's Almanac, "a penny saved is a penny earned." And as your children will learn as they invest their own savings, each penny invested for the long run can turn into dozens, even hundreds of pennies over that time!

I'll return to this stage in just a moment. We'll talk about getting them started, the actual savings system, how your children can generate extra income as they grow older, how and when they may begin to be involved with their investments and more. But for now, the important thing to realize is they must save 50% of income at this stage.

Stage 3 — Ages 18-21 (College Days), Save 10% of income.

These are the college years. And most kids have very little money at this time, since they have education expenses and since many are not working at all (at least during the school year), concentrating instead (or so we suppose) on their studies.

Yet even though money may be tight and making money is not a priority at this stage, they absolutely must save 10% of income during this period. There are two primary reasons for this.

First, even if they just save $10 a week during this period — because they're doing it from such a young age, those very small investments can turn into significant wealth over time.

For example, if your children invest $780 a year ($15 a week) during the ages of 18, 19, 20, and 21 and get the average market returns of 1950-2000 (13.2%), by the time they retire, those small investments ***all by themselves*** will be worth just over $1 million

If they get one of our Super-Strategy returns of as much as 18.8%, that total of $15 a week for 4 years could be worth *$9.58 million*!

But, of course, this program isn't about retirement. It's about helping your children develop good money habits that can help them create wealth over their entire lives. And it's about getting them started right away so they can begin to achieve significant wealth at a relatively very early age — so they can enjoy it with their families while they're young adults.

In this fashion, by beginning early and practicing these wealth-building habits their whole lives long, your children can actually build far greater wealth than $6.38 million by the time they themselves retire.

In fact, starting from the very earliest age, going by the modest income assumptions you'll see in a moment, and getting returns of 13.2%, they'd acquire over **$29 million** by the age of 65!

And at 18.8%… they'd acquire over ***$370 million!***

I'll show you the modest income assumptions and go into the investment returns these numbers are based on a little later. And you'll see that ***even if you subtract two or three percentage points*** from each of these annual returns to account for trading costs and taxes, your children can still end up with a fortune in the many millions of dollars.

At 10.2% (13.2%-3%), for instance, they'd end up with $8.4 million at 65, beginning with a few dollars a day from birth. At 15.8% (18.8%-3%), they'd end up with over $93 million.

Now bear in mind that by investing for the long haul and keeping trading costs and taxes down, these costs should actually consume less than one percentage point of total return (as I'll explain in the investment section, in Part V). But nonetheless, you can see that even if we knock off a full three percentage points from the historical long-term return of the market, we're still talking about a good deal of money — and even though we're working with moderate income assumptions. And it's all because your children begin to save and invest from an early age.

Now, granted, these numbers assume your children don't touch their accumulated wealth during their 30s, 40s, and 50s. And that means if they begin to use a portion of their wealth earlier, they'll end up with less.

And that's absolutely fine. In fact, it's what we expect. After all, you can't take it with you.

But by beginning to save and invest early, your children have the best chance of turning average or even below-average incomes into wealth in the millions of dollars by the time they reach their 30s, 40s, and 50s.

And they will also develop habits that will enable them to continue to grow their wealth even while they begin to put a portion of it to good use when they begin to raise their own families.

What's more this illustration of the wealth that can be built up through cradle-to-retirement investing does indeed *accurately* demonstrate the remarkable power of compounded interest over time.

After all, when you consider that Warren Buffet, Peter Lynch, and Mario Gabelli (who all began investing as children) have personal funds ranging from hundreds of millions to billions of dollars, these projections can seem rather *modest* by comparison!

But we're getting way ahead of ourselves. The point is, even if your children invested only $15 a week during their college years and never invested another dime, they could still end up with a multi-million-dollar sum!

That's the power of compounding *when you invest early*.

But the main reason to make sure your children invest 10% during their college years is something else. And it's just as important.

Keeping the Faith

Your children should continue to save a predetermined rate even during the lean college years because this is when they'll learn, that *even when money is tight*, if you've developed the right habits, you can always put a little something away to consistently build wealth.

After all, the great mistake most young adults make is they think they don't have "enough money" to invest when they're in their teens or twenties.

The Chief Financial Officer Who Wishes He Had Begun to *Invest* (Not Just "Learn" About Investing) During His College Days

A friend of mine is the chief financial officer for a $100 million company. He's very bright and knows the ins and outs of finance and accounting.

And yet he told me once that when he was in college — studying accounting and finance — someone advised him he should begin to invest just a few dollars at that time because it would eventually pay off big.

But his reaction was the same as mine was when I first began my career and passed up the chance to participate in a 401(k) program. He thought starting so early was unnecessary. He was sure he'd make good money one day, and at that point he'd be able to invest big chunks of money and grow rich quickly.

Yes, he's gone on to make a good living. But, like 99.9% of the population, he never got to the point where he could invest those huge "chunks" that would make up for the fast compounding of wealth he passed up by not investing just a few dollars back in his college days.

How Thomas Jefferson Could Have Left
an Even Greater Legacy If He Had
Learned to Manage His Money

Thomas Jefferson is considered a true genius. He was the principal author of the Declaration of Independence, one of the most important political documents in history.

During colonial times, he served in the Virginia House of Burgesses and also served as governor of that state.

He helped plan Washington, DC, paving the way for its transformation from a swamp into a world-class city along classic republican architectural lines.

After the colonies achieved independence, Jefferson became the first U.S. Secretary of State, the second Vice President, and the third President of the United States.

As president, he orchestrated the largest single land purchase in history, the Louisiana Purchase, which practically doubled the size of the country with the stroke of a pen.

He also planned the Lewis and Clark Expedition, which would bring important information back about the unexplored country west of the Mississippi.

In retirement, he founded the University of Virginia, and during his entire adult life he was an avid student of architecture, philosophy, and the arts.

Like Franklin, he was a true Renaissance man. But there was one practical area of his life he had considerable difficulty managing — money.

Jefferson was an idealist and a romantic, but he had great appetites too. He liked good wine, imported cheeses, fine books, tailored clothing from France, and quality furnishings and materials for his home, Monticello.

The trouble was, he often spent more than he made - and he almost never managed to save any money.

When Jefferson's father-in-law died, he and his wife inherited 11,000 acres and 14 slaves. In his writings, Jefferson made clear that he detested slavery as a moral and even economic wrong. Yet he felt he could not afford to maintain the property without the slaves, and in order to try to make the estate profitable he even bought more slaves.

To appease his conscience, he planned on freeing these slaves at his own death. Yet this man — who was so talented in so many ways — never got control of his money. And, because of that, he died broke and in debt, and was unable to free his slaves.

He's building wealth steadily now. But he realizes that if he had begun investing just 10% of his income in college (when he was supposedly *learning* about money!) — and gotten just the average market returns since then — he'd have perhaps *triple* the wealth he has today.

And, of course, if he had been on the *Seeds of Wealth* program since he was a child, he could easily be a millionaire today, before his 40th birthday!

The point is, the few dollars your children invest during their college years should multiply many times over by the time they're in their forties, fifties, and beyond. And, more importantly, by impressing upon your children the importance of saving 10% while they're in college, you'll help them learn there's never an excuse to not build wealth!

They'll always know how to enjoy the income they have, while using some of that income to continually grow their wealth.

What's more, because they'll be coming from a childhood during which they saved 50% of every dollar they made, saving just 10% (even of a very small income) will be a piece of cake!

Stage 4, Ages 22-28 (Single Working Adult), Save 15% of Income.

For the sake of illustration, from time to time we have to make assumptions about a typical child or young adult. Obviously, the case will be different for each person.

As children, some will be able to put away a little more than others. As young adults, not all will go to college. Others, meanwhile, will enter the workforce making an average salary, and some may start their careers making a great deal of money right off the bat.

This program works for everyone. But in order to _show_ you how the program works, I will use average incomes as examples. This is to demonstrate that even if your children never have "a lot of money" to invest they can acquire serious wealth by applying this system faithfully over time.

So, in stage 4 (ages 22-28) we are going to assume for the sake of argument that your children are single during this period. And during this time, they should save (no ifs, ands, or buts) 15% of their income.

(All the saving percentages, by the way, are *pre-tax* figures. More on this a little later, when we get into Better Budgets for Young Adults in Part IV.)

Now, again, even if they make just an average income as college graduates, saving 15% of their income by this time should not be difficult.

After all, they're making a great deal more money now than when they had to scratch by with very little income in college. They don't have to take care of any dependents. Saving 15% is still relatively easy when they compare it to the fact that they used to save 50% regularly. And they understand, from experience, the enormous benefits this practice yields for them.

I'll go into this stage in a bit more detail too in just a bit. For instance, I'll show you a budget and how a recent college grad making an average income for his age bracket and education level (about $725 a week) can easily support himself and save 15% of his income without great sacrifice.

For now, however, we'll keep in mind that you should strongly convey to your children in their late teen years before they leave the house, that once they're on their own they should save at least 15% of their income.

(They don't need to save a penny more than 15%, but if they have money to spare, it's likely they will want to put aside more because saving, investing, and building wealth will be ingrained habits by now.)

Stage 5, Age 29-30 (Married, No Kids), Save 15%.

When the day comes that your children marry, they're getting closer to the point that they may actually begin to *need* some of their acquired wealth to provide for their families. But between the time they marry and the time they have their first child, there is no reason for them to decrease their savings ratios. During this period, they should continue to save 15%. After all, as the old saying goes, "Two can live cheaper than one." (It's when a *third* arrives that things start to get expensive!)

In fact, when your children marry, if their spouse works too, this is an opportunity to save even more money and create even greater wealth. If both spouses save 15%, it's highly likely they can achieve a million-dollar nest egg by the time they're 40, and quite possibly much more. (On page 78, we'll talk more about the kind of wealth created under this scenario.)

Stage 6, Ages 31 Onward (Married with Children), Save 10%.

For the purposes of our income projections, we'll suppose that from the age of 31 onward, your children are beginning to have children of their own. At this point they only have to save 10% of income. That's still a great deal more than the average American saves (with a 3.7% savings rate as of mid-2003). But the 10% number is right in line with what *used* to be considered standard practice — before the era of the credit card.

And, again, if your children's spouses work too, it can be 10% of the combined income, and the wealth will grow all that much quicker. But (as I'll show you in detail a little later) even if only one spouse works, and makes just an average salary for a college graduate, the wealth should soon (within the next five to ten years) begin to approach seven figures.

And, again, the 10% savings will be second-nature and not a brutal sacrifice. It will be relatively easy after a lifetime of saving at higher ratios, and after many years of seeing those savings turn into incredible wealth through high-growth, long-term investments...

GETTING STARTED:

How to Turn These Few Dollars into a Fortune

Let's fast forward for a moment, and take a look at how those savings rates against even modest levels of income can lead to tremendous wealth over time — simply because you got your children to begin investing early.

The table that begins on the opposite page tells the story.

Examples of Wealth Built Up by *Seeds of Wealth Investor* Since Childhood at Different Rates of Return

Age	Income	Saving Rates	Invest	At 10.2% Returns	At 13.2% Returns	At 18.8% Returns
1	$730	100%	$730	$804	$826	$867
2	$730	100%	$730	$1,691	$1,762	$1,898
3	$730	100%	$730	$2,668	$2,821	$3,121
4	$730	100%	$730	$3,745	$4,019	$4,576
5	$730	50%	$365	$4,529	$4,963	$5,869
6	$730	50%	$365	$5,393	$6,031	$7,406
7	$730	50%	$365	$6,345	$7,241	$9,233
8	$730	50%	$365	$7,395	$8,610	$11,402
9	$730	50%	$365	$8,551	$10,159	$13,979
10	$730	50%	$365	$9,825	$11,914	$17,041
11	$730	50%	$365	$11,230	$13,899	$20,678
12	$730	50%	$365	$12,778	$16,147	$24,999
13	$1,300	50%	$650	$14,797	$19,015	$30,471
14	$1,300	50%	$650	$17,023	$22,260	$36,972
15	$5,200	50%	$2,600	$21,624	$28,142	$47,011
16	$5,200	50%	$2,600	$26,695	$34,800	$58,938
17	$5,200	50%	$2,600	$32,283	$42,337	$73,107
18	$7,800	10%	$780	$36,436	$48,808	$87,778
19	$7,800	10%	$780	$41,012	$56,134	$105,207
20	$7,800	10%	$780	$46,055	$64,426	$125,913
21	$7,800	10%	$780	$51,612	$73,813	$150,511
22	$37,828	15%	$5,674	$63,129	$89,980	$185,548
23	$37,828	15%	$5,674	$75,821	$108,281	$227,172
24	$37,828	15%	$5,674	$89,808	$128,997	$276,621

Age	Income	Saving Rates	Invest	At 10.2% Returns	At 13.2% Returns	At 18.8% Returns
25	$44,281	15%	$6,642	$106,288	$153,543	$336,517
26	$44,281	15%	$6,642	$124,449	$181,330	$407,673
27	$44,281	15%	$6,642	$144,462	$212,784	$492,206
28	$44,281	15%	$6,642	$166,517	$248,391	$592,632
29	$44,281	15%	$6,642	$190,822	$288,697	$711,938
30	$53,292	15%	$7,994	$219,095	$335,854	$855,279
31	$53,292	10%	$5,329	$247,315	$386,220	$1,022,402
32	$53,292	10%	$5,329	$278,414	$443,233	$1,220,945
33	$53,292	10%	$5,329	$312,685	$507,773	$1,456,814
34	$53,292	10%	$5,329	$350,452	$580,832	$1,737,026
35	$65,093	10%	$6,509	$393,371	$664,870	$2,071,320
36	$65,093	10%	$6,509	$440,668	$760,001	$2,468,461
37	$65,093	10%	$6,509	$492,789	$867,690	$2,940,265
38	$65,093	10%	$6,509	$550,227	$989,594	$3,500,767
39	$65,093	10%	$6,509	$613,523	$1,127,588	$4,166,645
40	$66,894	10%	$6,689	$683,475	$1,284,002	$4,957,921
41	$66,894	10%	$6,689	$760,561	$1,461,063	$5,897,957
42	$66,894	10%	$6,689	$845,510	$1,661,496	$7,014,720
43	$66,894	10%	$6,689	$939,123	$1,888,386	$8,341,434
44	$66,894	10%	$6,689	$1,042,286	$2,145,225	$9,917,571
45	$70,451	10%	$7,045	$1,156,362	$2,436,370	$11,790,444
46	$70,451	10%	$7,045	$1,282,075	$2,765,946	$14,015,417
47	$70,451	10%	$7,045	$1,420,611	$3,139,026	$16,658,685
48	$70,451	10%	$7,045	$1,573,277	$3,561,352	$19,798,887
49	$70,451	10%	$7,045	$1,741,514	$4,039,426	$23,529,448
50	$61,341	10%	$6,134	$1,925,909	$4,579,574	$27,960,271

Age	Income	Saving Rates	Invest	At 10.2% Returns	At 13.2% Returns	At 18.8% Returns
51	$61,341	10%	$6,134	$2,129,111	$5,191,021	$33,224,089
52	$61,341	10%	$6,134	$2,353,040	$5,883,180	$39,477,505
53	$61,341	10%	$6,134	$2,599,810	$6,666,703	$46,906,564
54	$61,341	10%	$6,134	$2,871,751	$7,553,652	$55,732,285
55	$68,951	10%	$6,895	$3,172,267	$8,558,539	$66,218,146
56	$68,951	10%	$6,895	$3,503,437	$9,696,072	$78,675,349
57	$68,951	10%	$6,895	$3,868,386	$10,983,759	$93,474,506
58	$68,951	10%	$6,895	$4,270,560	$12,441,420	$111,055,904
59	$68,951	10%	$6,895	$4,713,755	$14,091,493	$131,942,606
60	$59,728	10%	$5,973	$5,201,141	$15,958,331	$156,754,911
61	$59,728	10%	$5,973	$5,738,239	$18,071,592	$186,231,930
62	$59,728	10%	$5,973	$6,330,121	$20,463,803	$221,250,629
63	$59,728	10%	$5,973	$6,982,376	$23,171,786	$262,852,843
64	$59,728	10%	$5,973	$7,701,160	$26,237,223	$312,276,273
65	$59,728	10%	$5,973	$8,493,260	$29,707,298	$370,991,308

The table shows how your children can build a fortune of between $219,095 to $855,279 in a single generation, starting with a few dollars a day, and even go on to create a million-dollar-plus fortune within a few years after that.

Let me explain the numbers...

Average Returns Can Lead to Wealth Far Above the Average

13.2% is the average compounded annual return of the S&P 500 from 1950 to 2000 (which includes 9 official bear markets, including the bear market of the 1970s and the Crash of '87). The chart shows that just averaging this long-term total return of the stock market, your children can start by averaging a couple of dollars a day in savings through the pre-teen years, and end up with $335,854 by the age of 30.

At the same rate of return — and simply earning average incomes for college graduates — they become millionaires before their 40th birthdays.

But the market in this case is the S&P 500, which represents the 500 largest companies in the United States. While these are the biggest and most successful companies in the country, they are not necessarily always the ones that offer the greatest profits for long-term investors.

In fact, in 1999 and 2000, I warned repeatedly in investment newsletters that the S&P 500 was overvalued. In mid-2003, I think it still is. If you happen to agree, you would not put new savings into the S&P 500 at this time. There are better options.

Yet the performance of the S&P 500 from 1950 to 2000 shows the kinds of returns you can achieve when you invest in a market sector when it does offer value and the potential for strong, long-term growth. And, fortunately, the S&P 500 is not the only game in town. When it is overvalued and likely to fall or post meager returns over the next few years, there are other sectors of the market that are fairly valued or even *undervalued*. That means these value-laden sectors are more likely to post compounded returns in the low- to mid-teens over the long term.

Stratospheric Investment Strategies

For instance, James O'Shaugnessy studied the results of various investment strategies from 1952 to 1994. In his book *What Works on Wall Street*, he reported that investing in stocks with the lowest price-to-sales and high earnings growth rates posted compounded annual average returns of 18.4% during that period. When he updated the figures two years later, in his book *Retire Rich*, he found the performance of this strategy had actually improved, producing 18.81% annual returns between 1952 and 1996.

Christopher Graja and Dr. Elizabeth Ungar, meanwhile, in their book *Investing in Small Cap Stocks*, looked at the performance of different types of small caps (stocks with total market values in the bottom quintile, or lowest 20%, of the market) from 1975 to 1997. He found that small-cap value stocks returned about 18.8% during that time.

If your children target these kinds of strategies and get these returns, they would achieve a $855,279 fortune by age 30 from the same income and savings.

Later in this guidebook we'll also look at how your children can diversify into real estate investing. That will likely be when they're young adults. But if you're already a real estate investor, we'll show you how they can invest with you now in real estate — even while they're in grade school. And we'll show you how real estate can provide them a low-risk way to use the power of leverage (making money on borrowed money) to turn 4% to 5% annual increases in the value of their investment properties into the equivalent of 10-15% compounded annual returns on their original investments.

But, getting back to the stock market, there are other strategies that have provided even higher returns over long periods of time than the maximum 18.8% projection we use in the table on pg. 45.

For instance, O'Shaughnessy also reports that between 1952 and 1994, microcaps (stocks with market caps less than $25 million during this period) produced 20.38% compounded annual returns during this period. At the same time, Mary Buffet (the former daughter-in-law of Warren Buffet) tells in her book *Buffetology* how Buffet produced 23% compounded annual returns for his investors over a 32-year period...

Warren's First Seeds of Wealth

By the time Warren Buffet graduated from high school, he had made enough money from stock market investments to purchase a 40-acre farm!

Low, Middle, and High Projections

For the purposes of our projections, we won't use Warren Buffet's numbers or the return of micro caps. To keep it relatively conservative, we'll use 18.8% as our "high-performance" number. And we'll consider 13.2% middle-range returns because though that's the compounded annual average return of the S&P 500 between 1950 and 2000, your children will be focusing on investment strategies that have proven to outperform the S&P 500 during long periods of time.

Finally, to be somewhat conservative, we knock three percentage points off the 13.2% long-term return of the S&P 500 to get a 10.2% "lowball" estimate of possible returns. This is a tad less than the roughly 10.4% compounded returns posted by the S&P 500 during the entire 20th century (including the massive bear markets of the Great Depression). And yet, even at 10.2%, we see that your children can still end up turning just a few dollars a day into over $219,095 by age 30.

That's quite impressive, considering that most 30-year-olds are only just beginning to save and invest at that point. It's also a sizeable nest egg that can multiply into significant money from there. By his mid-40s, for instance, it would turn into over a million dollars.

And that's after investing for 46 years at a rate of return three percentage points *less* than the recent long-term market average. And it doesn't even include the steady portions of income they'd be adding to their investments along the way.

Ultimately, then, your children could easily achieve a seven-figure financial fortune by their mid-40s — even if the stock market over the next half century performs not nearly as well as it did in the last half of the 20th century.

Your Children Can Acquire Significant Wealth Even if They Make Average or Below-Average Incomes

You'll notice that for the income assumptions in our chart we use round numbers through the age of 21 and very specific numbers after that. That's because between the ages of one through 21 (while your children are at home and then in college) we use modest assumptions, which I'll explain in a moment. Then, from the age of 22 onward, we use 2002 U.S. Census Department figures for average earnings for college graduates working full-time, year-round.

Here's how it works:

From the age of 1 through the age of 12, we assume your children's average income is about $2 a day, or $730 a year. For the first 4 years that income would come from gifts from you, the parents, and from friends and relatives. Of course, it's quite possible they'll do better still.

At my youngest boy's baptism a few years ago, for instance, he received nearly $500 on that single day. Take into account the dollar allowance he got that year, the checks he received from his grandmother and a few uncles and aunts on Christmas and his birthday, a little household chore money here and there, and he is easily above the $730 mark.

Other years, he may "make" a little less, while other years he may make considerably more so that assuming a $730 average from the ages of 1 to 12 is very reasonable.

Allowing for Allowance

According to a Yankelovich Youth Monitor Survey, the average allowance for kids under 12 is about $5.90 a week—or just over $300 a year. Add $5 a week in chore money and that's another $250. Throw in $100 for miscellaneous holidays and $100 in birthday money, and you have well over $730 in "income" in a fairly normal year.

For the ages of 13 and 14, we assume the child makes an average of $25 a week, or $1,300 a year. This reflects the expectation that the child should begin to do some part-time work during these years. Again, the surveys bear this out. The average allowance for kids 12 to 17, according to the Nickelodeon/Yankelovich Youth Monitor Survey, was $16.60 a week, or $863 a year. For many of these children, some of that "allowance" may include chore money. Yet, if you add in holiday and birthday money and special occasion gift money and a few dollars they may begin to make around the neighborhood mowing lawns and such, it shouldn't be difficult to have your 13- or 14-year-old earn $1,300 in total income.

("Special occasion gift money," by the way, can include anything from cash gifts for Confirmations or Bar Mitzvahs to rewards for good report cards and cash gifts for graduation from grammar school, and jr. high school, etc.)

Combine all these different types of income together, and even if your 13- or 14-year-old only makes $20 a week during the 40 weeks of the school year, and triple that ($60 a week) during the 12 weeks of summer vacation, that still adds up to over $1,500 a year.

(In Part IV, we'll discuss ways children can learn to work, learn about money, and make money — spending a fixed portion and investing the rest — from the ages of 5 through 17.)

The High School Years

From the ages of 15 to 17, we assume the child makes $5200 a year. This boils down to an average of $100 a week. Not hard to do working one full day a weekend and a few extra days a week during the summer — at almost any job.

For instance, one of my brothers and I used to average over $100 a week working two weekend nights per week as busboys and then waiters in high school. And that was *in the mid-'70s!* Friends of ours, meanwhile, would often make $80 to $100 or more caddying Saturdays and Sundays. (A little later on, we'll cover the best employment opportunities for kids in this age group.)

During the college years, we assume the child averages $7,800 a year, or an average of $150 a week.

When I was paying for 2/3 of my college tuition and costs 20 years ago, I put in a few nights a week as a bartender and averaged over $200 a week. More recently, a friend of mine who graduated from college in 1997 got his classmates to subsidize his study time. He made about $1,000 a month by selling research reports for $100-$250 each. Combined with a few odd jobs over the summer, he was able to average over $200 a week while still getting good grades.

I give these examples only to point out that today to average $150 a week shouldn't be hard for any student with any gumption at all.

Average Assumptions for College Grads Working Full-time

Moving on to the working years, the income assumptions are again modest. We assume your children now make an average salary for a college graduate, according to their age bracket. (These averages are taken from the U.S. Bureau of the Census' 2002 figures.)

In addition, we'll look at how your children can continue to build significant wealth even if they make as much as a third *less* than the average college graduate. In this case, we'll assume your child has opted for a lower-paying job for one reason or another and only "makes his/her age." That is, he/she makes $22,000 at the age of 22, $23,000 at the age of 23... $30,000 at the age of thirty.

In this way, you'll see that even if your children make *substantially below the average for a college graduate*, they can still end up with net worths of over a quarter million dollars in their early 30s and even more than a million dollars by their early 40s. Simply because they started to build their wealth — and develop good money habits — early on.

What's more, even when we use the average incomes for college graduates, in the context of this program, these assumptions are still likely to turn out to be low estimates.

Why? Because any child who has gone through this program has had the experience of growing money, has developed the ability to follow a disciplined plan, and has a first-hand understanding of the importance of following a plan. And that means he or she is likely to be much _more_ than an "average" earner once reaching the workforce, anyway.

But we only use average income assumptions — from childhood, right on through college and into their working years as adults living on their own. At the same time, for our principal table, we only assume a single earner.

In effect, that results in income assumptions of perhaps 25-30% less than if one of the spouses worked full-time while the other worked half-time. It's also just half of what the numbers would be if there were two college-graduate parents working full-time. And it's *less* than half of what the numbers would be with one degreed professional (lawyer, doctor, architect, etc.) in the household working full-time.

So keep in mind that if your children wind up with incomes greater than the averages, they can achieve significant wealth even sooner. If they average 50% greater income than the average, they'll end up with 50% more in savings and investment. And (keeping investment return assumptions the same) that means they'll end up with 50% greater wealth than is shown in our tables.

At 18.8%, for instance, if your child makes 50% more than the assumed average figures, instead of having $855,279 at the age of 30 — he or she will have $1,282,918... Millionaire at the age of 30!

The point is, these aren't inflated numbers. Have your children follow the *Seeds of Wealth* program consistently, and it's very possible they could end up with many millions of dollars at a relatively young age...

The Average Investor Does Nowhere Nearly as Well

The stock market became more popular than ever, as the bull market made a record run from 1982 to 2000. Because of this, there were suddenly millions of people who knew very little about investing who believed the minute they got "enough money to invest," they were going to double their money every couple of years on Internet stocks — and end up filthy rich.

In mid-2003, we were three years into a nasty bear market. And now there are millions of investors who believe the whole game is rigged and you can't make money in the markets unless you're an insider.

Both of these ideas are extreme and therefore wrong. There are good and bad players in any area of life — and that includes public companies. If you steer clear of the hype, and consistently invest in a diversified way in good companies selling at good values, you can compound your wealth at double digit rates of return over the long term.

More importantly, between the extremes of greed and fear is a key point that most investors miss. It has to do with how you get rich in the first place.

Growing up at the right time — just as a bull market is starting, for instance — doesn't make you rich. Getting lucky on a hot biotech stock and making ten times your investment doesn't make you rich. In fact, making a lot of money at your job doesn't even make you rich.

Consistently keeping a portion of the money you make and knowing how to invest so it consistently grows through all sorts of markets... *that's* what makes you rich! But this is the crucial area about which most of America's young investors have absolutely no idea. They barely even save...

As of mid-2003, the personal savings rate in the U.S. is 3.7%. Over the last five years, it's averaged 3.2%. These are the lowest numbers since the Great Depression. And these low savings rates have been statistically "enhanced" recently. Since October 1999 the Bureau of Economic Analysis has begun to include government employee pension contributions in their calculations. It's the first time they've ever done that. Before that change was applied to 2000 figures, the savings rate actually went *negative* during one quarter of that year!

That is not a way to build wealth.

In fact, even if we assume the "typical investor" begins to save right out of college (which is not the case), and even if we assume a savings rate of 4% (above the average of the last five years), he doesn't come anywhere close to amassing the kind of wealth the *Seeds of Wealth Investor* does.

Here's a snapshot comparison that tells the story. All income assumptions for the typical investor and the Seeds of Wealth investor are the same — identical to those used in the previous table. Getting the same rates of return, the "typical investor" barely acquires a six-figure net worth by the time the Seeds of Wealth investor is already a millionaire.

Same Exact Income, Same Investment Returns...
Seeds of Wealth Investor Ends Up with 6 to 17 Times the Wealth!

Wealth Created at 10.2% returns

Age	Typical Investor	S. of W. Investor
20	–	$46,055
25	$8,046	$106,288
30	$25,438	$219,095
35	$56,260	$393,371
40	$109,101	$683,475
45	$195,542	$1,156,362
50	$336,429	$1,925,909

Typical investor, invests 4% from age 22 @ 10.2%

Seeds of Wealth investor, @ 10.2% since childhood

Wealth Created at 13.2% returns

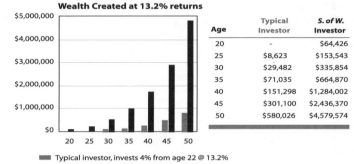

Age	Typical Investor	S. of W. Investor
20	–	$64,426
25	$8,623	$153,543
30	$29,482	$335,854
35	$71,035	$664,870
40	$151,298	$1,284,002
45	$301,100	$2,436,370
50	$580,026	$4,579,574

Typical investor, invests 4% from age 22 @ 13.2%

Seeds of Wealth investor, @ 13.2% since childhood

Wealth Created at 18.8% returns

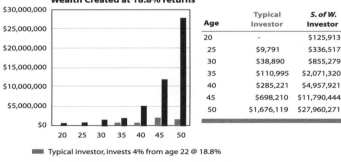

Age	Typical Investor	S. of W. Investor
20	–	$125,913
25	$9,791	$336,517
30	$38,890	$855,279
35	$110,995	$2,071,320
40	$285,221	$4,957,921
45	$698,210	$11,790,444
50	$1,676,119	$27,960,271

Typical investor, invests 4% from age 22 @ 18.8%

Seeds of Wealth investor, @ 18.8% since childhood

Assumes "typical investor" begins investing 4% of income from age of 22. This is a generous assumption on two counts: first, most investors don't start investing until after the age of 25. Second, the average savings rate for the past few years (1998-2002) has been 3.22%, significantly below 4%.

With *Seeds of Wealth* your children can end up with wealth dozens, even hundreds, of times greater than they would normally have. And it doesn't require them to get astronomical investment returns. The wealth builds up to a much greater degree simply because they begin to follow a sensible savings and long-term investment program far earlier than the typical investor.

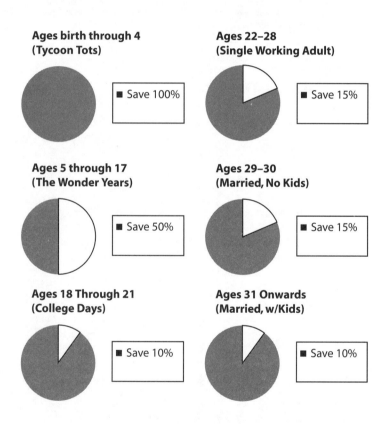

So let's begin immediately, since the sooner your children begin, the greater the benefits will be. We'll start by offering them a million dollars...

Getting Your Children to
Sign onto the Program

"Kids, how would you each like a million dollars?"

Try that at the dinner table. It's a guaranteed attention-getter.

The reactions will range from surprise to excitement to humor to skepticism. A general commotion will likely ensue. Simply repeat the offer because you're making it in all seriousness.

"I'm going to tell you kids how you can each make a million dollars by the time you're my age, maybe a little bit older, even if you never make a lot of money as grownups.

"In fact, I'm going to do more than show you, I'm going to actually help you make that million, starting today. You ready?

"First, I'm going to give each of you two dollars. It's my gift to you. And it's a small gift. But it's also the beginning of a great amount of wealth that you yourselves are going to create as you grow up. Sound good?

"Okay, here's how it works. One of the two dollars I'm giving to you now, you can spend however you please — on candy, Magic cards, combining it with some other money you have to buy something else… whatever you want.

"The other dollar you're going to save — permanently.

That means you're not going to spend it for any reason whatsoever for at least 30 years, maybe longer. So far, so good?

"Every other dollar you receive from now on — whether it be for allowance, a birthday present, Christmas present, chore money, or money you find in the street — you're also going to save half permanently and spend half however you like.

"You keep doing this, and I'll help you, and in a few months you should have a hundred or maybe even a few hundred dollars in your permanent savings. At that point, we'll count it out together and I'll invest it for you.

"By 'invest' I mean I'm going to buy a piece of a company, or companies, for you. You're going to own small pieces of businesses. What do you think of that?

"Now you're going to continue to save fifty cents of every dollar you get for as long as you live at home.

"Once you grow up and move out on your own, you'll make your own decisions. I will advise you now, though, (and I'll remind you later) that when you become a grownup, you should save and invest 15 cents out of every dollar you get. And if one day you decide to raise a family of your own, at that point you'd save and invest just 10 cents out of every dollar you get.

"Again, when you become young adults living on your own, you'll make those decisions for yourselves. But at least at that point, you'll know how to steadily create wealth. You'll know how to make sure you never lack money. And the chances are very good you'll actually soon have a great deal of money — as much as a million dollars or more when you're about my age.

"But that's far down the road. I only mention these future savings rates now so you can get the idea of how these habits will develop for you over time. For now, though, until you go to college or leave the house, you can spend half of every dollar you get however you like... and half you'll save.

"And keep in mind you're the ones who are going to benefit from this — because everything you put into savings and investment now you'll get back many times over in the future.

"In fact, the dollar you're going to put into savings right now will probably be worth somewhere around $40 thirty years from now, and maybe even $100, $200 or more. That's amazing, don't you think? That a single dollar can grow so much?

"Well, with time it can. And, what's more, the dollars you'll sock away as you're growing up can turn into a million dollars or more by the time you've got families of your own!"

You'll find the exact words to best express these ideas to your children. But this presentation should give you the general idea.

And in order to get them started immediately on the path to lifelong financial security, there's only one other thing you have to do...

The Two-Box System

The moment you first introduce the idea of saving and investing to your children, you're going to help make that idea a reality by doing two things. First, you'll give them two dollars so they can make their first allocation among spending money and savings. Second, you'll make sure they have two distinct boxes (or other receptacles) to put their money in.

These can be cardboard boxes, colored and designed by your child. They can be desk safes or piggy banks. One will be for their spending money (which is the same as "temporary savings"). The other will be for their permanent savings.

"The child is father of the man."
– William Wordsworth

And that's really all they need to _begin_ to build wealth and develop good money habits right away.

You'll explain how these two types of savings are to be used with an example — to make sure they understand the importance of always saving and investing before spending. To do that, you might say something along the following lines:

"One of these boxes is labeled 'permanent savings' and the other is labeled 'temporary savings.' They're both going to go on your dressers. Every time you get a buck, two bucks, twenty bucks, or a hundred bucks, half goes into the permanent and half goes into the temporary.

"I've just given you two dollars, so what's going to happen with those two?

"Right, one will go into the temporary savings and one will go into the permanent savings. From that permanent savings box you're going to grow a few dollars into a small fortune — or maybe even a big fortune — by the time you're around my age or a little older.

"The temporary savings you can spend whenever you want on whatever you want."

Now, it's time for an example to make sure they truly understand what you mean by "permanent savings."

"Let's say you get $20 from grandma, what do you do with it? Right, you put $10 in the permanent savings and $10 in the temporary savings.

"Now, what happens if you want to buy a new skateboard? Can you ever use money from your permanent savings to buy it?

"The answer is 'no.' You can buy the skateboard, but to do that, you'll have to get the money together from the temporary savings. The easiest way to do that is to set up a separate box for the skateboard. We'll call it the "Skateboard Fund" — and it's only to be funded from your temporary savings — *never* from the permanent.

The permanent savings are never to be <u>spent</u> for any

reason — at least until you're about my age. They're only to be invested so they can grow into a lot more money as you grow up.

"For instance, let's say the skateboard you want costs $80. You just got $20 from grandma so you put half, or $10, in the permanent savings. The other half, instead of spending it or putting it in the temporary savings box, you put into the new box for the skateboard — 'the skateboard fund.'

"About a month later, you get $100 over the holidays. Of this $100, you've got to put $50 into permanent savings. The other $50 you can spend, put it into your temporary savings, or into the skateboard fund.

"You spend $10 on candy and comic books and add $40 to your 'skateboard fund.' Since you had $10 in there previously, you now have $50 saved for the skateboard so far. You need just $30 more.

"A few weeks pass by, and you get $30 in birthday checks. That's the $30 you needed for the skateboard — but not so fast! Again, you have to put $15 of that into the permanent savings. Of the rest, you spend $10 on the movies and popcorn, and you add $5 to your skateboard fund. You've now got $55 put away toward the skateboard.

"Now you get another $60, this time from selling lemonade, washing cars, and doing chores around the house. $30 goes into permanent savings. You spend $5 on Magic cards... and add $25 to the skateboard fund. You now have $80 for the skateboard. That means you can buy it, *except...*

"You need $5 more for sales tax!

"You pick up $20 in allowance over the next couple of months, you put $10 in permanent savings, you spend $5 on candy, and $5 goes in the skateboard fund, giving you $85 total in the fund, enough to cover the skateboard and tax!

HOW TO BUY A SKATEBOARD AND GROW RICH AT THE SAME TIME

Income	Source	Add to Perm. Savings	Spend from Temp. Savings	Add to Skateboard Fund		Balance in Skateboard Fund	Balance in Perm. Savings
$20	Grandma	$10	$0	$10	→	$10	$10
$100	Holiday	$50	$10	$40	→	$50	$60
$60	Chores	$30	$5	$25	→	$75	$90
$30	Birthday	$15	$10	$5	→	$80	$105
$20	Allowance	$10	$5	$5	→	$85	$115

*Temporary savings is for spending money. The skateboard fund is an example of a special savings box — funded strictly from temporary savings/spending — that does not interfere with permanent savings.

"Now you can go ahead and buy the skateboard — it's all yours! You deserve it because while you've put the money together for this purchase, you've also added $115 to your permanent savings (equal to the $85 you put in the skateboard fund plus the $30 you spent on candy, comics, movies, popcorn, and Magic cards).

"Now, why go to all this trouble?

"Because by doing this you get your skateboard and get to buy some other small fun things as well — the candy, etc. But the $115 you invest at the same time is going to multiply anywhere from 30 to 40 times, maybe even 100 or 200 times in the next 30 years or more.

"The 'permanent savings,' in other words, is the part that's going to create a lot of money for you by the time you're about my age, long after you've retired the skateboard!"

A Fun-Filled Childhood

Let's take a break from the numbers for a bit. The numbers we just used aren't complicated, but there were a lot of them. So let's just leave numbers aside for a moment and talk about the most important thing — the reason you're doing this in the first place.

You're doing this to help your children live more successful lives as adults. The focus is on getting them to start creating their own futures today. But that doesn't mean for a moment that by involving your children in this program you're asking them to *forfeit a normal fun-filled childhood!*

On the contrary, these habits should help your children enjoy what they do have all the more without contracting the dreaded "Gimme Disease."

Preventative Medicine for the "Gimmes"

The Gimme Disease is a condition that a lot of middle-class kids get when they have everything handed to them on a silver platter. The more you give, the more they demand.

The end result is often an unhappy, spoiled child. And later that child can become an adult who is never satisfied — who never has enough "things."

I don't suggest for a moment that your children should work for every toy they get. You should treat them as the beloved kids they are and absolutely give them gifts for birthdays, holidays, good report cards, special achievements, and special occasions.

I would advise you to be careful not to overdo it, but certainly give them things they want and need — that you approve of and can easily afford — and give to them with love.

But at the same time, you're also going to give them a little balance, instruction, training, and discipline in handling money and material things. That's all. But that is a great deal.

As adults, they'll avoid the out-of-control spending habits that lead to unhappiness and plunge so many households into serious debt.

By helping your children follow this program with common sense and balance, they will still have plenty of fun-filled memories of playing with their friends, getting new toys, showing off their hip new clothes, or whatever the case may be. They'll just have a better financial future as well.

You're not going to *deprive* your children. You're simply setting good boundaries for their sakes.

This Course Is About Saving and Investing — We Don't Expect Your Children's Lives to Be Centered Around That

Before we continue, one other idea bears repeating at this point. This course is focused on helping your children build wealth and develop good money habits. But that doesn't mean we expect your instruction to them will be focused strictly on money.

In doing research for writing this program, I was surprised at how little truly useful material there is on helping children build secure financial futures. What's more, most of the few books and tapes I did find on this area shared a problem in that they seemed to assume that money was going to be all that the parents and children ever talked about.

This program will work well for children who are entrepreneurial from a very early age...

But it's also equally effective for children who show very little interest in money matters, and for children who show great interest in things other than money.

In other words, if your children are scientists in the making, or artists, or teachers, or scholars — that's great. You can let them follow the paths of their own talents and interests — without having to worry about their financial futures.

This course will help them painlessly build up financial competence, responsibility, and, yes, wealth at the same time. And it will do it without trying to take over their lives as the subject that should become their primary concern.

One of the fundamental ideas behind this course, in other words, is that natural-born merchants and deal makers shouldn't be the only ones who have "enough" money in their lives. Others who practice good money habits should also have the benefit of being able to turn savings into security and even wealth, over time.

This course will help children who are not business people by nature to gain a measure of control over their financial destiny. And that can enable them to pursue their own dreams and make a positive impact on society in accordance with who they are — without the fear of ending up broke, dependent, or in debt.

Another way to look at it is you'll enable your children to become their own patrons for their own particular geniuses. For hundreds of years, rich art patrons like the Medicis and the popes of Rome sponsored the Da Vinci's and Michelangelos so they could practice their craft. Today, your children can learn to be their own benefactors — whether their art ultimately becomes painting or teaching or trying to find new cures in a medical lab.

By mastering steady wealth creation techniques early on, they can pursue their dreams with confidence even and especially if those dreams have nothing to do with money...

"Annual income twenty pounds, annual expenditure nineteen pounds six, result happiness. Annual income twenty pounds, annual expenditure twenty pounds ought and six, result misery."

— Charles Dickens

Wealth, Security, and Good Money Habits

You have already told your children everything they need to know to begin to build wealth and achieve financial security by a very young age. As they continue to follow the program and as they see their wealth steadily grow over time, saving and investing will become self-reinforcing habits.

But to help them get started, let's also give them a glimpse of the future. Let's show them the pot of gold at the other side of the rainbow.

Depending on how old each of your children is, the method for doing this will vary. If he/she's just 5 years old, broadly explaining what we've already discussed can do the trick for now. "You'll save half of every dollar you get... I'll invest it for you for now, later you'll invest it with my supervision... And by the time you're my age you'll have a great deal of money!"

That's really all most 5-, 6- or 7-year olds will need. You automatically have authority with them. They trust you, as well they should.

However, for the more inquisitive tikes and for older children, it may be appropriate to go into a bit more detail right away.

One way to do that is to show them the table on page 45. Show them exactly the amounts of money they can achieve, with very little savings, at different rates of return over a number of years.

It's important to realize, however, that the table on page 45 shows the wealth accumulated if you begin this program from day one of a child's life. The following abbreviated tables give you an idea of the wealth achieved if your child begins the program at different ages — 5, 10, and 15.

Not surprisingly, the *Seeds of Wealth Investor* who starts the earliest builds 6- and 7-figure nest eggs at the youngest age.

Yet the ones who start a little later still do very well. In fact, in the course of 30 years, they make a bit more than the early starters make in 30 years — simply because their 30-year projections include more "higher-earnings" years. But by the same token, by the time the earliest starters get to their age, they'll have even more.

Wealth Accumulated By Seeds of Wealth Investor Beginning to Invest at Age 5		
Age	At 10.2% returns	At 13.2% returns	At 18.8% returns
5	$402	$413	$434
10	$3,119	$3,456	$4,178
15	$10,725	$12,421	$16,573
20	$28,341	$35,205	$53,884
25	$77,500	$99,226	$166,069
30	$172,309	$234,890	$451,937
35	$317,334	$477,197	$1,116,865
40	$559,899	$935,156	$2,699,330
45	$955,527	$1,787,936	$6,445,787
50	$1,599,511	$3,374,265	$15,312,848
55	$2,641,804	$6,318,115	$36,289,693
60	$4,339,029	$11,793,835	$85,933,192
65	$7,092,153	$21,966,343	$203,401,089

For the child who starts the *Seeds of Wealth* program at 5, getting the average market return (and always using the conservative average assumptions discussed previously), he/she winds up with $234,890 by the age of 30. That's a little over $100,000 less than the *Seeds of Wealth Investor,* who began as an infant, ends up with at the age of 30.

Still, by the time the *Seeds of Wealth Investor* follows the program for a full 30 years, at the age of 35 his/her wealth reaches $477,197 at average market return of 13.2%. And at the superior return of 18.8%, he ends up with over a million ($1,116,865) after 30 years of following the program.

Still a great deal of money at a very young age — and without ever having had a great deal of money to invest.

For kids who begin the program at 10 years old, the

projections are as follows:

Wealth Accumulated By Seeds of Wealth Investor Beginning to Invest at Age 10			
Age	At 10.2% returns	At 13.2% returns	At 18.8% returns
10	$402	$413	$434
15	$6,310	$6,765	$7,713
20	$21,165	$24,691	$32,918
25	$65,837	$79,683	$116,458
30	$153,354	$198,563	$334,538
35	$286,529	$409,672	$839,056
40	$509,835	$809,641	$2,041,931
45	$874,163	$1,554,629	$4,890,140
50	$1,467,277	$2,940,595	$11,631,617
55	$2,426,898	$5,512,010	$27,578,548
60	$3,989,762	$10,295,448	$65,319,420
65	$6,524,523	$19,181,145	$154,621,327

By starting at 10 years old instead of 1 day old, the 30-year-old *Seeds of Wealth Investor* has accumulated about $136,000 less than his/her earliest-starting peers accumulate by their 30th birthdays (assuming they all get the average market return of 13.2%). Nonetheless, your child has built up nearly a $198,563 nest egg in just 20 years.

At the same time, by the time he/she's followed the program for 35 years — a little more than a generation — even at average market returns, he/she's amassed over $1.5 million. At the 18.8% returns, meanwhile, he/she'll have amassed close to $5 million by his/her mid-forties, without ever having earned an above-average income!

For the *Seeds of Wealth Investor* who starts at the age of 15, the picture is as follows:

Wealth Accumulated By Seeds of Wealth Investor Beginning to Invest at Age 15		
Age	At 10.2% returns	At 13.2% returns	At 18.8% returns
15	$2,865	$2,943	$3,089
20	$15,567	$17,587	$21,976
25	$56,740	$66,479	$90,564
30	$138,569	$174,019	$273,265
35	$262,500	$364,050	$694,060
40	$470,782	$724,839	$1,698,819
45	$810,694	$1,396,998	$4,078,210
50	$1,364,126	$2,647,592	$9,710,291
55	$2,259,256	$4,967,375	$23,031,985
60	$3,717,310	$9,283,083	$54,560,581
65	$6,081,733	$17,299,363	$129,161,960

At the age of thirty, at long-term average market returns, the *Seeds of Wealth Investor* who started at 15 years old has a little more than half the amount accumulated by his/her 30th birthday as *Seeds of Wealth Investors* whose parents began the program for them at 1 day old.

Nonetheless, this "late starter" has still amassed over $174,000 in just 15 years — again, investing from just an average income. And by the time he/she's kept with the program a full 30 years, even at long-term average market returns, he/she's built up well over a million dollars ($1,396,998).

Finally, at 18.8%, this same *Seeds of Wealth Investor* reaches the million-dollar mark at the age of 38, even though he began to save and invest only at the age of 15. What's more, by the time he/she's followed the program for 30 years, at this higher rate of return, your child ends up accumulating wealth in excess of $4 million by his/her mid-forties.

Not bad for a "late starter!"

Better Paid, More Savings and Investments... More Wealth Sooner

Okay. Why sell ourselves short? We'll leave the average projections for a single-worker household aside for a moment and look at the kind of wealth that will be created if your children are in two-earner families.

Under these assumptions your child follows the *Seeds of Wealth* program from infancy through the age of 27, just as in our table on page 45. From the age of 28, however, we assume your child marries someone who also works and earns the average income for a college graduate. In effect, with a two-earner household, the income assumptions from 28 to 65 are doubled.

Seeds Of Wealth Fortune Created For Two-Earner Couples					
Age	Income	Invest	At 10.2% Returns	At 13.2% Returns	At 18.8% Returns
27	$44,281	$6,642	$144,462	$212,784	$492,206
28	$88,562	$13,284	$173,837	$255,910	$600,523
29	$88,562	$13,284	$206,208	$304,728	$729,203
30	$106,584	$15,988	$244,859	$363,050	$885,287
35	$130,186	$13,019	$472,541	$756,005	$2,189,745
40	$133,788	$13,379	$856,308	$1,501,548	$5,294,575
45	$140,902	$14,090	$1,482,829	$2,890,412	$12,645,273
50	$122,682	$12,268	$2,503,067	$5,474,401	$30,042,857
55	$137,902	$13,790	$4,152,540	$10,267,881	$71,200,177
60	$119,456	$11,946	$6,839,842	$19,185,389	$168,602,667
65	$119,456	$11,946	$11,196,830	$35,749,735	$399,079,024

*Assumes young adult has been saving and investing since childhood and so begins married life with anywhere from $144,462 to $492,206 already accumulated. From that point, the two-earner couple saves and invests twice as much as in the single-earner projections on page 45.

The above scenario could equally apply to a *below-average* estimate of the type of income your child might make as a single-earner professional. (The average income for degreed professionals in 2001 was $113,725, according to the Bureau of the Census. That's *almost twice* the $59,683 figure for college grads.)

Alternatively, this scenario would also cover a situation where your child makes, say, 50% above the average and his or her spouse makes perhaps half the average income in a part-time job.

Either way, the two-earner projections are still very feasible. And, with this kind of household income and following the *Seeds of Wealth* program, your children can become very wealthy very quickly.

At one extreme, getting superior returns of 18.8%, they can acquire fortunes in the hundreds of millions of dollars. At the other extreme, even if your children net a full three percentage points less than the long-term average of the stock market, they will still do very well indeed.

Getting just 10.2% annual compounded returns, for instance, this would make them millionaires by their early forties and could ultimately leave them with a retirement nest egg of over $11 million — even after getting _below-average_ returns for their entire invest-ment careers!

And none of this takes into account, by the way, the home equity your children would build up as competent managers of their own money. Nor does it take into account the appreciation of other assets they may acquire (such as a business, art, or collectibles) outside of their financial investment activities.

It's impossible to predict exactly what income your children will make or what investment returns they'll get. Yet, as we'll see in the next section, there are steps you can take to increase the likelihood of average to above-average returns. And there are steps you can take to put your children on a regular saving and invest-ment program from a very early age that will leave them far, far better off than the average investor.

And, as we've already seen, the sooner your children begin, the better. The more wealth they'll build up over time and the sooner they'll develop important money management habits.

But whether your children today are 1, 5, 15, or 25, if you get them to start planting the seeds of their own wealth today, they can have a lifetime of financial security and abundance ahead of them.

Wealth Accumulated By Age 50	
Begin Seeds of Wealth program at age:	Wealth Accumulated at 10.2% returns
15 years	$1,941,285
10 years	$2,044,436
5 years	$2,176,669
1 day old	$2,503,067
Begin Seeds of Wealth program at age:	Wealth Accumulated at 13.2% returns
15 years	$3,542,419
10 years	$3,835,423
5 years	$4,269,093
1 day old	$5,474,401
Begin Seeds of Wealth program at age:	Wealth Accumulated at 18.8% returns
15 years	$11,792,877
10 years	$13,714,203
5 years	$17,395,434
1 day old	$30,042,857

*The above tables show the wealth accumulated by age 50 for Seeds of Wealth Investors beginning at different ages and getting different rates of return.
** All tables assume two-earner income from age 28 onwards.

How Savings Can Grow into Wealth

For children under 12, what we've discussed so far should give them enough of an explanation of why they're saving and how those savings will be invested and grow into significant wealth over time.

To recap, they're using their savings to buy small pieces of companies. And as those companies make money, your children make money as part owners of the companies. Over time, the amount of money a company makes each year tends to grow, and that means the value of those companies grow. In turn, the value of your children's "shares," or pieces of companies, grows.

That should suffice until about the teen years. At that point — perhaps a bit sooner, depending on the nature of your child — a little more detailed explanation of how and why investments grow in value may be in order. To explain this, we have to begin with the financial force that Albert Einstein allegedly called...

"The Most Powerful Force in the Universe"

Legend has it that Albert Einstein was once asked what was the most powerful force in the universe. He answered, "Compound interest!"

No doubt, Einstein was joking. People were probably expecting him to say something like nuclear energy or gravity. But, when it comes to money, what he said was absolutely right. Nothing grows money over time like compound interest.

To explain this all-important concept, we should naturally first explain the concept of interest. That's a pretty easy one.

Interest is simply when your money makes money. If you lend $1 to someone and he/she gives you $1.10 back, you made ten cents interest (or 10%). If he/she pays you back $1.20, you made 20 cents interest on a dollar — or 20% interest.

The idea of compound interest is a little trickier. But basically it's pretty straightforward.

Compound interest is when the interest on your money makes interest. Even at the same interest rate, compound interest makes your money grow by a greater amount each year.

And that can make a very big difference over time...

How to Turn a Penny into $21.4 Million

If you take a penny and double it every day for a month, do you know how much you would come up with?

A hundred dollars?

A thousand dollars?

How about a million dollars?

Not even close.

Starting with just a single penny, if you double it every day for 31 days you end up with...

$21,474,836.48 — Over Twenty-one million dollars!

This is an example of the power of compound interest. The original penny turned into 2, but then those 2 turned into 4, and the 4 turned into 8, and so on... The growth of your money <u>accelerated</u> or sped up because not only was your original penny collecting interest — but all the pennies you received as interest also began to earn interest. And so the growth built up — or compounded.

That's how you get the term compound interest.

And that's how you get rich.

Now, it's just about impossible to double your money (or get 100% interest) every year — let alone every day. But the power of compounding still applies whether the interest rate is 100% or 10%. And, even at 10%, compounding will make your money grow by a larger amount each year.

Let me give you a quick example...

Compound Interest Adds Up in a Big Way

You lend someone the same $1 we talked about, and he pays you the same $1.10 after a year. You've made 10% interest. Now let it compound.

When he pays you back, you lend him the money again — but this time you lend him $1.10. The next year he owes you $1.21. You made 10 cents interest in the first year and 11 cents interest in the second year.

Why?

Because in the second year you were collecting interest

on your interest, too. You got 10% not of a dollar, but 10% of $1.10 — and that equals 11 cents.

So now you have $1.21. During the third year, that $1.21 earns just over 12 cents in interest. Because now it's the original dollar and the 21 cents you received in interest that are earning interest.

It's compounding in other words. And every year the amount of interest you earn on that original dollar will increase. As a result of the compounding, your investment grows geometrically over time — like a snowball rolling down a hill, becoming bigger and bigger.

But instead of a lot of snow, you end up with a lot of dough — money, that is!

Interest Collected On A Single Dollar Invested At 10%		
Number of Years	Value of $1 Compounded at 10%	Yearly Interest
1	$ 1.10	$ 0.10
2	$ 1.21	$ 0.11
3	$ 1.33	$ 0.12
4	$ 1.46	$ 0.13
5	$ 1.61	$ 0.15
10	$ 2.59	$ 0.24
20	$ 6.73	$ 0.61
30	$ 14.75	$ 1.59
40	$ 45.26	$ 4.11
50	$ 117.39	$ 10.67
100	$13,780.61	$1,252.78

Notice that your original investment has grown by more than two-and-a-half times by year 10, by nearly seven times by year 20, by more than 100 times by year 50, and by more than thirteen thousand times by year 100! And the reason for this accelerated growth is that the amount of interest earned on your original single dollar investment goes up every year.

At the end of 50 years, you're getting over $10 in interest every year on the original one-dollar investment. By year 100, you're getting yearly interest equal to over twelve hundred and fifty-two times your original investment!

And here's another important point about compounding: Every percentage point counts a great deal.

Why? Because if, for instance, you double your interest rate — over time you'll end up with <u>far more</u> than double the wealth.

Let's take a look at how that works by looking at what happens to a single dollar when compounded at 20% annual returns.

<u>How to Turn a Dollar into $82.8 Million</u>

The following table compares the growth of a single dollar at 10% versus 20% annual compounded interest rates.

	Double the Interest Rate Creates More Than Double the Wealth			
Number of Years	Compound Total @ 10%	Yearly Interest earned on $1 at 10%	Compound Total @ 20%	Yearly Interest earned on $1 at 20%
1	$1.10	$0.10	$1.20	$0.20
2	$1.21	$0.11	$1.44	$0.24
3	$1.33	$0.12	$1.73	$0.29
4	$1.46	$0.13	$2.07	$0.35
5	$1.61	$0.15	$2.49	$0.41
10	$2.59	$0.24	$6.19	$1.03
20	$6.73	$0.61	$38.34	$6.39
30	$17.45	$1.59	$237.38	$39.56
40	$45.26	$4.11	$1,469.77	$244.96
50	$117.39	$10.67	$9,100.44	$1,516.74
100	$13,780.61	$1,252.78	$82,817,974.52	$13,802,995.75

*All figures refer to an original investment of a single dollar.

Compare the growth of a single dollar at 20% with the growth of that dollar at 10% and you'll notice some important differences. By year 10, even though you're getting double the interest rate, you have more than doubled the wealth — about 2.4 times the wealth. And the farther along the time scale we go, the greater that difference becomes.

By year 20, getting just twice the interest rate, you end up with nearly six times the wealth. And by year 100, twice the interest rate ultimately results in more than six thousand times the wealth!

In fact, by this time, you've turned that single dollar into over $82.8 million!

That's the power of compound interest.

The Snowball (or "Doughball") Effect

Compound interest begins to work right away. The second year you're already making more interest than the first year, and the third year you're making more than the second year and so on... even though you're always receiving the same interest rate.

The longer you stay the course, in other words, the greater the wealth build-up becomes.

That's why, by beginning to invest small amounts regularly during childhood, you can build up great wealth by the time you're about the age your parents are now.

Time, in other words, is your greatest strength as young investors. You have your whole lives ahead of you. And that means you can take maximum advantage of the power of compound interest.

And you don't have to wait 100 years to build significant wealth. After all, you're going to be investing more than a single dollar.

By investing a few hundred dollars a year from a very early age... and then a few thousand dollars a year as you get older... the miracle of compounding will create 6- and 7-figure wealth for you that much sooner.

In the tables on pages 45, you can see how you can acquire hundreds of thousands of dollars by the time you're in your 30s, and millions of dollars by the time you're in your 40s.

It's simply a matter of investing modest amounts from an early age and letting the power of compound interest — and time — do their thing.

Don't Let the Snowball Melt

I highly recommend the exact saving ratios in this course, for reasons I'll go into in a moment. However, these ratios are obviously not set in stone.

Nonetheless, *if*, for whatever reason, you decide to tell your children they must save only 40% of income while at home, you must stick to that ratio.

You can't constantly change the ratio, and you can't make it a "sometime" thing.

The whole point of discipline is to follow a program consistently. If the savings guidelines end up being vague or if the whole idea of saving is initially introduced as "optional," your children won't have clear lines to follow. And the chances of them developing good money habits are significantly reduced.

The essence of discipline in any area of life is to follow a program even on the occasions you'd rather not.

How many Olympic champions would come to stand at the top of the podium if they trained only when they felt like it? And how many great scholars, scientists, and Nobel Prize winners would rise to the top of their fields if they studied only when it was easy and there was nothing else to do with their time?

Point is, there are always options. There are always different things you can do with your time *and* with your money.

The people who tend to achieve the most in different

areas of life tend to be those who have developed the discipline to make the hard choices when necessary — because they understand dedication and consistency are necessary to achieve their goals.

In a similar fashion, *you* have to be consistent in laying down the guidelines for your children. And you have to show like-minded dedication in guiding your children along.

Now, having said that, I would strongly urge you follow precisely the savings and investment program outlined above — without modification. They have been carefully thought out, and tested. And I believe these saving ratios are the best for a number of reasons.

First, they are significant percentages so they will help your children build real wealth that much sooner.

Second, by getting your children to save 50% during childhood, over time you will help make saving and investing at least as important in his mind as spending.

Third, by beginning with what some might initially consider a high rate (50%), your children will be able to undertake the subsequent lower rates of savings with relative ease.

Fourth, 50% savings as a child should really not be much of a sacrifice since (as explained) children at this stage have 100% disposable income... and because spending greater amounts of money does not lead to greater happiness. In fact, the development of the idea that the amount you spend is connected to your level of happiness is ultimately likely to lead to unhappiness.

Fifth, a 15% savings rate as a single adult (or married adult without children) is very doable without great sacrifice, as will be shown in our Better Budgets for Young Adults section. (Also, consider the fact that many rapidly developing countries such as Chile and China have income levels 1/6 to 1/30 that of the U.S., yet they also have personal savings rates of 20% or more!)

Sixth, a 10% savings rate for married couples with families used to be the standard, and should be absolutely no problem for a person who has developed good saving, investment, and money management habits over the course of a lifetime.

In short, while these ratios may at first blush seem high (especially in a society where young people have far more experience with credit cards and consumer loans than with saving), they are designed to help create maximum wealth over time — even working from very modest resources, or income.

What's more, the different savings ratios coincide with different stages in a child's and young adult's life so that the process is not a burden. It becomes automatic and not a cause for missing out on any of the really good things life has to offer.

Also note that if you're especially ambitious to help your children achieve financial security early on, that doesn't mean you should *increase* these ratios.

First, arbitrarily increasing the ratios can be a discouraging experience (they've done what you've asked them to, but now you want more). Second, you can and should impress upon your children that they can always save and invest more if they like. They just can't save less.

The ratios are minimums, in other words, not maximums.

For instance, when one of my sons was seven and received $440 for First Communion, he readily agreed to have us invest about $350 of it for him. Since he had no plans to spend $220 (though we would have let him do that if he wanted to — it's part of the deal), he was content to have us invest an extra-large portion of the "windfall income" for him.

Be firm in your commitment, and your children will be firm in theirs. The result, over time, will be significant compounding wealth for your children.

Out of Balance

According to the 1999 Youth & Money Survey sponsored by the American Savings Education Council, only 18% of students between the ages of 16 and 21 own stock or a mutual fund. However, 28% use a credit card.

"For Each Hundred"

"Percent" comes from the Latin *per*, meaning "for," and *centum*, meaning "hundred." Together, then, percent means "for each hundred."

"Annual" is another English word that comes from the Latin. It comes from *annus*, meaning year, so "annual" means yearly. Put percent and annual together, and you can understand how interest is charged.

If someone lends you money for one year at 10% interest, that simply means that, at the end of the year, for each hundred cents they lent you, you will pay them back that hundred cents plus 10 cents — or ten per cent interest. And if they lend you a hundred dollars, you pay them back the hundred dollars plus ten dollars interest.

If they lend you $200, meanwhile, the same idea applies. You simply pay them back the original $200 plus ten dollars for each hundred. Since they lent you two hundred, the interest you pay them is equal to two tens, or $20.

PART III

Cultivating Good Habits — and Nipping Bad Habits "in the bud"

Separating the Good from the Bad

Okay, you've given your children a clear idea of the wealth they can build by always putting away a portion of their income. You've set up the two-box system and you've clearly spelled out the savings rates they are to follow. You're committed to monitoring their progress and you're ready to regularly take their permanent savings — every time they have $100-$200 or so — and invest it for them.

You've taken some very important steps, in other words, to help your children begin to develop good money habits. Now, to make sure these actions have the maximum positive effect on their futures, you want to make sure they don't offset the good habits with bad habits.

There are two primary *bad* money habits: borrowing and overspending.

You can consider these to be two sides of the same coin. After all, if you overspend, you will likely have to borrow. And if you're constantly borrowing money, you are spending future income. And that means you're spending more than your current income.

Still, let's look at these damaging money traits separately to keep the ideas as uncomplicated as possible.

An Example of Good Debt: Borrowing to Buy a Home

Until recently homeownership was often the only serious wealth-building device for most middle-class people. Today, more people are investing in the stock market than ever before so that's changing. Nonetheless, home ownership is still a central part of wealth accumulation for a great many people. And if you're a homeowner, you are likely to be *much* better off than non-homeowners.

According to a recent Harvard study, for instance, homeowners 55 years or older have a median net wealth *33 times* greater than renters in the same age bracket!

Also, among people who make $50,000 or more a year, the median net worth for home-owners was *more than four times* the net worth of renters in the same income bracket.

This difference is principally due to the build-up of home equity. And it supports the case that mortgage debt is highly beneficial whenever the interest and property taxes you end up paying are equal or very close to what you would have paid in rent. Because, when you basically convert rent money into mortgage payments, you end up controlling a great deal of borrowed money virtually interest-free.

Yes, you're paying interest payments and property taxes along the way. But they are both tax-deductible. And so the net cost to you of your mortgage payments (including principal, interest, and property taxes) should be very close to what you would have paid in rent anyway. *And you've got to live somewhere!*

So, you put $20,000 down on a $100,000 house, and what do you get?

You get *tax-deferred* (and usually tax-free) compounded capital gains year after year on the full $100,000. (In effect, over time you make money not only on your down-payment, but on the money you borrowed. That's low-risk leverage, and it can help turn 4-5% annual gains on the value in your home into 10-15% gains on your initial investment.)

You get asset diversification (away from financial assets and cash).

You also get (if you have a fixed-rate mortgage) the assurance your "rent" won't go up. (In fact, one day, if you live in the house long enough, it will actually go down 80-90% or more — to just the property taxes and maintenance.)

And you get to be the owner of your own home... That's a great deal!

In the investment section, we'll talk more about the benefits of home ownership as an important wealth-building component. We'll also talk about how buying rental properties can be a low-risk, high-return investment for your children when they're young adults (or even now, if you, the parent, are already a real estate investor).

For now, however, whenever the subject of debt comes up, you can let your children know home ownership is one of the *few* examples of good debt.

Another Example of Good Debt: Financing College Education

College education can be the single best investment your children ever make. For one thing, they can learn things that can inspire them to make more of their lives. For another, it's necessary if you want to enter a professional field such as law, medicine, or architecture. And, last but not least...

Statistics show beyond a shadow of a doubt that college graduates tend to make much more money than non-college grads.

A Big Earnings Advantage

According to the U.S. Bureau of Census, the average earnings for high school graduates (all age groups) in 2001 were $32,906. The average earnings for all college grads, meanwhile, *were more than 80% greater than that figure — $59,683!*

That's a huge difference. In fact, the annual earnings advantage is *almost three times* the annual cost of the average public university (about $8,500 per year for tuition and room and board in 2000). What's more, the cost of college is incurred usually for four years (though you may finance it over a longer period), but the earnings advantage lasts for an entire working lifetime.

Multiply that average annual earnings advantage ($26,777) over a 44-year working career (from age 22 through 65), for example, and you have more than an extra million dollars in income!

To take the comparison a little further, you can pay 25% tax on those extra earnings, spend half of the rest, and invest half of the rest at, let's say, 10%... and at the end of 44 years, you'll have an extra $6,553,410.

On the other hand, if you had foregone college altogether and invested $37,500 over four years (the current average cost for four years of room, board and tuition at a public college), you now end up with $2,259,002.

Not bad, but by going to college you ended up more than $4.2 million richer (approximately $6.5 million minus approximately $2.3 million) at the end of your working career.

Plus, you had, on average, an additional $10,041 (after taxes and additional savings) to spend each and every year of your working life.

Plus, hopefully, you had good experiences in college and are a bit smarter because of the education.

There's no doubt about it. College pays off big — in many ways. But even if you weigh it *only* in financial terms, it's likely to be an excellent investment.

And that's why it's one of the few good reasons to

borrow money. The long-term monetary rewards are likely to be much higher than the cost of borrowing money to finance your college education.

Car Loans: An Exception to the Debt Rule

The one type of loan that is not an investment, and yet represents a reasonable cause for taking on some debt — is a car loan. Since cars are a necessary item for most people, a car loan can be a prudent debt — as long as the car is "bought right," and the loan is a good deal.

In the Smart Money Tips for Young Grownups section, in the appendix to this guidebook, we'll talk about

---

Not All Debt Is Created Equal

There are two types of debt: good and bad. Good debt helps you make money (with low risk). Bad debt costs you money. And the more your debt costs you the worse it is.

Good debt can be a mortgage to buy a house. Another form of good debt could be the mortgage you take out to buy a house, apartment building, or commercial property you're going to rent to others. Yet another form of good debt can be the money you borrow to pay for your college education.

Bad debt is money you borrow to buy "stuff" that tends to decrease in value over time, instead of increase in value — much as a good investment does.

---

how you can do just that. We'll discuss how to help your children determine how much car they need and can truly afford without cutting into their savings.

We'll discuss ways to buy good cars at below-market prices, how to get together a down-payment for a car without touching the investment nest egg, and how they can get someone else to pay for the depreciation of a "like-new" car.

We'll also tell you ways you can make sure that first second-hand car your child buys is mechanically sound (even if you or your children are not mechanics), we'll look at ways to get good financing deals, how to save on car insurance, and why leasing is usually a very *bad* idea.

For now, however, we'll simply concede that borrowing to buy a car is one of the few non-investment uses of debt that can be a reasonable thing to do.

The Good, the Necessary, and the Bad

We've talked about home mortgages and college loans being examples of good debt, since they are for investments that historically have provided returns far above the cost of the loans. We've also talked about car loans as possibly a "necessary" debt, the cost of which can be kept in check by taking steps to buy the right car at the right price (depending on your child's income at the time) and getting the right financing for the car.

So, now that we've talked about the good and the necessary... It's time to talk about the ugly... The kind of debt that <u>doesn't</u> make you money, that actually eats away at your wealth — and your chances for *future wealth* — the kind of debt that is far too prevalent in America today...

Bad Debt: Consumer Loans

In order to develop good money habits, we can't only talk about the bright side of things. We also have to try to steer our children away from widespread *bad habits.* And just as loans to buy a home are usually good debt, consumer loans are almost always very ***bad*** debt! And, unfortunately, they're bad habits that have become a way of life for many people.

According to the Federal Reserve's Flow of Funds report, U.S. households increased their borrowing 130% between 1997 and 2002, from $333 billion to $768 billion. At the same time, however, they increased their income by only 29%, from $6.9 trillion to $8.9 trillion.

Total assets of households, meanwhile, fell by $973 billion between 1999 and 2002. Yet total liabilities (or debts) soared by $1.9 trillion during the same period.

That's a very unhealthy combination. But the fact is, things are only getting worse.

As of 2002, consumer debt in the U.S. exceeded $1.76 trillion. That's a 425% jump since 1980, versus only a 291% increase in personal income over the same period. And debt is continuing to grow faster, increasing by 3.5% in 2002— versus only a 2.8% rise for income.

These borrow-and-binge habits are reflected in the fact that the national personal savings rate has plummeted to the lowest levels since the Great Depression.

But it doesn't have to be this way. Boom times like the '90s don't have to mean binge times. And times of slow economic growth and recession (like 2001-03) don't have to mean you have to borrow just to get by.

By teaching your children good money habits early, they can take advantage of boom times to grow their wealth, not their debt. And they can be well prepared to weather any economic threats that might arise during recessions. And the first step to reaching this level of financial security is to recognize why consumer debt is almost always "bad debt."

What Department Stores and Credit Card Companies Don't Want You to Know

If you get used to carrying credit card balances and revolving consumer loan balances every month, you might as well get used to the idea of living paycheck to paycheck and struggling to get buy.

Kill the idea of consumer debt once and for all, however, and you've eliminated a major obstacle on the route to major wealth.

To understand why I say that, let's take a look at what consumer loans are, in essence, and how they hurt your long-term chances for financial success.

Consumer loans are loans you take out to buy things you consume or use for personal purposes, not for a home and not for the purpose of making a profit. These can

---

include installment loans on furniture, personal computers, and appliances. Or they can be credit card debt you accumulate on everything from nights out on the town to clothing purchases.

The thing to always remember about consumer debt is, almost without exception,...

Consumer debt increases your costs and reduces your wealth.

It accomplishes these dual dastardly deeds in two ways...

Interest and Depreciation: Bad Debt's Henchmen

Consumer debt increases the costs of things. The moment you buy something on credit, you pay the normal price plus interest. But it's not just the cost of the item that increases — your *cost of living goes up, too!*

The nature of debt is that you're buying something with money you don't have. And since you're going to pay for it over time, your monthly payments must now go up.

And this is the insidious way that consumer debt begins to diminish your wealth. Your monthly disposable income is now reduced by the new monthly payments you must make to pay off the debt. And that's even while the thing you bought on credit immediately loses value.

A Good Investment Tends to Rise in Value. Even the Best Consumer Goods, However, Tend to Fall in Value

Let's say you buy a $1,000 jumbo-screen TV on credit at

13.77% interest (the average credit card interest rate in mid-2003, according to *Consumer Reports*). If you pay it off over a year, you pay a total $1,138. At the end of that year, however, if you wanted to sell the TV, you'd probably be lucky to get $700 for it.

That's the nature of consumer goods. They depreciate (or lose value) very quickly. An investment, on the other hand, generally *gains* value over time.

That doesn't mean you're not going to buy "stuff." Of course, you will and you should. Just don't borrow to do it. If you want a $1,000 jumbo TV, create a temporary savings box for that purpose, *without* interfering with your permanent savings. And the moment you have the $1,000, buy it.

This will simply ensure that you're buying things you can afford, and that you're always growing your wealth at the same time. Why? Because you'll always continue to add to your investments, but you won't be adding to your debts.

Don't Become a Debt Junkie

To get a good idea of how quickly consumer goods depreciate, you can always try the following experiment.

The next time you see a "great deal" advertised in the newspaper, a magazine, or on TV, try to sell the same item yourself at the same price.

For instance, let's say see you see a state-of-the art stereo system going for $1,600. Normally, one with that kind of speakers, CD player, etc., etc., would easily run $2,000.

Don't buy it. Just write an ad that you're selling the stereo system and put it up at your local neighborhood supermarket, but offer the same stereo for $1,600.

If you get some calls, just direct them to the advertisement so they can follow up on the deal themselves. But chances are you won't get a single inquiry. In fact, if you put the ad up at $1,000, you'd be lucky to get one or two inquiries.

That's because the *resale* value of a consumer good is almost always far less than the *retail* value. After all, when buying at retail, a customer usually gets a warranty. And if he knows and likes the store, he has a certain amount of confidence that the product should be of decent quality.

But once that product passes into a consumer's hands, it plunges in value. Unlike an investment, which should rise in value over time, the longer you own a consumer good, the more value it is likely to lose.

Now, the fact is, the $1,600 stereo may indeed be a good deal. *But only if you already were in the market for a stereo in the $2,000 price range.*

In other words, if you had already planned on spending about $2,000 on a stereo of similar quality — and you had saved the money out of your temporary savings — then the sudden appearance of this deal is a good thing.

Go ahead and buy it. You will save about $400 off of what you were likely going to spend, <u>and you'll be using money you had already budgeted and put aside for the purchase</u>.

But don't imagine for a moment that it's an investment.

That stereo is still going to lose a good chunk of value the minute you take it out of the box.

The lesson is: don't be suckered by "great deals" and "limited-time-only" offers to make purchases *<u>you weren't planning on making</u>*! And, especially, don't be suckered in by these come-ons to buy consumer goods on credit.

Credit cards and installment plans aren't paid off with Monopoly money. They cost you real money, and actually cost you more than a purchase on cash terms would.

What's more, if you get into the habit of buying on credit, you can easily find yourself accumulating a lot more things than you otherwise would.

The result is you'll end up with a lot of "high-priced junk" and a lot of high-cost bills taking a big bite out of your paycheck every month

Overspending Is the Mortal Enemy
Of Wealth Accumulation

One of the reasons America is "dissaving" (or spending more than it earns) is sky-high credit card debt balances. Credit cards were designed to make *purchasing* things easier. Not more affordable, just easier to acquire.

Credit cards make things more expensive, but people treat them as if they make things more *affordable*. "It'll only be $50 a month, and I can have it *now*," is the thought. But ultimately, at $50 a month, they end up paying much more than the price of the product.

The only way to actually make things more affordable, is to buy it at a discount or to *make more money*. Credit cards do neither of those things for you. They make things more expensive and cut into your future income.

Credit cards, in other words, are the compulsive spender's self-destructive weapon of choice.

This is why you need to make sure your children don't follow the financial example of the crowd. And it's why it's so important to nip consumer spending on credit in the bud. Otherwise, the more your children earn, the more they'll spend. Just as is happening all across the country today.

But we know it's almost impossible to accumulate wealth without consistent savings. And your children can't save if they develop out-of-control spending habits. Instead, they'll live day to day. If their earnings should fall for whatever reason, they'll have nothing to fall back on.

Continued on pg. 108...

Don't Pay $20,624 for a $2,000 Computer

Over time, regularly buying consumer goods on credit has a very, very high cost.

Let's say you buy a $2,000 brand-new computer on credit. The one you had serves your needs but the new one will do things for you faster and quicker.

First, over 36 months and at a 12% interest rate, say, your new computer will end up costing you not $2,000 - but approximately $2,500. (It would be $2,498 to be exact, but we'll use round numbers to keep it simple.)

Second, at the end of that 36 months, that computer will be worth, on the resale market, perhaps a third of the original list price - or say about $700. Your total cost, then, to use this computer for three years was $1,800 ($2,500 - $700 = $1,800.).

If, however, you waited, let's say, a year to be able to buy the computer for cash, you would have been better off. First, you would have been exercising discipline, waiting to make sure you can afford something before you can buy it. Second, after three years, the computer ends up costing you $1,300 ($2000-$700 resale value), not $1,800.

Take that $500 difference and compound it over 30 years at the 13.2% long-term returns of the market, and the impulse buy on credit could actually end up costing you much more — $20,625 over the course of thirty years!

Now add the long-term costs for other credit purchases year after year, and you can begin to see today's debt habits can literally end up costing you millions of dollars in future wealth.

Far too often we read stories of famous athletes and entertainers who have made millions of dollars in their career only to end up penniless and in debt. (See page 8 for examples.) Sometimes it may be because they had no financial training themselves and ended up relying on others who turned out to be incompetent or dishonest. Other times, it's because they simply could never get a handle on their spending.

So, the moral is — there are only two ways to make sure your children don't overspend:

Number one — make sure the first thing they do with their income is save their fixed percentage (half, while they're at home).

Number two — teach them to never borrow for consumption.

Credit Cards Are Negative Investments — Practically Guaranteed to Eat Away at Your Wealth

There are hundreds of thousands of people today who hold "safe" government bonds paying in the neighborhood of 4% even while they constantly have credit card balances with interest rates of 13%-16% or more. They could get, in other words, three or four times the returns of a government bond — *guaranteed* — simply by paying off their credit cards.

But the reason most people don't pay off their credit card debt is because purchasing on credit has become a *habit*. They can avoid hard choices *now*, even though they will eventually pay more for what they buy on credit and even though the debt they take on today will reduce the amount of money they'll be able to spend tomorrow.

Never Ever, Ever, Ever, Ever, *Ever*
(Did I Say "Never"?)
Let Your Children Borrow from
Their Permanent Savings

Perhaps the best way to make sure your children don't develop bad habits once they're adults living on their own, is to make sure they don't borrow money while they're kids, growing up at home. At the same time, it should be made clear to them that, under no circumstance whatsoever, are they to borrow from their permanent savings.

If they want something but don't have the money for it at the moment, they must learn to exercise patience and discipline. Chances are they'll learn that just about everything they come to feel they "have to have" is something they don't really have to have at all. And it's often something they'll soon forget about as they get enthusiastic about some other new thing.

Look back to pages 64. for a discussion on how your children can save for large purchases out of their temporary savings and never encroach on the all-important, inviolable, permanent savings.

The Third Box:
Special Purchase Funds

(To be financed strictly from temporary savings)

Instead of letting your children borrow to buy things they really want, you can do them a much better service by teaching them to save up for it. And one of the best ways to do that is to use a separate savings box that *does not interfere at all with the permanent savings*.

A few years ago, my children began this idea on their own. They wanted to buy a CD-burning, Internet-connected, Playstation II with DVD. The product cost $299 and my oldest son convinced his two youngest brothers it was something they should get, so he started his own savings box for it.

For every $1 they got, 50 cents still went into the permanent savings and 50 cents went into the temporary savings. But from time to time he and his brothers would go into their temporary savings (_never_ their permanent savings) and take out a dollar or 2 to put it into the Playstation II box.

Within nine months, they had the $299 plus tax, just a few months after the product was released. They now owned the Playstation free and clear — and they did it while continuing to build their own future long-term wealth.

The Choices We Make Define Who We Are

Fairy tales are beautiful things for children. But when adults believe in them, the results can be disastrous.

That's why part of the responsibility of a parent is to gradually wean our children off fairy tales as they grow older and help prepare them for the real world.

In matters of money, however, so many children become young adults while still entertaining fantastic notions about earning, spending, and saving.

Well, the fact is, you _can't_ have it all. You can have plenty. You can have all that you need. And you can even have _more than enough_. But you can't have it all.

Life involves choices. You can't have an athlete's physique and eat bags of potato chips each night. You can't become a scholar and spend all your free time watching TV. You can't build wealth while spending money on every impulse, borrowing money, and constantly spending more than you earn.

The word "decide," comes from the Latin *decidere*, meaning "to cut off." Whenever we choose to do or have something, we choose not to do or have some other thing. Even if we're not consciously aware of that fact, that's the way it works — for everybody.

Ultimately, we define who we are by the decisions we make. And the sooner your children learn to balance their short-term desires against their long-term goals, the better the chance they have of making decisions that will serve them well in both the short and long run.

Consumer debt and spending sprees are usually ways to satisfy short-term desires at the expense of long-term goals. The more people give into short-term impulses, including but not limited to short-term debt and spending impulses, the less control they have over their lives in the long run.

The Deal on Debt, in Brief

Let's summarize what you can tell your children about debt.

Consumer debt — Very, very bad. Never, for no reason.

Mortgage debt — Fine. As long as you 1) buy right

(more on that in the real estate section, in Appendix B), and 2) don't buy more house than you can comfortably afford.

College debt — No problem. Just reduce your college costs first (see Smart Money Tips for Young Grownups, in the appendix). And make sure money isn't the only thing invested during the college years. The willingness to study and take advantage of the college opportunity must be there, too.

Car debt — Okay. Unlike mortgages and student loans, car loans aren't likely to make you richer or smarter. However, given that a car is usually a necessity, the loan can be a prudent one if you keep your car payments within 5% to 8% of gross income. But be sure to do research and determine _separately_ the value of the car you're buying, available financing terms, and the value of your trade-in if you have one. (More on this in the car section, in Appendix C.)

Investment debt — Depends. This can be a sensible choice. It depends on how much, how it's arranged, how well you and the lender understand the risks, and whether or not you have a plan in place to limit the risks. But unless you have an incorporated business, the only investment debt most people should consider is for real estate.

All other debt. As a rule of thumb — _fogeddabout it!_

For children in their pre-teen years, all they really need to know at that point is that debt for consumption helps many people become poor — but never helps anyone get rich (except for the lenders!).

The Power
Of Compounding Wampum

In 1624 Peter Minuit reportedly bought Manhattan Island from the local Indians for the equivalent of $24 in trinkets. If the Indians had invested those trinkets at 8% annually, by 2000 they would be worth more than $88.6 trillion dollars. That's more than twice the value of all the goods and services produced in the entire world in 1999!

When you make a good investment, you get the power of compounding working for you. When you borrow to buy "stuff" that doesn't go up in value, the power of compounding is working against you.

It won't end up costing you $88.6 trillion, but it will increase the cost of the stuff you buy. And it can eat away at your chances of building a good amount of wealth by a very young age.

SEEDS OF WEALTH

PART IV

Tilling The Earth
(or they've got to rake it in
before they sock it away)

Jobs for Junior

So far, we've discussed the importance of creating a regular savings and investment program at the earliest possible age. We've discussed how to incorporate this practice with the teaching of other good money habits — from avoiding wealth-destroying debt, to creating temporary savings funds for special purposes. Now it's time to take a look at the income side of the equation.

How can you see to it that your children "make" total income roughly in line with our projections on page 45. As we've already demonstrated, our income projections for ages 22 onwards are conservative because they are simply average income numbers for college grads as reported by the U.S. Bureau of the Census — and it's very possible your children will make more than the average once they've been practicing good money habits since childhood.

But let's focus on the income side through the pre-teen, teen, and college years. And let's begin with allowances. Then we'll move onto chore money and part-time and spot jobs.

Once again, the goal here is to show you how easy it is for your children to make the incomes shown in our average income projections. This way, you can see more clearly how your children can save and invest roughly in the amounts (or more) shown in the projections on page 45 , and — ultimately — create the kind of wealth shown in the same projections...

Allowance: To Give or Not to Give?

What are the pros and cons of allowance? Should you give your children one? If so, how much?

According to a T. Rowe Price survey, only 39% of children under 16 report getting an allowance. The Youth & Money Survey by the American Savings Education Council, meanwhile, also reports only 39% of children say they receive an allowance or other money from their parents on a regular basis.

The argument against allowance is that your children may get the mistaken notion that you can get something for nothing. But as long as the allowance is moderate and they regularly save a portion of it, you shouldn't have to worry about spoiling them.

On the one hand, they're your kids after all and *deserve* to be spoiled a little bit! On the other, with the discipline of saving half their income — including their allowance — you're not just giving them an allowance, but a chance to regularly exercise that discipline and build wealth at the same time.

So if you don't give them allowance, try to make sure you give them at least a part of their birthday and holiday gifts in the form of cash. And try to see to it

"Financial attitudes and habits developed when young — whether positive or negative — can last a lifetime and have a dramatic impact on an individual's ultimate economic security."

— 1999 Youth & Money Survey, sponsored by the American Savings Education Council.

they have enough opportunities to do paid chores around the house to make up the balance of what they need to meet their income and savings targets.

And if you do decide to give your children an allowance... What's a reasonable amount of allowance? Well, let's start with some averages...

A Few Dollars a Week Can Go a Long Way

In the Nickelodeon/Yankelovich Survey, children 5-6 averaged $2.57 a week in allowance, while the overall average for kids ages 6-15 was $5.85 a week. In the T. Rowe Price Survey, for the 774 children ages 5-16 who did report an allowance, the average was $6.92 a week.

Depending on your income range and the age of your children, then, you might round off these figures and use $3 to $7 as a reasonable range. If you can swing it,

I don't see how it could be construed as excessive — since even the maximum is only a little more than a single hour of minimum wage pay, once a week. What's more, $182 of that $364 in annual allowance ($7 x 52 = $364) will go into permanent savings.

For the record, my wife and I give our kids considerably less. We like to give them some money as a no-strings allowance, but we also like to keep them a bit motivated to do extra work about the house if they want to accumulate money to buy a particular toy, game, or other item.

We happen to give our nine- and eleven-year-olds allowances of $2 and $3 each a week. And once they turn 12, they'll get four dollars, just as their older brother did. When each one reaches the age of 14 (as the oldest recently has), that's it for allowance. Still, at that point, they will continue to have _extra_ opportunities to make chore money at home, especially since they'll be older and presumably capable of more challenging jobs, like painting, minor carpentry, a little heavier yard work, etc.

But whether you give your children $5, $8, or $12 a week, it's important to take note of how much they're "making" in total income and, by extension, how much they're saving. If, for instance, you notice that over the course of the last six months or so, your child has only given you $100 from permanent savings to deposit, he's a bit behind schedule as far as depositing around $365 for the entire year goes (half of $730 in guideline income).

In that case, if his birthday or the holidays are coming up, you might give him a little more in cash gifts. At the same time, you can make an extra effort to make a few more age-appropriate chores available to him.

And speaking of chores, since they will be most children's first paid work experience, let's talk about them now...

"Work is the grand cure for all maladies and miseries that ever beset mankind."

– Thomas Carlysle

Home Improvement

There are two kinds of chores: paid and unpaid. Unpaid chores are the kind kids should do for no money at all — but simply because it's work that has to be done and they're part of the family. In our house, these chores include taking out the garbage and the recycle, walking and feeding the dogs, setting and clearing the table, patrolling the backyard for litter, and each keeping his own room in order and generally picking up after himself.

Clearly identifying unpaid chores is very important so that children know that family is about cooperation and sharing responsibility, and not negotiating for something for every bit of work someone might do within the house. But paid chores can be very helpful to children for a number of reasons.

Making sure there are enough paid chores available will help ensure your children can meet income, savings, and investment guidelines. It also gives them the chance to be a little ambitious if they want to be.

There can be assigned paid chores and optional paid chores. The assigned paid chores are work children are expected to do on a regular basis, but will also get paid for. Optional paid chores let them earn more *on their own initiative.*

Paid chores, by age group, might include those listed in the table.

And don't forget the fringe benefits of giving your children the opportunity of doing some paid chores: you can also give your spouse and yourself a break. Instead of you two doing everything — or trying to find good help (hard to do, as they say) — let your kids do some of the chores, handle a little more responsibility, earn some extra money, add to their savings, and plant a few more seeds of wealth.

Picking Up a Few Extra Bucks at Home	
Age	Chores
5-7 and up	Water plants Patrol yard for litter Clear lawn of small objects before someone else mows
8-10 and up	Wash cars Hose down garbage pails Sweep garage, patio and driveway Pull weeds

11-13 and up	Mow lawn
	Give dogs baths
	Wash windows
	Scour tubs
	Clean refrigerator
14 and up	Shovel
	Rake
	Paint
	Light handyman work
	Trim hedges
	Clean air conditioning vents
	Do lawn-edging

Pumping Up the Income:
Outside Work Usually Starts During the Teen Years

We're almost halfway through this course, and the kids have been picking up some extra money by doing chores around the house, but they've yet to bring home an actual paycheck. It's time to get 'em to work.

Through the age of 12, we assume the average child doesn't work, apart from the occasional chore. But once a child becomes a teenager, we can assume they're ready to accept a little bit of responsibility in the form of formal work, or "job." And so for the ages of 13 and 14, we assume the child has an annual income equal to $1,300.

To make a total of $1,300 at 13 or 14 requires an average income of $25 a week. Some of that we expect to still come from allowances, birthday, and holiday money. But most of it should come from part-time or spot jobs — whether it's occasional baby-sitting, mowing lawns, raking leaves, or shoveling walks.

So, if your 13- or 14-year-old gets a $5 allowance and still receives $100 in holiday money, $100 in birthday money, and $150 in chore money, that adds up to just over $600 a year he receives apart from a job. That means, to *"Work spares us from three evils: boredom, vice, and need."*
— Voltaire

meet our income projections of $1,300 at age 13 or 14, he now only needs to make $700 in formal jobs, or about $14 a week.

And even if he receives $100 or $200 less in allowance and other personal money, this simply means he has to make an additional $100-$200 over the entire year, or another $2 to $4 a week in job income. That would bring the total job income needed to $18-$20 a week for a 13- or 14-year-old — still a very modest figure.

So, whether your 13- or 14-year-olds pick up a good deal of money at home, or a modest amount, they can reach a total income of $1,300 a year with just a couple of hours of work a week.

On the following page are a few examples of how total income of $1,300 for a 13-14-year old might be achieved:

Below-average Allowance, Gift, and Chore Income

Allowance ($2 a week)	$ 104
Birthday Money	$ 50
Holiday Money	$ 50
Household Extra Chore Money	$ 50
Income from Outside Job (averaging $21 or 3 to 4 hours a week)	$1,092
Total Income	$1,346

Average Allowance, Gift, and Chore Income

Allowance ($5 a week)	$ 260
Birthday Money	$ 100
Holiday Money	$ 100
Household Extra Chore Money	$ 100
Income from Outside Job (averaging $16 or 3 to 4 hours a week)	$ 830
Total Income	$1,390

Above-average Allowance, Gift, and Chore Income

Allowance ($7 a week)	$ 364
Birthday Money	$ 150
Holiday Money	$ 150
Household Extra Chore Money	$ 150
Income from Outside Job (averaging $10 or 2 hours a week)	$ 520
Total Income	$1,334

Lean, Teen Earning Machines

In 1998 Teenage Research Unlimited (TRU) conducted a survey of 2,044 youngsters ages 12 to 19. The report showed the following breakdown of the teens' weekly income: 12-15 years — $32, 16-17 — $95, and 18-19 — $151 a week. This works out to an average weekly income for the teenagers of about $84, or $4,368 a year. In our assumptions, 13 and 14-year-old teenagers make less than a third of that, while teenagers from 15 through 19 make anywhere from 19% to 79% more than that. The overall result is that throughout the entire teenage years (13-19) we're right on target.

Adjust TRU's 1998 estimate of $4,368 upwards by just 3% a year over the last 5 years to partially account for inflation, and you'd have an average teenage annual income of $5,063 today. That's about 5% above the average income for teens (13 through 19) used in our assumptions.

What's more, I think anyone who has worked as a teen would attest to the fact that earning the kind of money we use as guidelines here should be a very doable task today.

> *"Go to the ant, thou sluggard; consider her ways, and be wise. Having no guide, overseer or ruler, she provides her meat in the summer, and gathers her food in the harvest."*
> — Proverbs, 6:6-8

Making $1,300 at 13 and 14 — total (including gift, home chore and allowance income) — translates into making an average income of between $3.60 and $4.00 a day. That should not be difficult — especially when you consider that special events like graduation from junior high school could bring in a few hundred dollars in gift money from a single occasion. And events like Confirmation or Bar-Mitzvah by themselves could bring in an entire year's worth of this level of income, or more, in a single day.

Bigger Teens, Bigger Income

The income assumptions we use for the high school years—ages 15 through 18—are an average of $100 a week. For college years—ages 18 through 21—we assume average income of $150 a week.

These expectations should be quite doable. By high school most children are fully grown physically. By the age of 16, they're eligible for grownup privileges like drivers' licenses. In fact, in most states they can even get married at that age. At the very least, then, they should be ready for part-time employment at this point.

Even if it's just one full shift during the weekend or a couple of 4-hour shifts during the week, income in the $5,200 range should not be hard to achieve for a teenager.

Go to your local golf course, and you'll likely find teenage caddies who are making over $100 a weekend.

Under the spreading chestnut tree
The village smithy stands;
The smith a mighty man is he
With large and sinewy hands.
And the muscles of his brawny
arms Are strong as iron bands.
His brow is wet with honest sweat,
He earns whate'er he can,
And looks the whole world in the
face, For he owes not any man.
— Henry Wadsworth Longfellow

Go to a popular local restaurant, and you can find high school kids making the same kind of money working as bar backs and bussing tables, and college kids making even more as waiters, bartenders, and valet parkers.

Three years ago, before he headed off for college, my nephew made about $200 a month part-time working at a gym, and another $200 or so doing odd jobs for his father, an independent businessman. Throw in the few hundred a year I paid him for watching our dogs when we went away ($25 a day)... and he easily came in at about the $5,200 guideline for 17-year-olds in our program.

A friend of his worked weekends at a record store. And because he closed up, he got a whopping $8.25 an hour. That's $132 a weekend, or just over $5,200 ($5,280) for working two shifts 40 weekends a year — giving him a full 12 weeks off as a high-schooler.

Yet another friend delivers pizzas for $7 an hour. With tips, he averages at least $10 an hour. If he only takes off 8 weeks during year, he makes in the neighborhood of $7,360.

Ask the Busy Man, He Has Time...

There's a saying, "Ask the busy man. He has time." I believe it's true. Getting good grades and making an average of $100 a week in high school and $150 or more per week in college is not an either-or situation. Your children can excel in school, learn while they earn at a part-time job, and have fun.

To do it requires discipline and balance. But this is, after all, part of what you're helping your children learn through the lifelong practice of responsible financial habits.

Making A's — and a Little Bit of Money — in College

In college, the combination of a job that averages just 12 hours a week at $10 an hour and then full-time work for eight weeks in the summer at the same hourly rate would more than cover our earnings assumptions. With simply this kind of average college job, your child would make $120 a week for 40 weeks ($4,800) and $400 a week for eight weeks ($3,200), for a total annual income of $8,000.

Your children, in effect, would meet these guidelines even without one of the "higher paying" college jobs (like bartender or waiter). They'd also do it while still enjoying at least four full weeks off without work or study.

They'd be right on target, in other words, without having to work the kind of hours that might interfere with their ability to study or enjoy some free time.

Staying on Track: Income and Savings During the Teen and College Years			
Age	Income	Savings	Comment
13	$1,300	$650	Living at home, save 50%
14	$1,300	$650	Living at home, save 50%
15	$5,200	$2,600	Living at home, save 50%
16	$5,200	$2,600	Living at home, save 50%
17	$5,200	$2,600	Living at home, save 50%
18	$7,800	$780	In college, save 10%
19	$7,800	$780	In college, save 10%
20	$7,800	$780	In college, save 10%
21	$7,800	$780	In college, save 10%

Now, no one is going to earn exactly these amounts. Some will earn less and some will earn considerably more. But they are reasonable guidelines.

And that means if your children simply average these modest incomes, follow the *Seeds of Wealth* savings ratios, and get approximately the long-term average return of the stock market, they should have a good chance of building a nest egg in excess of $200,000 to $300,000 by the time they begin to raise families of their own.

And that's even if they never have a high-paying job.

But it's quite possible your children could earn significantly more than this. For instance, if the pizza delivery person we spoke about a moment ago, continues to work weekends during the school year *and* works full-time over the summer, he'll end up with over $10,500 during his senior year — even after taking four weeks off during the year.

While he's living at home, then, that translates into after-tax, 100% disposable income of more than $9,500, and over $4,250 in yearly savings.

A college student, meanwhile, can average $200-300 or more a week by working two busy nights a week as a bartender. (That's the kind of money I made *more than 20 years ago*, when I worked my way through college.) That's as much as $15,000-plus a year again, almost twice the above projections.

The Best Jobs for Students
Let Them Learn While They Earn

Okay, hopefully we've established that these income assumptions of $5,200 at 15 and up to $7,800 at 21 are realistic. So let's take a look at some jobs at which your children might work in high school and college to make this money.

The first thing to consider is that few people work for money alone. There are many other benefits to a good job. In fact, if a paycheck is the *only* reason you do your job, you're likely to be very unhappy at it — and probably not very good at it (unless you're paid a ton of money, and you may not even be happy then).

This is especially true for young people, because ideally they should be learning while they're earning. They should be learning in a broad sense — about responsibility. They should be learning in a social sense — about what it takes to deal with different kinds of people on a professional level. And they should be learning in a specific sense — a skill or set of skills that may come in handy later on in life.

Now, at just about any job, your children will learn in the first two ways (how to be responsible and how to deal with people on the job). But not all jobs offer the chance to learn useful skills as a fringe benefit. Working the "frialator" at McDonald's, for instance, is probably not a job skill your children will apply later in life.

At the same time, McDonald's doesn't pay much. But at a different job in roughly the same industry for instance, working as a waiter at a good restaurant your child can earn three or four times the minimum wage.

The best-paying jobs for teenagers, in fact, are generally service-industry jobs that include a significant tip component — busboy, waiter, car-valet, food-deliverer, caddy, etc. Yet, unfortunately, all these jobs offer little in the way of also teaching kids advanced skills.

On the other hand, teens can work in environments

where they may learn very specific, advanced skills. At an office job, for instance, they might learn computer, accounting or other skills. On a construction site, they might learn about building and, indirectly, about engineering, architecture, and real estate. At a hospital, about medicine. And at a law office, about law.

But these jobs are much harder for teens to get, and they are likely to pay high-school-age students minimum wage — or even less if these jobs are offered as part of an internship program. Still, these are the preferred jobs — especially if your teen has a strong desire to have a career in a specific field.

The chance for a serious student/aspiring doctor to work in a hospital as a teenager may be worth a great deal more than the money he/she may give up by not working in a higher-paying, but less intellectually engaging job. And at this point, your children can afford the trade-off.

> *"Far and away the best prize that life offers is the chance to work hard at work worth doing."*
>
> — Theodore Roosevelt

For instance, if you cut our income projections in half during high school (while keeping all other income projections the same), at the average long-term market return of 13.2%, your child will still wind up with $310,679 at the age of 30.

That's less than the $335,854 we'd expect if he/she earned exactly our assumed figures. But it's still a great deal of money for someone so young — especially since we're assuming he/she's never made an above-average income.

And, of course, if his/her lower-paid internship has helped in pursuit of a career as a doctor, lawyer, architect, or other professional, your child will likely make much more during his/her 20s than our assumptions. In fact, the average income for degreed professionals of all age groups in 2001 was $113,725 — almost twice the $59,683 figure for college grads. By the age of 30, then, he/she could end up with much more than $335,854.

What's more, taking higher-skill/lower-paying jobs during high school and college doesn't have to mean your child has to fall short of the guidelines.

In the mid-90s, for instance, I hired a young woman straight out of college to work in the publishing company I was running. One of the reasons I hired her was because she had an excellent attitude toward work. And she developed that attitude by working while she was in college.

During her college years, she worked 20 hours a week at an art gallery, making $120 a week during the school year. She worked full time during the summer and made twice that for about 13 weeks. As a full-time student, then, she made nearly $8,000 a year, even though she made only $6 an hour.

What's more, she graduated with the highest GPA in her major, and she was the president of her sorority. She loved working at the gallery, learned a little bit about art, about small business, and about selling — earning money at the same time, and getting close to a straight-A average. Today, she runs her own marketing business.

So if your 17-year-old makes just $7 an hour in a brokerage office and works an average of 16 hours a week, that's $5,824 a year. Add in chore money, high school graduation gift money, and other money gifts for holidays and birthday, your child has kept well above the income averages even while working in a lower-paying, yet skill-enhancing job.

The ideal, then, is to find a skill-enhancing job that also permits your child to make at least the guideline incomes. But if it's off by a thousand or two, it doesn't matter. Frankly, he/she's likely to more than make up for it later as a working adult.

Finally, it's not strictly a choice between high-level skills or high hourly earnings. There is one way, in fact, that a young person can build high-level skills while still making very good money — in fact, far above the guidelines used here. And that's to be an entrepreneur.

Teen Entrepreneurs Can Get the Best of the Working World's Benefits: Higher-level Skills and Pay

If your teen works at a car wash, he/she might make $6.00 an hour. If he/she starts his/her own neighborhood car wash business, he/she might make two or three times that much. And he/she can also learn some very valuable skills that can come in handy in many different lines of businesses later on.

Granted, washing cars isn't exactly high tech. But running any business requires valuable skills that you generally don't learn in school and you don't learn in most "jobs."

More than anything else, running your own business successfully takes judgment and the willingness to take calculated risks. And those are qualities that are best developed through experience.

At the same time, running your own business requires you learn some diverse, important skills — marketing, customer relations, and, at the very least, rudimentary accounting.

Then, there are teen businesses that also require technical skills on top of managerial skills. Let's say, for example, that your teenage child is a computer whiz. If he/she learns how to market his/her services, he/she can turn that talent into a very profitable business.

By charging small businesses and individual PC users $20 to $25 an hour for debugging and putting together systems, putting up websites, and other tasks that are beyond the normal computer user, your child can offer a very valuable service at a fraction of what the customer might normally pay.

Along the same lines, let's say your child is an aspiring performer. Rather than work at a fast food restaurant, perhaps he/she might teach himself magic tricks and market his/her services to children's parties and the like. He/she'd hone his/her performance skills while learning the very valuable skill of selling him/herself as a performer.

And even if your child is like 99% of the kids out there (and probably 90% of adults) not yet sure about what career to pursue running a business can pay off big.

With a little practice, just about anyone can learn to paint, for instance. Your child can begin with his/her own room and maybe graduate to painting the outside of your garage. Then his/her first job might be something as simple as a picket fence.

But, soon he/she can be making more than he/she would at most jobs while learning how to manage his/her supplies, advertise his services, figure out the rates he/she should and can charge, maybe even learn to work with partners and employees, and devise ways to work more efficiently.

Young Entrepreneurs at Work

Entrepreneurship, of course, doesn't have to start in high school. It can start much earlier. What greater business starter is there, after all, than the old lemonade stand? Not every kid has to have the ambition of Lucy from the Peanuts comic strip to benefit from entrepreneurship. (Lucy not only sold lemonade, but also occasionally converted the stand to a psychiatrist's booth, where you could have your problems analyzed for just a nickel!)

Five and six-year olds don't have to do it for the ambition. They can and probably will do it simply because it's fun! And, again, the child who is encouraged to follow through on these ideas and actually sets up the stand is likely to gain not only fun memories but another small seed of confidence as well.

Babysitting is another entrepreneurial activity that is often practiced by responsible kids as young as 13 or 14. But, again, it's not enough to know how to watch after a child (though that *is* paramount!). The successful baby sitter also has to know how to get all the business he/she wants.

If he/she'd like to make some money baby sitting, in

other words, he/she shouldn't just wait for the phone to ring. You can help your child learn how to *make* the phone ring. (He/she can do that by spreading the word amongst the parents of his/her friends who have younger siblings, by posting notices at day care centers and supermarkets, and offering references upon request in each ad.)

Examples of these kinds of opportunities abound... rather than work at a cookie store, for instance, why not bake and sell cookies?

An important thing to keep in mind about any business to attract new customers, always try to get your potential customers to think about the *benefits for them* of the servies you offer.

For instance, if you want to convince Mr. Smith to hire you to mow his lawn, don't tell him how you want to earn money. When you talk to him, keep in mind the things *he* wants — and how the service you offer him can help him get those things.

For instance, after working hard all week, Mr. Smith will be able to do the crossword on Sunday, rather than push a lawnmower around the yard. And he'll be proud of the way his lawn always looks so neat and well taken care of. He'll never have to worry about it getting too high because he didn't have the time to mow the lawn this week...

Good business is about finding profitable ways to give your customers what they want. That way, you'll get repeat business, new customers from referrals, and you won't have to spend all your time looking for new customers.

From ABCs to CEOs

Dollar Digest, an online money magazine for kids, recently ran a story about two young girls, 11 and 12, who turned their passion for baking cookies into a profitable business.

The same magazine has a story about a 13-year-old boy who distributed flyers throughout his neighborhood offering a variety of junior handyman services, including trimming trees, mowing lawns, painting, staining decks, gardening, caring for dogs, and pool cleaning. He made $150 in his first three weeks — at just 13 years old!

Then there are the two 11-year-old cousins from Minnesota who sold home-grown sweet corn and made nearly $500 each their first year, then experimented by setting up a stand and *doubled* their profits the second year.

But my favorite is the story of the 15-year-old who has been selling recycled golf balls since she was seven. Her grandfather, an avid golfer, brings them to her each week and she sells them for $3-$5 a dozen.

She's now hired an assistant to help her sell the balls. And she's learned how to wash the balls in a washing machine, too (throwing them in with a few towels to protect the washing machine), a productivity-boosting change that saves her about 3 hours in labor every week.

Here are some examples of some businesses your own children might run on the following pages.

29 Businesses for Kids

Business and Age Group	Business & Marketing Tips
Ages 5-8	
Ye Olde Lemonade Stand	Use homemade recipe, display fresh lemons on counter, use extra-large colorful plastic cups; especially good to do when there's foot traffic going by your house - from a parade, church letting out, charity race, or other social event
Garage sales	Advertise your best specific items (bicycles, TV) on flyers in neighborhood, and if you have toys to sell, advertise those in flyers near the local schoolyard; have colorful balloons tied to your mailbox to make your house easy to spot
Selling homemade baked goods	Take custom orders, hand out mini recipe books with each order; set up this and the lemonade stand when you have a garage sale
Ages 9-10	
All of the above, plus... Walking dogs for neighbors	Offer this service to older neighbors and single people who work long hours and can't always get home to take care of their dogs during the day
Recycling cans	Save all your cans and bring to recycling center once every two weeks or so; also ask neighbors if you can take cans from their recycle bins they put on the curb
Ages 11-13	
All of the above, plus... Delivering papers and flyers	Go to local PennySaver office and offer services; also go to restaurants, real estate agencies, and other local businesses that may from time to time want to advertise their businesses with flyers in the neighborhood

29 Businesses for Kids (continued)

Business and Age Group	Business & Marketing Tips
Ages 11-13	
Stuffing envelopes and applying postage (letter-shopping)	Many small businesses need to do mailings of 100 to 200 people or so. They may send out a newsletter, sales offer, or business update to clients. Draw up a flyer describing the services you offer and distribute it to all local businesses.
Selling sodas and bottled water at beach	Make sure you have plenty of diet soda; have a big cooler with ice nearby (maybe in the car, or with a friend or sibling watching it), then walk the beach with a knapsack with the beverages and dry ice inside
Washing Cars	Pass flyers out in neighborhood and offer to wash people's cars in their own driveway. Pass flyers out at office buildings and offer to wash people's cars while they're at work.
Taking care of pets, taking in mail and watering plants for people while they're away	Drop off stacks of flyers at local travel agencies; also pass them around the neighborhood
Shining shoes	Offer services in office buildings on a regular basis - once or twice a week during the summer, or even on Saturday mornings during the school year for offices, like banks that are open.
Retrieving, restoring, and reselling golf balls	Most golf courses are closed one day a week for maintenance. Ask head groundskeeper if you can patrol the fairways for balls. Offer to rake the sand traps in return.

29 Businesses for Kids (continued)

Business and Age Group	Business & Marketing Tips
Ages 14-15	
All of the above, plus... Grocery shopping and delivery	Offer this service especially to older neighbors and to neighbors who might be disabled
Tutoring	If you excel in a particular subject or subjects, bring proof of that to local guidance counselors and let them know you're offering tutoring services to their students; also leave flyers with local recreation centers, daycare centers, and supermarkets
Window washing	Leave flyers at homes and one-story office buildings
Babysitting	Leave flyers at daycare centers, super-markets, and health spas
Snow shoveling	Offer services door to door, but also get a head-start on the competition by handing out flyers at the beginning of winter and handing them out again just before major snow storms are expected. Work with a partner and get an early start, before the snow starts to pack down; get a wide shovel; if you live in an area where it snows a lot, a snow blower could turn out to be a very profitable investment
Magician/Juggler/Party entertainer	Advertise services with flyers in daycare centers and supermarkets, near kids' stores in shopping centers
Mowing lawns	Offer services door to door (look for big lawns) and via flyers distributed near lawn and garden centers; set up regular schedule so that you can mow even when your customers are not home; just bill them later

29 Businesses for Kids (continued)

Business and Age Group	Business & Marketing Tips
Ages 16 and Up	
All of the above, plus…	
Painting	Place flyers near local hardware stores; go door to door to houses that look like they need a paint job
DJ	Advertise services in your high school newspaper, in the junior high school's newspaper; post flyers near local recreation centers and music stores
Newsletter publisher	Pick something your peers or other kids are mad about and then tell them all they want to know about it in a newsletter; for instance, you could have one on Pokemon, computer games, World Wide Wrestling, or Hip-Hop music
Videotaping parties	Distribute flyers around schools and shopping centers, especially near winter holidays and graduation time
Photographer	Distribute flyers around daycare centers and supermarkets, offer services for portraits as well as birthdays, graduation, and other special occasions
Catering for kids' parties	Distribute flyers around daycare centers and supermarkets
Light computer repair	Advertise services in local PennySaver, post flyers near local computer retailers, distribute flyers to local small businesses
Light handyman work	Distribute flyers door to door in the neighborhood, at supermarkets, and near local hardware stores
Landscaping	Post flyers at supermarkets and near local home & garden centers; distribute flyers door to door in the neighborhood
Local moving	Leave stacks of flyers with local real estate agencies and even with local U-Haul and other truck and van rental offices, since people who rent vans often need help with the actual move

Let Your Children Work Part-time for You And You Could Possibly Save Thousands in Taxes!

If you own a business, having your children work for you can provide a good source of income and work education for them. And it can also provide substantial tax savings for you!

For instance, my oldest son recently turned 14 and now handles the routine database and product fulfillment functions of one of my businesses. Soon, if he so chooses, he could also help out with research. He could also see what's involved in putting together editorial and marketing copy. He could help bid out needed services (from printing to shipping), and much more. At the same time, he'd continue to sharpen his overall computer skills and learning to deal with customers and suppliers.

It's a good learning opportunity for him and a chance to earn, at the very least, enough to meet the age-specific income guidelines in this program.

If you're self-employed or have your own business, this can also be a great deal for you. First off, you get to spend a little more time with your children. Second, you can save a good deal of money in taxes.

Have Your Children Work for You And Save Up to $19,740 or More in Taxes!

For example, let's say you pay one of your children a total of $4,700 during the year. That's right under the IRS minimum-income reporting requirement. At that level, your child won't have to pay taxes or even file a tax return. At the same time, because he's under 18 years of age, working for a parent, and making less than $4,701, you don't have to pay social security taxes on the wages you pay him. Nor does he.

The taxes he pays on that $4,700, then, is zero. And yet you get a deduction on that $4,700. Even if you were at the lowest marginal tax rate of 10%, that would save you $470 a year. At the maximum marginal tax rate of 35%, meanwhile, it would save you $1,645 a year!

And if your child works for you for 4 years in this way, you save $6,580. And if three of your children end up working for you in the same way, you save a total of $19,740.

Now, compound that for, say, 20 years at 10% — *and you've added $120,728 to your retirement nest egg to boot!*

To take full advantage of this great money-saving technique for you, and income-producing technique for your child, you can't be a corporation or a partnership in which one of the partners is not the child's parent. However, the technique works wonderfully for sole-proprietorships, including Limited Liability Corporations (which are state, not federal, legal entities), and unincorporated family partnerships in which both partners are the child's parents.

What's more, you can still take partial advantage of this technique even if your business is a corporation or partnership in which one of the partners is not your spouse. You will have to pay Social Security taxes on wages you pay to your child, but you still get the benefit of "income shifting" for income tax purposes.

In effect, in the case where you pay your child $4,700, for example, you deduct that from your corporate or partnership income, and it is transferred to the tax liability of your child, whose effective income tax rate in this case is zero! Even in this way, then, you can save thousands of dollars while your child is exempt not only from paying federal income taxes, but even from having to file.

Simply have your child file a W-4 with you when he starts to work for you. Since he knows he'll make less than $4,701 during the year, he'll mark "exempt" on line seven and then submit it to you for your records. You won't have to withhold any federal income, since you both know he won't owe any. And again, if you're an unincorporated sole-proprietorship, limited liability company, or partnership where both partners are the child's parents, you won't have to pay Social Security, Medicare, or Federal Unemployment taxes either.

Simply keep good records yourself to document that all work your child does for you is legitimate.

Also, keep in mind that many accountants may not be familiar with this technique. But if you go to www.irs.gov and download Publication 15, Circular E and look at pages 7-8, under "Family Employees," you'll see it all in black and white.

How Your Children Can Continue to Save and Build Wealth Once They Leave the Nest

We've discussed how easy it should be to follow the *Seeds of Wealth* savings ratios.

Saving 100% of income from the ages of 1 through 4 is simple — you do it for them.

Saving 50% from 5 through 17 should not be a problem at all since, living at home, they have 100% disposable income. And I don't think anyone can make a convincing argument that a child who gets to spend $730 out of $730 received in a given year is twice as happy as a child who spends $365 of that amount, and uses the rest to build wealth.

And, finally, saving 10% while in college should be a snap compared to the discipline of having saved half of all income while growing up.

So how do we prepare our children to save 15% of their income once they're young adults, on their own — and answering to no one but themselves?

The key is to _show_ them the future. Make sure, as they're growing up, that they understand the likely, highly positive future consequences of their current actions.

Preparing Your Children to Maintain Good Money Habits When They Become Independent Adults

As your children become teens and eventually high-school seniors, they should be familiar with the table on page 45, and fully understand how just a few dollars a day at long-term average market returns can result in a six-and even seven-figure fortune over time. At the same time, this theoretical knowledge should be reinforced by experience — by seeing their own funds grow over the years, through disciplined savings and investment.

And then, of course, there is your example. If you're a regular saver and long-term investor — and you let your children understand that fact — it will be easier for them to follow in those footsteps.

But the consistent habits formed over many years of saving and investing through the *Seeds of Wealth* program — and letting them know from about the time they're 16 that they should save 15% once they've graduated from college and are living on their own — should suffice.

You can also point out to them — just for a bit of *extreme* perspective — that the personal savings rate in countries like Chile and China are over 20% — even though the average per-capita income in these countries is one-fifth and one-thirtieth of that in the U.S. (The high savings rates are one of the reasons the economies

> *"I am indeed rich since my income is superior to expenses, and my expense is equal to my wishes."*
>
> — Edward Gibbon

of these countries have been growing twice as fast as the U.S. over the last 15 years or so.) So saving 15% for a person living in one of the richest countries in the world — while they're still single and have no family to support — should not be a problem.

But to show how it can work, let's take a look at what a budget might look like for your children once they're in their mid- to late-20s. We'll assume they are making an average salary for full-time working college graduates (per the U.S. Census figures). And we'll see how they can fit 15% into their budget and still have more than enough money to live comfortably and without great sacrifice.

BETTER BUDGETS FOR YOUNG ADULTS

Saving 15% on an Average Income Requires No Great Sacrifice

According to the U.S. Census, the average income in 2001 for a college grad, aged 25-34 who worked full-time year-round was $48,787.

The following table shows how your children, making this average income, can easily save 15%, pay all taxes and bills, and still have a good amount of money left over to handle unexpected expenses and even live it up a little.

In the following example, the amount saved is $7,318 (15% of $48,787). We assume 2003 tax rates, using the single independent filer column.

(1) Gross Annual Income		$48,787
	Deductions:	
(2)	IRA	$3,000
(3)	College Loan Interest	$1,500
(4)	Standard Deduction & Exemption	$7,700
(5)	Taxable Income (line 1 minus lines 2, 3, & 4)	$36,587
	Taxes:	
(6)	Federal Inc. Taxes	$4,007
(7)	State Inc. Taxes (5%)	$1,829
(8)	Social Security, Medicare	$2,799
(9) After-tax income (line 1 minus lines 6, 7, & 8)		$40,152

Annual Expenditures	
IRA	$3,000
College Loan (assumes $1,500 interest, $1,500 principal)	$3,000
Rent	$7,200
Groceries	$3,900
fuel/electric	$900
Phone	$900
gas for car	$720
car payments	$2,400
car insurance	$1,200
Extra savings (for total savings of 15% of gross income)	$4,318
Clothes	$900
Total Annual Spending	$28,438
ANNUAL SURPLUS	$11,714

We also assume that at this point your adult child has no 401(k), Keogh, SIMPLE IRA or SEP IRA available to him, so he can shelter only $3,000 maximum from income taxes in a traditional IRA. We also assume he's making payments of $250 a month on a college loan, and half of that represents interest so it's tax-deductible.

Other than that, he only gets the standard deduction ($4,700 for a single taxpayer) and a single exemption ($3,000). This leaves us with taxable income of $36,587.

147

After paying federal and state income taxes and Social Security and Medicare taxes, we're left with after-tax income of $40,152 (gross income of $48,787 less total taxes of $8,635).

We assume he shares a $1,200 a month apartment with a roommate, so his share of the rent is $600 a month, or $7,200 a year.

His share of the groceries come to $75 a week ($3,900 annually), and his share of the energy bill is $75 a month (or $900 annually).

Younger folks tend to talk a bit more on the phone, so his share of the phone bill — even with free Internet — is $75 a month. We then assume he drives his car 12,000 miles in the year, which, at an average of 25 miles per gallon, means he has to buy 480 gallons of gasoline. At $1.50 per gallon, that's $720 a year. Insurance for a four- or five-year-old car is also $600 (with a slightly higher deductible, if need be). The extra savings of $4,318 is simply the portion of his total savings that is represented below the tax line. Combined with the tax-deductible $3,000 in the traditional IRA, it pushes total savings to $7,318 or 15% of total income. He spends $900 a year on clothes.

After all this, not living a deprived existence by any means, he still has almost $12,000 in surplus to take care of miscellaneous expenses!

Plenty of Cushion

If we give our assumptions a bit of a stress test, we

might suppose he has to spend $500 on car maintenance and another $500 on medical insurance premiums. That still leaves him with over $10,000 for miscellaneous expenses — ranging from the purchase of a stereo to the occasional movies, dinner and economy ski weekends.

On the other hand, if he does have a 401(k) available to him, he can shelter *all* his savings from income taxes — and pick up an extra $1,079 in disposable income!

Any way you look at it, for a college graduate making simply the average income, it is not at all difficult to live well and still save 15% of income.

Yet, the national savings rate is less than 4% — even though people are making more money than ever before. That's why it's important to help your children develop good money habits early on, so they will continue to build wealth instead of debt when they're adults living on their own.

Your Children Can Easily Continue to Build Wealth Even with Incomes Just Over $700 a Week

If we lower our income assumptions by more than 40%, it is still clear that your child can always continue to save money according to the *Seeds of Wealth* guidelines. They can continue to build wealth, in other words, even when they're just starting out in the workplace and may be making a more modest income.

According to the U.S. Bureau of the Census, the average income for college graduates age 18-24 was $37,828 in 2001. (Now of course, there are almost no college graduates under the age of 21, so this average is actually skewed on the low side. Still, we'll use it to see how your child can continue to save and create wealth even with a modest income.)

(1) Gross Annual Income	$37,828
Deductions:	
(2) IRA	$3,000
(3) College Loan Interest	$1,500
(4) Standard Deduction & Exemption	$7,700
(5) Taxable Income (line 1 minus lines 2, 3, & 4)	$25,628
Taxes:	
(6) Federal Inc. Taxes	$2,324
(7) State Inc. Taxes (5%)	$1,281
(8) Social Security, Medicare	$1,961
(9) After-tax income (line 1 minus lines 6, 7, & 8)	$32,262
Expenditures	
IRA	$3,000
College Loan	$3,000
Rent	$4,800
Groceries	$3,900
fuel/electric	$900
Phone	$900
gas for car	$720
car payments	$1,200
car insurance	$1,500
Extra savings (for total savings of 15% of gross income)	$2,674
Clothes	$900
Total spending	$23,494
SURPLUS	$8,768

All the assumptions remain the same as in our first table. In this case, however, since your child is just starting out, we assume he shares an $800 apartment (instead of a $1,200 apartment) so that his share of the rent is $400. We also assume he's driving a less-expensive car, and pays only $100 a month on the car loan (roughly in line with the monthly payments on a $5,000 car loan at 8% over five years).

Yet, at the same time, because he's only 22 or so, we increase the amount he has to pay in car insurance by $300, or 25%.

After those adjustments, even at the lower income, he has over $8,700 in surplus for miscellaneous expenses and the occasional night out on the town — all while saving 15% of gross income, as planned.

And if we make the assumption that he *does* have a 401(k) or other plan with a higher tax-deduction limit available to him? In that case, he can shelter all of his savings from taxes, adding another $401 to his disposable income!

Realistic Wealth Creation

With the above examples, you can see that if your child happens to make *above* the average incomes for college graduates in his age group, he'll have even more disposable income after saving 15% of his income. And, because of the habits he'll have been developing since childhood, he may well decide to invest a portion of that surplus as well.

After all, as we stated when we introduced the savings

ratios on page 27, the ratios are minimums — not maximums.

But now that we've seen how your children can painlessly generate investment capital, the stuff fortunes are
made of, at different levels of income, let's talk about
how they can invest those savings for high returns...

PART V

How To Make The SeedsGrow

Going for High Returns

Okay, we've talked about earning income. That, as we said earlier, is like tilling the earth. We've also discussed having your child follow firm savings ratios throughout different stages of his youth. And that's like planting the seeds. So now it's time to make the seeds grow. The way to do that is to invest. And for our purposes, specifically, we want to invest for the long term.

So to complete the *Seeds of Wealth* program, we'll now talk about investment strategies that can help your children grow their wealth at high rates of return over the long term.

Neither a Trader nor a Timer Be

The first thing we need to stress is *what you absolutely don't want to do with your children's investment funds.* And that is, you don't want to trade in and out of stocks... or try to "time" the market on a weekly, monthly, or even yearly basis.

You want to invest for the long term. And by that I mean you should anticipate holding every investment you make for your child at least 5 years, and as long as 25-30 years or more.

We'll address the issues of when to buy and when to sell toward the end of this section. But the point I'd like to make here is that you don't want to gamble with your children's funds.

Yes, you're going to take on some risk. That's inevitable because there is risk involved in every investment. But you won't be recklessly gambling because the best way to go for relatively high returns while reducing risk is to make diversified investments in stocks for the long term.

Here's the proof...

The Longer You Invest, the More Volatility Evens Out

The stock market has posted positive total returns 73 out of the last 100 years. Using the past century as a guide, then, you have a 73% chance of making money if you get the overall returns of the stock market in any given year.

But that's on a year-to-year basis. Longer-term, your chances of making money are much better. In fact, if you go out long enough, they're practically 100%. In fact, during the entire 20th century there was not a single 15-year or 30-year period when the stock market posted negative total returns.

What's more, the volatility of returns (or the degree to which returns vary) is also much smaller during longer periods. And since volatility in stocks is basically the same as risk, that means your risk is generally smaller when investing for the long term.

What's more, this fact (that volatility tends to decrease significantly the longer your investment time frame) will even permit your children to target investments that traditionally *are* a bit more volatile and *profitable* over the long run. In other words, your children can go for the extra reward because they'll be eliminating much of the extra risk (volatility) by investing for the long term!

(A little later, in a brief separate section on page 193, I go into the volatility issue in a little bit more detail for those who have a propensity to crunch numbers... or who need a little convincing before they'll sit still and let long-term compounding do its magical best for their children.)

But the fact that we'll face lower volatility isn't the only reason we're going to invest for the long haul. There are a few other very important reasons, including...

Trading Is Expensive

Every time you buy or sell a stock, there are costs involved. First there's the spread. The spread is the market maker's cut. The market maker is a guy or company that pretty much makes sure you can buy or sell your stock any time. He's always going to sell you the stock for more than the price at which he'll buy it from you. And he'll always buy the stock at a price that's less than what he'll sell it to you for. That difference between the buy and sell price is the spread — his margin of profit.

On a stock from a big company like GE, the spread might be less than one-quarter of one percent of the share price. On a small company like Gasonics International (a growing small cap in the semiconductor industry), on the other hand, it might be closer to 10%. For each stock — whether it's a big-spread or small-spread stock — the spread fluctuates a bit. Yet, whatever it is, you're going to pay something every time you buy and sell it.

A bigger cost than the spread, usually, is the commission. Even with deep-discount brokers, commissions can add up. Buy and sell 12 stocks a year instead of buying and holding two, and the costs can really add up.

Even on Scottrade (one of the lowest-cost, highly rated online brokers), these ten extra "round-trips" (buys and sells) will increase your children's commission costs somewhere in the neighborhood of $140. On E-Trade, meanwhile, they can cost you $300 to $350 or more.

Those numbers are way too much, especially considering that for the ages of 1 through 12 your children will likely average around $365 a year or so in new investment capital.

Put an Extra $69,030 in Your Pocket

What's more, even when your children become adults with tens of thousands or hundreds of thousands of dollars in their portfolios, they're still likely to be far better off investing for the long term — rather than jumping in and out of the market.

First off, if your children cut their commissions and spread costs just $200 a year over the course of 30 years, say, and we compound those savings at the long-term market return of 13.2% a year... they end up putting an extra $69,030 in their pockets.

Second, but perhaps even more importantly, by not jumping in and out of stocks, they'll be better able to follow a disciplined plan of investing. And that's the best way to produce superior returns over the long run. And there's a lot of proof to back that up...

Don't Try to Time the Market...
Your Children Will Likely Be Far Better
Off Making Long-term Investments
in Good Companies at Good Prices

In 1950, the average portfolio turnover in the typical mutual fund was 20%. That means if a fund manager began the year with 100 stocks in his portfolio, by the end of the year 20 of those stocks would have been sold (replaced or just sold for cash) and 80 would still be there.

Today, according to the Investment Company Institute (the mutual fund trade industry association), turnover in the average mutual fund is nearly 100%!

Mutual fund managers today rarely hold a stock for an entire year. Instead, they are now buying and selling stocks five times as often in a given year as they did 50 years ago. That certainly increases costs...

Yet there is _no_ evidence that they're getting any closer, as a group, to "beating the market!"

According to the New York institute of Finance, over 70% of mutual funds fail to do better than the S&P 500 (also referred to here as "the market"). Wall Street money manager, analyst, and author James O'Shaugnessy, meanwhile, has studied the long-term performance of mutual fund managers and found that, on average, about 80% fail to beat the market. Other studies by groups ranging from AT&T to Ibbotson Associates have gotten similar results.

Now, since most individual investors invest through mutual funds, that means most individual investors fail to beat the market too. But that's not necessarily *terrible* news.

On the one hand, since all investors together *make up the market*, it's impossible for all investors together to beat the market. What's more since "the market" doesn't take costs into account (while all investors must pay costs, like commissions, spreads and taxes), it's to be expected that most investors would "underperform" the market by at least a little bit.

And if you're not among the 20% to do better than the market, you might be among the 30-40% or so who underperform the market, but just by one or two percentage points a year. And that's really not so bad.

After all, if you'd done that over the last 50 years, that means you're still averaging 11.2% or 12.2% annual returns. And following the *Seeds of Wealth* program from infancy, those rates of return will still turn into between $251,039 and $289,466 by the age of 30.

Not bad, considering your children will have averaged just over $1 a day in savings and investment in the pre-teen years, just over $2 a day from the age of one through 21, and we're basing the adult savings and investment numbers on assumptions of only an average salary.

What's more, people who *very actively* trade in and out of the market tend to do much worse than falling short of the market by a percentage point or two. In 1999, in fact, a study by the National Association of Securities Dealers Administrators showed that *56 cents of every dollar* day traders invest is eaten up by trading costs! And that was in a bull market!

At about the same time, the government released a survey that showed that 77% of all day traders lose some or all of their money.

So the evidence suggests that most people who jump in and out of the market actually end up making things far worse, not better.

But the evidence also suggests *that over the long term* there are methods of investing that have proven to con-sistently beat "the market," or the S&P 500. We'll take a look at some of those methods in a little bit...

First, however, let's decide how much we're going to invest in stocks, long-term bonds, short-term bills, real estate, gold, and other assets... In other words, we have to make an "allocation" decision!

Allocation — Alloshmation!

Allocation is how you divvy up your money among your different types of investments.

The ratios can get real fancy. For instance, if we're deciding how to cut up the pie just among stocks, bonds, bills, and gold, it might be 50-30-15-5 if we're relatively conservative investors. Or something like 80-10-5-5 for an aggressive investor...

But for the first 25 or 30 years of our *Seeds of Wealth* investment program, our allocation ratio is going to be very easy to remember.

Are you ready for it?

It's 100% stocks. And zero in everything else.

I told you it would be easy to remember!

The exception to this is if you, the parent, are a real estate investor and would like to include your children's savings in some of your property investments. We'll reveal a technique you can use to do that in Appendix B of this guidebook.

But as concerns securities, let me show you why 100% stocks is the best way to go when your children are just beginning to build wealth and are investing for the very long term...

Stocks Beat All Other Major Financial Assets Over the Long Term — Hands Down!

In the short term, stocks are more volatile than bonds, bills, or gold. Yet, as we discussed, over the longer term most of that volatility evens out. And the result is stocks end up producing a higher return relative to their risk than any other asset class. We'll prove that in the next few pages. But for the moment, let's just see by how much stocks beat the other asset classes on the basis of returns alone.

What we'll see is that stocks win by a large margin. And the longer you intend to invest for, the greater the advantage you'll likely gain by investing in stocks...

The charts on this page show that a single hundred-dollar investment in gold at the beginning of the 20th century was worth just $1,404 at the close of it. But a hundred dollars in U.S. Treasury bills was worth $6,335 one hundred years later.

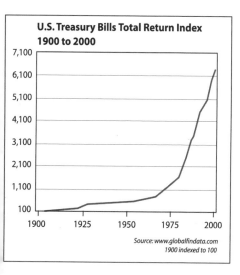

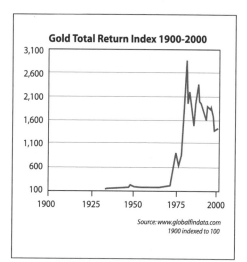

The additonal two charts on this page, show that long-term government bonds, turned $100 on January 1, 1900 into $9,038 by January 1, 2000, and that triple-A rated corporate government bonds did better still — turning $100 into $19,194 in the course of a century...

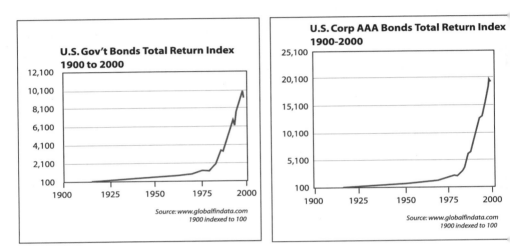

But stocks beat them all — and by a very big margin.

A hundred-dollars invested in the equivalent of the S&P 500 at the beginning of the 20th century was worth...

$1,612,548!

Over 1.6 million!

Over the last 100 years, in other words, stocks beat gold by better than 1,148 to 1, Treasury bills by more than 254 to 1, government bonds by more than 178 to 1, and blue-chip corporate bonds by more than 84 to 1!

What's more, during any 30-year period that

occurred during, or even partially overlapping, the 20th century, stocks beat all these other assets classes **99 out of 100 times!**

The only time it failed to beat all other major asset classes, in fact, was from 1874 to 1904, when corporate bonds edged stocks out *by less than 1/5th of a percentage point* in compounded annual returns!

During the last hundred 30-year periods, stocks, on average, created more than triple the wealth created by corporate bonds, and more than four times the wealth created by government bonds, government bills, and gold.

But stocks don't produce much higher returns only with a 99% consistency over 30-year periods, they also do it with *** less risk per unit of reward.*** In other words, when adjusted for the gains they produce, stocks are even less risky!

Getting More for Less: Taking Advantage of Stocks' Higher Risk-Adjusted Returns

There is no question about it. When investing for the long term, no financial asset beats stocks. But there's something else to keep in mind, too...

Because risk is largely measured by how much your returns are likely to vary, stocks become a less risky investment the longer your time frame is. But besides the concept of risk, there is also the very important concept of "risk-adjusted returns."

Risk-adjusted returns measure how well you get paid

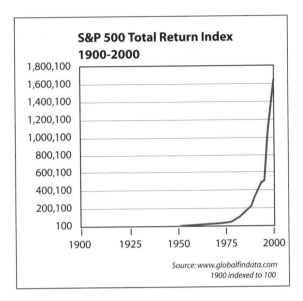

**S&P 500 Total Return Index
1900-2000**

1,800,100	
1,600,100	
1,400,100	
1,200,100	
1,000,100	
800,100	
600,100	
400,100	
200,100	
100	

1900   1925   1950   1975   2000

Source: www.globalfindata.com
1900 indexed to 100

for taking on a little extra risk. If you increase your risk by 2%, for instance, but increase your potential for profits by 5%, your risk is falling relative to your potential returns. And, when investing for the long term, you want to get the highest possible returns relative to risk.

And guess what investment category wins here...

Stocks again. Hands down.

In *Stocks for the Long Run,* Jeremy Siegel put it this way: "It is widely known that stock returns, on average, exceed bonds in the long run. But it is little known that in the long run, the risks in stocks are *less than* those found in bonds or even bills!"

This is not only because the volatility of stock returns tends to stabilize the longer your investment horizon (though it does). It's because volatility decreases while returns are still far above the average.

In fact, as Siegel points out again, money invested in stocks *even* at the peak in August 1929 accumulated to a greater sum over the next 30 years than money put into bonds over the same period. And from 1960 to 1990 (the worst 30-year period for stocks since World War II), stocks created *three times* as much wealth as bonds.

Stocks, then, are the way to go for your children because even in worst-case scenarios, they have proven to produce much higher returns over the long run — and higher risk-adjusted returns too.

How to Measure Risk Against Reward

We've said it before; we'll say it again: every time you make an investment, you take on risk. And there are different types of risk, too, such as "default risk" (or the risk someone won't pay you back), interest-rate risk, and reinvestment risk, to mention just a few. But the key thing to keep in mind is that when you take all the types of risk into account, the degree of total risk can vary greatly, depending on the investment.

So let's take a look at risk in different asset classes and begin by first taking a quick look at what is considered the least risky investment of all — U.S. Treasury bills.

A Treasury bill is a "promissory note" (or I.O.U) the government gives you in return for money you've lent them for a short period of time — ranging from 12 weeks to a year. That I.O.U. states that, at "maturity" (or the date the loan is to be paid off in full) the government will pay you back what you lent it, *plus* interest.

Because there is almost zero chance the government won't pay you back and because a Treasury bill is a short-term and "liquid" investment (meaning you can cash it in anytime), it is usually considered the least risky financial investment you can make.

Now, this notion of the "least risky" investment is useful for those who may need their money soon and so can't take any short-term risk or "volatility." But, for the purposes of comparing risk-adjusted returns, it's also very useful because the T-bill will serve as our "risk-free rate of return."

It's a "risk-free rate of return" for a few reasons. First, because the loan is for such a short term that inflation isn't likely to hurt its value much. Second, because the government can (if they were in an extreme cash crunch) raise taxes to get money to pay you back, or they can issue long-term bonds to meet their short-term obligations (meaning pay your bill).

So, in a nutshell, this means that anytime you make an investment in anything riskier than a Treasury bill, you'll require a higher return.

Otherwise, why take the higher risk?

This is why a company has to pay you a higher interest rate than a T-bill pays when they want you to lend them money (which is the same as buying one of their bonds). You have to get paid the amount of interest you would get paid if you bought a T-bill _plus_ a little (or a lot) more to compensate you for the extra risk you're taking on.

This is also why, throughout history, corporate bonds have paid more than government bonds. It's also the reason stocks have paid more than corporate bonds. ... because the only reason to take on higher risk is for the prospect of higher returns...

How to Get Paid a Lot More To Take on a Little More Risk

Over the short term, stocks are the riskiest major financial investments. That's generally why they pay the most. But do the extra returns make up for the extra risk? In other words, over the long term, have stockowners been

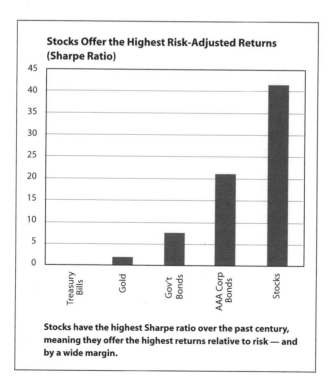

Stocks Offer the Highest Risk-Adjusted Returns (Sharpe Ratio)

Stocks have the highest Sharpe ratio over the past century, meaning they offer the highest returns relative to risk — and by a wide margin.

properly paid for the extra risk they've taken on over the last century?

The question is important because, if the answer is "no," we can't justify taking on the extra risk involved in stocks. Fortunately, we have a way to quickly answer this question. To do that, we're going to use something called "the Sharpe ratio."

The Sharpe ratio (developed by Nobel prize winner William Sharpe) is the most common measure of risk-adjusted returns used in the financial industry. To calculate the Sharpe ratio, you take the average return of an investment, subtract the risk-free rate of return, and then divide that number by its standard deviation (the amount its returns generally bounce up and down).

The result of this equation is the measure of return you get per unit of additional risk. The higher the number the better.

The chart on the previous page shows that when we gauge gold, Treasury bills, Treasury bonds, AAA Corporate Bonds and stocks for the entire 20th century, stocks score the highest Sharpe ratio. And that means they don't only offer the biggest returns in absolute terms, they also offer the biggest returns relative to the risk they entail.

The Tale of the Tape: The Bad and the Beautiful of the Stock Market's Long-term Performance

Now that we've established that stocks beat all other

asset classes over the long term — both in straight-out profits, and in risk-adjusted returns — let's take a look at the kind of returns we might expect as a long-term investor in stocks over the next 30 years or more.

The table on the next five pages shows the total returns of the U.S. stock market from 1871 through 2000:

Performance of America's Largest Stocks 1871-2000					
Year Ending	S&P 500 Index	Capital Gain	Div. Yield	Total Return	Total Return Index
1871	4.75	NA	5.23%	NA	1.00
1872	5.07	6.74%	6.03%	12.77%	1.13
1873	4.43	-12.62%	6.71%	-5.91%	1.06
1874	4.55	2.71%	6.68%	9.39%	1.16
1875	4.36	-4.18%	6.57%	2.39%	1.19
1876	3.58	-17.89%	7.11%	-10.78%	1.06
1877	3.25	-9.22%	4.73%	-4.49%	1.01
1878	3.44	5.85%	4.90%	10.75%	1.12
1879	4.92	43.02%	4.26%	47.28%	1.65
1880	5.84	18.70%	4.43%	23.13%	2.03
1881	6.02	3.08%	5.06%	8.14%	2.20
1882	5.84	-2.99%	5.42%	2.43%	2.25
1883	5.35	-8.39%	6.00%	-2.39%	2.20
1884	4.34	-18.88%	6.39%	-12.49%	1.92
1885	5.2	19.82%	4.22%	24.04%	2.39
1886	5.64	8.46%	3.70%	12.16%	2.68
1887	5.27	-6.56%	4.67%	-1.89%	2.63
1888	5.14	-2.47%	3.91%	1.44%	2.66
1889	5.32	3.50%	4.04%	7.54%	2.87
1890	4.6	-13.53%	4.37%	-9.16%	2.60

Performance of America's Largest Stocks
1871-2000 (continued)

Year Ending	S&P 500 Index	Capital Gain	Div. Yield	Total Return	Total Return Index
1891	5.41	17.61%	4.01%	21.62%	3.17
1892	5.51	1.85%	4.09%	5.94%	3.35
1893	4.41	-19.96%	4.89%	-15.07%	2.85
1894	4.3	-2.49%	4.58%	2.09%	2.91
1895	4.32	0.47%	4.06%	4.53%	3.04
1896	4.22	-2.31%	4.01%	1.70%	3.09
1897	4.75	12.56%	3.55%	16.11%	3.59
1898	5.65	18.95%	3.48%	22.43%	4.39
1899	6.02	6.55%	3.47%	10.02%	4.83
1900	6.87	14.12%	3.82%	17.94%	5.70
1901	7.95	15.72%	3.72%	19.44%	6.81
1902	8.05	1.26%	3.84%	5.10%	7.16
1903	6.57	-18.39%	4.57%	-13.82%	6.17
1904	8.25	25.57%	3.57%	29.14%	7.96
1905	9.54	15.64%	3.31%	18.95%	9.47
1906	9.84	3.14%	3.82%	6.96%	10.13
1907	6.57	-33.23%	6.13%	-27.10%	7.39
1908	9.03	37.44%	4.27%	41.71%	10.47
1909	10.3	14.06%	4.17%	18.23%	12.38
1910	9.05	-12.14%	5.03%	-7.11%	11.50
1911	9.11	0.66%	4.95%	5.61%	12.14
1912	9.38	2.96%	4.85%	7.81%	13.09
1913	8.04	-14.29%	5.38%	-8.91%	11.93
1914	7.35	-8.58%	5.50%	-3.08%	11.56
1915	9.48	28.98%	4.32%	33.30%	15.41
1916	9.8	3.38%	5.73%	9.11%	16.81
1917	6.8	-30.61%	9.30%	-21.31%	13.23
1918	7.9	16.18%	7.16%	23.34%	16.31
1919	8.92	12.91%	5.26%	18.17%	19.28
1920	6.81	-23.65%	7.27%	-16.38%	16.12
1921	7.31	7.34%	5.77%	13.11%	18.23
1922	8.78	20.11%	5.63%	25.74%	22.93
1923	8.55	-2.62%	5.93%	3.31%	23.69
1924	10.16	18.83%	5.08%	23.91%	29.35
1925	12.46	22.64%	4.38%	27.02%	37.28

Performance of America's Largest Stocks
1871-2000 (continued)

Year Ending	S&P 500 Index	Capital Gain	Div. Yield	Total Return	Total Return Index
1926	13.49	8.27%	4.96%	13.23%	42.21
1927	17.46	29.43%	4.30%	33.73%	56.44
1928	24.35	39.46%	3.48%	42.94%	80.68
1929	21.45	-11.91%	4.56%	-7.35%	74.75
1930	15.34	-28.48%	5.47%	-23.01%	57.55
1931	8.12	-47.07%	9.08%	-37.99%	35.69
1932	6.89	-15.15%	5.66%	-9.49%	32.30
1933	10.1	46.59%	3.47%	50.06%	48.47
1934	9.5	-5.94%	4.13%	-1.81%	47.59
1935	13.43	41.37%	3.34%	44.71%	68.87
1936	17.18	27.92%	4.41%	32.33%	91.14
1937	10.55	-38.59%	8.34%	-30.25%	63.57
1938	13.21	25.21%	3.41%	28.62%	81.77
1939	12.49	-5.45%	4.48%	-0.97%	80.97
1940	10.58	-15.29%	6.25%	-9.04%	73.65
1941	8.69	-17.86%	7.92%	-9.94%	66.33
1942	9.77	12.43%	5.69%	18.12%	78.34
1943	11.67	19.45%	4.97%	24.42%	97.47
1944	13.28	13.80%	4.67%	18.47%	115.47
1945	17.36	30.72%	3.69%	34.41%	155.21
1946	15.3	-11.87%	4.44%	-7.43%	143.68
1947	15.3	0.00%	5.48%	5.48%	151.56
1948	15.2	-0.65%	6.25%	5.60%	160.04
1949	16.76	10.26%	6.68%	16.94%	187.16
1950	20.41	21.78%	6.86%	28.64%	240.75
1951	23.77	16.46%	5.91%	22.37%	294.62
1952	26.57	11.78%	5.39%	17.17%	345.20
1953	24.81	-6.62%	5.84%	-0.78%	342.49
1954	35.98	45.02%	4.31%	49.33%	511.45
1955	45.48	26.40%	4.13%	30.53%	667.62
1956	46.67	2.62%	4.21%	6.83%	713.19
1957	39.99	-14.31%	4.55%	-9.76%	643.56
1958	55.21	38.06%	3.23%	41.29%	909.28
1959	59.89	8.48%	3.16%	11.64%	1015.10
1960	58.11	-2.97%	3.37%	0.40%	1019.13

Performance of America's Largest Stocks 1871-2000 (continued)					
Year Ending	S&P 500 Index	Capital Gain	Div. Yield	Total Return	Total Return Index
1961	71.55	23.13%	2.86%	25.99%	1283.99
1962	63.1	-11.81%	3.30%	-8.51%	1174.73
1963	75.02	18.89%	3.11%	22.00%	1433.17
1964	84.75	12.97%	3.04%	16.01%	1662.62
1965	92.43	9.06%	3.06%	12.12%	1864.16
1966	80.33	-13.09%	3.64%	-9.45%	1687.98
1967	96.47	20.09%	3.08%	23.17%	2079.12
1968	103.86	7.66%	2.99%	10.65%	2300.56
1969	92.06	-11.36%	3.48%	-7.88%	2119.24
1970	92.15	0.10%	3.36%	3.46%	2192.52
1971	102.09	10.79%	2.99%	13.78%	2494.58
1972	118.05	15.63%	2.71%	18.34%	2952.17
1973	97.55	-17.37%	3.64%	-13.73%	2546.96
1974	68.56	-29.72%	5.37%	-24.35%	1926.83
1975	90.19	31.55%	4.08%	35.63%	2613.34
1976	107.48	19.17%	3.87%	23.04%	3215.47
1977	95.1	-11.52%	5.08%	-6.44%	3008.44
1978	96.11	1.06%	5.44%	6.50%	3204.05
1979	107.94	12.31%	5.55%	17.86%	3776.26
1980	135.76	25.77%	4.67%	30.44%	4925.88
1981	122.55	-9.73%	5.65%	-4.08%	4724.89
1982	140.64	14.76%	4.87%	19.63%	5652.45
1983	164.93	17.27%	4.29%	21.56%	6871.17
1984	167.24	1.40%	4.64%	6.04%	7286.23
1985	211.28	26.33%	3.82%	30.15%	9483.28
1986	242.17	14.62%	3.47%	18.09%	11198.85
1987	247.08	2.03%	3.66%	5.69%	11835.78
1988	277.72	12.40%	3.70%	16.10%	13741.44
1989	353.4	27.25%	3.31%	30.56%	17940.89
1990	330.22	-6.56%	3.74%	-2.82%	17435.11
1991	417.09	26.31%	2.91%	29.22%	22529.07
1992	435.71	4.46%	2.87%	7.33%	24181.42
1993	466.45	7.06%	2.71%	9.77%	26542.77
1994	459.27	-1.54%	2.89%	1.35%	26901.28
1995	616.71	34.28%	2.31%	36.59%	36744.60

Performance of America's Largest Stocks
1871-2000 (continued)

Year Ending	S&P 500 Index	Capital Gain	Div. Yield	Total Return	Total Return Index
1996	740.47	20.07%	2.01%	22.08%	44856.99
1997	970.43	31.06%	1.61%	32.67%	59509.95
1998	1229.23	26.67%	1.34%	28.01%	76177.85
1999	1469.25	19.53%	1.14%	20.67%	91920.79

Performance of America's Largest Stocks
1871-2000 (continued)

Beginning of Year to Beginning of Year	Arithmetic Average Annual Return	Compounded Average Annual Return	Standard Deviation
1871-2000	10.79%	9.34%	17.58%
1901-2000	11.97%	10.36%	18.46%
1901-1950	9.64%	7.78%	20.89%
1933-2000	13.95%	12.60%	17.24%
1950-2000	14.30%	13.2%	15.72%
1970-2000	14.44%	13.4%	15.18%

Average annual capital gain since 1950	10.55%
Average annual dividend yield since 1950	3.80%
One-time $1000 investment on 1/1/1950, by 1/1/2000 turns into	$ 491,150
invested since 1/1/1950, by 1/1/2000 turns into	$1,000/year $4,151,766

The table shows that during long periods of the 20th century, the stock market has usually produced double-digit compounded annual gains. The notable exception to this is surrounding the Great Crash and Bear Market of 1929-1933, when the market fell 89% peak to trough.

But even then, compounded at 7.78% annually, each dollar you invest doubles every 9¹/₄ years. That's not so bad a downside for the long-term investor, especially considering that the alternative — according to today's most common practices — would be simply to continue to spend income faster than you can make it and build even more debt.

What's more, if you actually began the *Seeds of Wealth* program just before a crash and subsequent market performance *exactly like* that of January 1929-January 1958, you'd average much better returns on a per-dollar basis than 7.23%. In fact, you'd compounded average returns well in the double digits again!

Before I explain why — and how this goes right to the heart of the great advantages of children as long-term investors — let me *show* you.

The following table combines our modest *Seeds of Wealth* income assumptions and actual market returns from the beginning of 1929 through the end of 1958.

How to Build Over $300,000 in Wealth by the Age of 30... Even If You Began to Invest Just Before the Greatest Stock Market Crash of All Time

Age	Income	Savings Rates	Invest	Year	Total Return	Wealth
1	$730	100%	$730	1929	-7.35%	$676
2	$730	100%	$730	1930	-23.01%	$1,083
3	$730	100%	$730	1931	-37.99%	$1,124
4	$730	100%	$730	1932	-9.49%	$1,678
5	$730	50%	$365	1933	50.06%	$3,066
6	$730	50%	$365	1934	-1.81%	$3,369
7	$730	50%	$365	1935	44.71%	$5,403
8	$730	50%	$365	1936	32.33%	$7,633
9	$730	50%	$365	1937	-30.25%	$5,579
10	$730	50%	$365	1938	28.62%	$7,645
11	$730	50%	$365	1939	-0.97%	$7,932
12	$730	50%	$365	1940	-9.04%	$7,547
13	$1,300	50%	$650	1941	-9.94%	$7,382
14	$1,300	50%	$650	1942	18.12%	$9,488
15	$5,200	50%	$2,600	1943	24.42%	$15,039
16	$5,200	50%	$2,600	1944	18.47%	$20,897
17	$5,200	50%	$2,600	1945	34.41%	$31,583
18	$7,800	10%	$780	1946	-7.43%	$29,958
19	$7,800	10%	$780	1947	5.48%	$32,423
20	$7,800	10%	$780	1948	5.60%	$35,062
21	$7,800	10%	$780	1949	16.94%	$41,914
22	$37,828	15%	$5,674	1950	28.64%	$61,217
23	$37,828	15%	$5,674	1951	22.37%	$81,855
24	$37,828	15%	$5,674	1952	17.17%	$102,558
25	$44,281	15%	$6,642	1953	-0.78%	$108,348
26	$44,281	15%	$6,642	1954	49.33%	$171,715
27	$44,281	15%	$6,642	1955	30.53%	$232,810
28	$44,281	15%	$6,642	1956	6.83%	$255,807
29	$44,281	15%	$6,642	1957	-9.76%	$236,834
30	$53,292	15%	$7,994	1958	41.29%	$345,917

The table shows that even if your children began to invest on the eve of the Great Crash of '29 and legendary bear market of the early '30s, they would end up with well over $300,000 by the age of 30!

That's after the worst bear market of all time... and assuming they've never earned an above-average income!

The Double-Whammy Stress Test

Now, let's give our suppositions an even greater stress test. And let's significantly _reduce_ our income at the same time. The table below shows the same modest income assumptions through the age of 21, but from 22 to 30, we assume your children just make their age — $22,000 at 22, $23,000 at 23, etc.

The net result is, under this scenario, their total income from the ages of 22 to 30 adds up to $234,000. That's 40% less than the $388,181 in total earnings under the scenario where we use Bureau of the Census 2001 average income figures for college grads.

Now let's see what happens...

How to Build Over a Quarter Million Dollars In Wealth by Age 30... Even If You Make a Below-Average Income, And Begin to Invest Just Before the Greatest Stock Market Crash of All Time

Age	Income	Savings Rates	Invest	Beginning of Year	Total Return	Wealth
1	$730	100%	$730	1929	-7.35%	$676
2	$730	100%	$730	1930	-23.01%	$1,083
3	$730	100%	$730	1931	-37.99%	$1,124
4	$730	100%	$730	1932	-9.49%	$1,678
5	$730	50%	$365	1933	50.06%	$3,066
6	$730	50%	$365	1934	-1.81%	$3,369
7	$730	50%	$365	1935	44.71%	$5,403
8	$730	50%	$365	1936	32.33%	$7,633
9	$730	50%	$365	1937	-30.25%	$5,579
10	$730	50%	$365	1938	28.62%	$7,645
11	$730	50%	$365	1939	-0.97%	$7,932
12	$730	50%	$365	1940	-9.04%	$7,547
13	$1,300	50%	$650	1941	-9.94%	$7,382
14	$1,300	50%	$650	1942	18.12%	$9,488
15	$5,200	50%	$2,600	1943	24.42%	$15,039
16	$5,200	50%	$2,600	1944	18.47%	$20,897
17	$5,200	50%	$2,600	1945	34.41%	$31,583
18	$7,800	10%	$780	1946	-7.43%	$29,958
19	$7,800	10%	$780	1947	5.48%	$32,423
20	$7,800	10%	$780	1948	5.60%	$35,062
21	$7,800	10%	$780	1949	16.94%	$41,914
22	$22,000	15%	$3,300	1950	28.64%	$58,163
23	$23,000	15%	$3,450	1951	22.37%	$75,396
24	$24,000	15%	$3,600	1952	17.17%	$92,560
25	$25,000	15%	$3,750	1953	-0.78%	$95,558
26	$26,000	15%	$3,900	1954	49.33%	$148,521
27	$27,000	15%	$4,050	1955	30.53%	$199,151
28	$28,000	15%	$4,200	1956	6.83%	$217,240
29	$29,000	15%	$4,350	1957	-9.76%	$199,963
30	$30,000	15%	$4,500	1958	41.29%	$288,885

Even beginning to invest just before a market like 1929 and after, and with all these restraints on our income assumptions, we still end up with over $288,000!

I think you'd have to concede that's pretty remarkable...

We've just given ourselves a *double-whammy* — income a third below the average *and* we're beginning to invest just before the greatest all time market crash. Yet we *still* end up building over a quarter-million dollars in wealth by the age of 30!

How is this possible?

It all has to do with your children's uniquely powerful advantages as young investors...

Harnessing Your Children's Great Advantages As Young Investors

Throughout childhood and into young adulthood, our children are just beginning to build their wealth. Throughout most of this period, they don't have a great deal at risk. And they also have at least a 30-year time horizon as investors (though probably longer, since they may not need to touch a significant part of their wealth until their 40s, 50s, or later).

That combination means they're in a much better position than the average investor to ride out the market's ups and downs and still end with a nest egg in the hundreds of thousands, even millions, of dollars, by the time they begin to raise families of their own.

Your children, in other words, aren't going to be "lump-sum" investors, risking a great deal at once. And they're not going to try to "time" the market, jumping in and out — something, as we said, that is futile for even most adult *professional* investors.

Instead, as *Seeds of Wealth* investors, your children will invest steady, small sums over a long period of time — far longer than a single market cycle. And that means, though they initially suffered temporary losses of a few hundred dollars in the above "worst-case scenario," they also continued to invest at *the very bottom* of the market and each time the market began a new bull cycle!

The reason your children would have had such great success during one of the worst market periods in history was not because they were "buy and holders" in January 1929 — but because they were "buy and builders."

In the Accumulation Phase of Your Investment Career You Can Better Withstand the Market's Volatility

If your children had had a lot of money in 1929, buying and holding would have been a big mistake. If they had a half-million or million dollars that they might be in need of soon, they would have been better off using trailing stops (selling whenever a particular investment falls by a certain percentage). But trailing stops work best for investors in or approaching the "wealth preservation" stage of their investment careers.

Your children, by contrast, are just beginning the "wealth accumulation" phase. They're adding new money to the market (in a diversified fashion) all the time, as a fixed percentage of their income. As their income goes up, the amount they invest goes up.

And because, in this case, a major market drop happened early in the wealth-accumulation phase, it actually helped them far outperform traditional buy and holders.

Let me show you what I mean.

Seeds of Wealth Investors Are
Not Static Index Investors

Going by a standard "total return index," the stock market averaged 8.4% average annual returns from January 1929 through December 1958. At that rate, each dollar you invest doubles in value about once every $8^1/2$ years.

Considering that you get those total returns in the wake of the greatest bear market ever, that's not too shabby. Nonetheless, these returns are far below the 10.36% compound average annual returns for the entire 20th century. And they're even farther below the 12.6% compounded average annual returns since the end of 1933 (near the market bottom), the 13.2% compound annual returns from 1950 to 2000, and the 13.4% returns from 1970 to 2000.

Yet a standard total return index assumes a single amount invested at the beginning of the period. It does not take into account contributions, or variations in the size of contributions during the period. The standard index, in other words, bears little resemblance to the experience of most investors, who are constantly bringing new money into the market and pulling some money out.

It reflects even less the experience of the young *Seeds of Wealth Investor*, who is a disciplined saver and investor who begins averaging about $1 a day through the age of 12, then steadily increases his average contributions over the years as his income rises. When you take this into account, the advantages of our young *Seeds of Wealth Investor* are astounding.

In fact, while the market posted 8.4% compounded annual returns during this period (on the basis of a standard total return index), our *Seeds of Wealth Investor* got "dollar-weighted" compounded average annual returns equivalent to 13.39%! That's very close to the total index return of 13.4% annually from January 1970 to January 2000, the best 30-year period in history!

Compare the final wealth figure in the following table (the last cell in the bottom right-hand corner of the table), with the final wealth figure in the table on page 175 and you'll see they're the same.

How to Get Returns Equivalent to 13.39% Compounded Annually, Even Investing Just Before the Greatest Stock Market Crash and Bear Market of All Time!

Age	Income	Savings Rates	Invest	Wealth Built Up at 13.39%Compounded Avg. Annual Returns
1	$730	100%	$730	$828
2	$730	100%	$730	$1,766
3	$730	100%	$730	$2,831
4	$730	100%	$730	$4,038
5	$730	50%	$365	$4,992
6	$730	50%	$365	$6,075
7	$730	50%	$365	$7,303
8	$730	50%	$365	$8,695
9	$730	50%	$365	$10,273
10	$730	50%	$365	$12,063
11	$730	50%	$365	$14,092
12	$730	50%	$365	$16,394
13	$1,300	50%	$650	$19,327
14	$1,300	50%	$650	$22,652
15	$5,200	50%	$2,600	$28,634
16	$5,200	50%	$2,600	$35,418
17	$5,200	50%	$2,600	$43,110
18	$7,800	10%	$780	$49,769
19	$7,800	10%	$780	$57,319
20	$7,800	10%	$780	$65,881
21	$7,800	10%	$780	$75,589
22	$37,828	15%	$5,674	$92,148
23	$37,828	15%	$5,674	$110,924
24	$37,828	15%	$5,674	$132,215
25	$44,281	15%	$6,642	$157,456
26	$44,281	15%	$6,642	$186,077
27	$44,281	15%	$6,642	$218,531
28	$44,281	15%	$6,642	$255,333
29	$44,281	15%	$6,642	$297,064
30	$53,292	15%	$7,994	$345,917

After investing for 30 years at 13.39% returns, the wealth achieved is identical to that achieved after 30 years if your child began *Seeds of Wealth* just before the Crash of '29 (see page 175.).

As we've explained a bit already, the principal reason your children would do so well, even beginning just before the greatest bear market of all times, is that *they are in the <u>wealth-accumulation</u> phase of their investing careers.* And that's one of your children's great advantages as investors.

The following very simple graphic shows the difference between two investors at opposite ends of their investment careers.

Wealth Accumulation Phase ◄──► Wealth Preservation Phase

The younger you are, the closer you are to the left of this line. The older you are, the closer you are to the right.

In the very earliest points in the Wealth Accumulation phase, you don't have much capital to risk. And even as you add capital, you can withstand market volatility better than older investors. That's because you have a much longer time horizon — and hence a longer time *not only to make up for any temporary losses, <u>but to add new exceptional gains</u> <u>when investing at the bottom of new market cycles</u>.*

This is why, by the time your children are in their mid-20s to early 30s, they should begin to diversify into other asset classes, beginning with real estate investments. (Usually that means first buying their own home, then later possibly buying real estate strictly for investment.)

At around this stage, once they've accumulated a significant amount of wealth, they can also begin to use other strategies to "preserve," or protect, some of the wealth they've achieved. These strategies might include an initial "loss limit" and a wider, subsequent trailing stop, among other things. We'll address these a little more starting on page 307.

The Moral of the Math

Before I wrap this section up, let me make one point as clear as I possibly can...

I am not advocating that you put your children's savings into the S&P 500 or any other index regardless of the level at which the index is trading. On the contrary, as we'll cover in more detail, you should generally put new money into the value end of the market—especially when investing for the long term. And that, in fact, is why your children did so well in the above scenario.

Just a couple of years after they started investing, the market did turn into a value index. Consequently, even though the market suffered manic ups and downs in the '30s, your children were basically loading up their portfolio with shares bought at low prices relative to past highs and relative to future earnings.

As the market and economy began a sustained recovery in the late '30s, the value of their investments bought at low prices soared during the '40s and '50s.

However, following the *Seeds of Wealth* investment strategy we're about to cover, you would not have put new money into the S&P 500 in 1929 and 1930 since there were clear signs that the market was overvalued and therefore overdue for a correction. Principal among those signs were the facts the market was selling at a record price-to-earnings ratio and had risen at a record rate, virtually uninterrupted, for the previous five years.

Instead, by focusing on value, in 1929 and 1930 you would have sought other sectors of the market that were already selling substantially below former highs and at good or reasonable prices relative to past earnings and probable future earnings.

In short, the point of the 1929 investment scenarios is to emphasize that children are in an ideal position to go for maximum long-term gains and weather market volatility better than other investors.

And that's a major reason you should ***never put off starting your child's Seeds of Wealth savings and investment program today just because you think the broad market might be overvalued and ready for a major fall! Instead, focus on putting new money into mutual funds representing sectors of the market that offer the best value at the moment.***

Don't Waste Time with
"Psychic Hotline" Investing

No one has a crystal ball. We can't pretend to pick the tops and bottoms of markets — not in 1929-1933, and not in 1999-2003. But you can make sure you put your new savings into the value end of the market.

Warren Buffet doesn't make more money investing in the market than anyone else because he pretends to be able to predict the market. Far from it. He basically makes money, he says, because he buys good companies at good prices and usually buys these companies with an eye for the long term.

And that, in effect, is what your children are going to do — through a careful selection of low-cost, no-load mutual funds.

In the first edition of *Seeds of Wealth*, published in 2000, I said the market was overvalued and that a "severe correction is likely in the next few years." Writing today, in mid-2003, I still think the market is overvalued. Nonetheless, I continue to invest for myself and my children.

My "new money" and their "new money" go into sectors of the market I believe *are not* overvalued at the moment. But money we already have in good investments will not be pulled out because I have a hunch about what will happen to the broad market tomorrow, next week, or next month.

On page 307, we'll talk about when to sell an investment — both for an adult who's more in the wealth preservation phase of his or her life and for a child who's in the wealth accumulation phase. But for now, the point I'd like to emphasize is this...

Trying to Predict the Market in the Short Term Is a Sucker's Game

Only a handful of professional investors can play the "prediction game" successfully. And, frankly, I don't want to spend my days reading stock market charts and trying to guess its direction because what the statistics show more than anything else is that most professionals who trade on that basis do far worse than they would do by simply buying an index fund.

We've already shown how 70%-80% of professional mutual fund managers fail to beat the market in a typical year, and since most investors invest via mutual funds, they also fail to beat the market. In fact, many of them do a great deal worse.

A few years ago, for instance, Morningstar took a look at 1,000 growth mutual funds over a 6-year period and found that the average return for those funds were 12.01% annually during that time. *Yet individual investors in those funds averaged only 2.2%!* Why? Because they were trying to time the market!

Short-term timing is not a game that should be played by most investors. After all, Ibottson Associates reports that a dollar invested in the stock market in 1926 was worth $1,114 by 1995. Yet, if you took out the best 35 months of that period, it was worth just $10.16!

By the same token, the University of Michigan looked at the 7,802 trading days between 1963 and 1993. They found that one dollar invested at the beginning of the period turned into $24.30 at the end of it. But if you take out the best 90 days, it was worth only $2.10!

Finally, even if you were an excellent market timer, chances are you'd lose more than you would gain by jumping in and out of the market.

Jeremey Siegel, in fact, reports that if you had gotten out of the market just one month after each peak since World War II and then gotten back into the market just one month after each bottom, you would have gotten about 0.6% less return annually than if you stayed put.

<u>Focus on value rather than trying to guess peaks and troughs... buy when an important sector of the economy is severely undervalued. Sell when that sector is severely overvalued and there are clearly better values elsewhere.</u>

The Trouble with Timing

The trouble with jumping in and out of the market is that — unless you have a crystal ball — for every fall of the market you miss, you may miss an equal or greater rise. Ultimately, you will certainly increase your trading and tax costs... and the chances of your improving your performance are miniscule!

What's more, *Seeds of Wealth* is designed to help any young person steadily build a great deal of wealth over time. You don't have to be a market expert to build a great deal of wealth over time through disciplined saving and value-focused investment.

And even if your children have their hearts set on becoming firemen, nurses, or schoolteachers (jobs that generally don't pay very well), there's no reason they shouldn't be able to build a significant amount of wealth by the time they're ready to start families of their own.

By following the principles laid out in this program, they can still build 6- and even 7-figure wealth at a very early age — without becoming "market mavens" or spending all their free time pouring through financial reports.

And that applies even if the broad market's about to go through a correction. That's because they'll be putting new money into sectors that have already corrected. They'll also be ready to buy the broad market after it has corrected and sells once again at low or reasonable multiples of earnings.

This isn't to say they'll buy into the broad market exactly when it bottoms. That's very unlikely. But they don't have to buy at the exact bottom either.

Even if they buy it just a third below where peak buyers buy the market, that means they'll make 50% when the market gets back to the former peak, while peak buyers will just be breaking even.

For example, let's set the market index to 100 and suppose it goes down by 10 points a year for 5 years then recovers by 10 points a year for 5 years. People who bought at 100 in the beginning waited 10 years to get even. People who bought at 67 on the way down, made 50% in less than 7 years. Not killer returns, but not bad for being very early. People who waited for value and then for signs the market was recovering might have also missed the bottom. But even if they bought at 67 on the way up, they made 50% in just over 3 years. And, presumably, for the first 7 years of the broad market's correction and recovery, they invested in other sectors offering more value and the prospect of better long-term returns.

In short, your children should buy diversified groups

of funds — but each representing a sector selling at good prices and with the prospect for long-term earnings growth.

They should sell only if 1) the reason they originally bought an investment has changed, 2) if the investment becomes severely overvalued relative to its own earnings and relative to other sectors of the market, or 3) if their chosen fund is significantly underperforming its sector over a long period of time. (More details on when to buy and sell on page 307.)

The need to make good investments for your children as soon as they have the money — and not wait until you think you've heard the "all clear" sound in the broad market — is very much the point I was making on page 175.

That's where we saw how even if your children began this program and mistakenly invested in an overvalued sector just before the Crash of '29, they would have ended up with over $345,000. And even if they began the program and had income 40% below the average as college-graduate adults, they still would have amassed a fortune of $288,885 by the age of 30.

Well, to hammer home the point again — because it's a very important one — we're going to put our assumptions through another stress test. We'll see what happens if your children begin to invest just before a 30-year market like that which occurred leading up to and in the wake of the next greatest bear market of all time — that of 1972-74.

Even If the Market Were to "Peak" Again Tomorrow, Your Child Can Build a Nest Egg of Over $400,000 by the Age of 30

The following table takes us back to the 2nd greatest market peak of all time — that of 1968. It shows your children would still get incredible results even if they began the *Seeds of Wealth* Program in the year Richard Nixon was elected president and the "Go-Go" market of the '60s was topping out ...

Thirty years later, your children would end up with over $412,000 each by the age of 30! That's equivalent to a dollar-weighted compounded average annual return of 14.52%.

And your child continues to build this wealth even after inflation, the legendary bear market of 72-74, stagflation, and the crash of '87!

And even if we reduce the adult income assumptions by a quarter to 75% of the national income averages, the *Seeds of Wealth Investor* still ends up with $309,519 after 30 years!

That's over $300,000 by age 30, even with below-average income *and* in the wake of the 2nd greatest bear market of all time!

Moral: No matter how you feel about the current state of the overall market, begin your children on the *Seeds of Wealth* savings and investment program today! Simply focus on putting new money into sectors of the market that offer good value for long-term investments.

How to Build a Half-Million Dollar
Fortune Investing Right Through
The 2nd Greatest Market Crash of All Time

Age	Income	Savings Rates	Invest	Beginning of Year	Total Return	Wealth
1	$730	100%	$730	1968	10.65%	$808
2	$730	100%	$730	1969	-7.88%	$1,417
3	$730	100%	$730	1970	3.46%	$2,221
4	$730	100%	$730	1971	13.78%	$3,357
5	$730	50%	$365	1972	18.34%	$4,405
6	$730	50%	$365	1973	-13.73%	$4,115
7	$730	50%	$365	1974	-24.35%	$3,389
8	$730	50%	$365	1975	35.63%	$5,092
9	$730	50%	$365	1976	23.04%	$6,714
10	$730	50%	$365	1977	-6.44%	$6,623
11	$730	50%	$365	1978	6.50%	$7,443
12	$730	50%	$365	1979	17.86%	$9,202
13	$1,300	50%	$650	1980	30.44%	$12,851
14	$1,300	50%	$650	1981	-4.08%	$12,950
15	$5,200	50%	$2,600	1982	19.63%	$18,603
16	$5,200	50%	$2,600	1983	21.56%	$25,774
17	$5,200	50%	$2,600	1984	6.04%	$30,088
18	$7,800	10%	$780	1985	30.15%	$40,174
19	$7,800	10%	$780	1986	18.09%	$48,363
20	$7,800	10%	$780	1987	5.69%	$51,939
21	$7,800	10%	$780	1988	16.10%	$61,207
22	$37,828	15%	$5,674	1989	30.56%	$87,320
23	$37,828	15%	$5,674	1990	-2.82%	$90,372
24	$37,828	15%	$5,674	1991	29.22%	$124,110
25	$44,281	15%	$6,642	1992	7.33%	$140,337
26	$44,281	15%	$6,642	1993	9.77%	$161,339
27	$44,281	15%	$6,642	1994	1.35%	$170,249
28	$44,281	15%	$6,642	1995	36.59%	$241,615
29	$44,281	15%	$6,642	1996	22.08%	$303,073
30	$53,292	15%	$7,994	1997	32.67%	$412,692

For Anyone with "Get-rich-quick" Fever

To measure volatility, you take an average of all yearly returns over a certain period of years. Then you calculate how much, on average, each yearly return differs from that average. That average difference is called the standard deviation, and it's the most common measure of risk in the stock market.

For the 20th century, the simple average total return for one-year periods was about 12%. And the average standard deviation was about 18.5% for one-year periods. That means the returns in any given year "deviated," or strayed from the average, by about 18.5%.

Now, statistically, a single standard deviation either side of the mean (or average) should cover 68.26% of possible outcomes in a "normal" or random distribution of outcomes.

In other words, about 2/3 of the time the returns in any given year should be between —6.5% (the 12% average minus the 18.5% standard deviation) and 30.5% (the 12% average plus the 18.5% standard deviation).

Now, statistics also show that given a "random" or normal distribution, two standard deviations from either side of the mean should cover 95.44% of possible outcomes. So, in any given single year in the stock market there is a roughly 95% chance that you'll get between — 25% (12% - 18.5% x 2) and 49% (12% + 18.5% x 2).

From roughly negative 25% to positive 49%... That's a big swing! On a year to year basis, in other words, the stock market can be very volatile.

But when you measure the market over 15-year periods, you get a very different result.

Longer Investment Horizons Make for More Stable Returns

During the 20th century, the average annual return of the S&P 500 for 15-year periods was 9.5%. And the average standard deviation over rolling 15-year periods was just 4%.

That means the "normal range" of returns you might expect over a 15-year periods is much narrower than for a typical one-year period. During most 15-year periods, in fact, you would have a 95% chance of annual returns ranging between 1.5% (9.5% - 4% x 2) and 17.5% (9.5% + 4% x 2).

But here's the great news for your kids: during 30-year periods, the standard deviation, or risk, is even less.

During all 30-year periods in the 20th century (spanning the crash of '29, the Depression, two World Wars, the bear market of '73-'74 and the crash of '87), the average annual return was less, just 8.8%. But the standard deviation was much less too: just 2.1%. And that means that in any given 30-year period you have a 95% chance of getting annual returns between 4.6% (8.8% - 2.1% x 2) and 13% (8.8% + 2.1% x 2).

Now that's a 95% chance that *in the worse case scenario,* you'll double your money about every 15 years... and a 95% chance that *in the best case scenario* you'll double your money about every 5 1/2 years.

Those are pretty good odds — when you consider that your odds on a year-to-year basis were that you would lose money more than 1 out of every 4 years, and that in the worse case scenario, you'd lose 25%!

And, remember, this is just for the S&P 500. Since your children are long-term investors, they can target strategies that have proven to be more volatile yet also more profitable over the long term. And these other strategies — whether small cap, value, growth, or international — also have decreasing volatility over longer periods of time.

The moral of the story? Your chances for greatly compounding your wealth while reducing risk are best when investing over the long term.

And that plays right to your children's strong suits as young investors with a very long time horizon.

What to Buy, What to Buy?

At this point we've established four important things about your children as investors.

- They should be 100% in stocks

- They should be long-term investors

- They should always put new money into sectors of the market that 1) promise to be important areas of the economy for many years and 2) are selling at good values

- And, given that they're in the wealth-accumulation phase of their investing careers, they should stay fully invested through bull and bear markets (again, with an eye toward reasonably priced investments with "new money," especially)

Now, let's take a look at the best ways to invest in the overall market. Then we'll see if there are certain strategies we can follow to help us do better than the overall market.

In other words, even though we've pointed out that 70% to 80% of professional managers fail to outperform the market, we'll explore strategies that have proven to outperform the market when followed _over the long term_. And these are strategies that play to children's natural strengths as investors.

But whether our goal is to get the returns of the overall market with a minimum of bother or to go for returns higher than the overall market, our first step to understanding the investment strategies we're about to discuss is to understand exactly what "the market" is.

There Is More to the Market than the S&P 500

The S&P 500 is the most common market index used today. This index has been around "officially" for only about 50 years. Yet analysts have "reconstructed" the index as far back as 1871 to track the equivalent performance of the U.S.'s 500 or so largest companies. The Dow Jones Industrials Average (the next most popular index) is inferior in this regard, since, when it started out in the late 1800s, it consisted of only 12 companies in the index — and so was much less representative of the overall market.

The S&P 500 is, in fact, what most financial analysts and other market commentators usually mean when they talk about "the market." It's also what we've been referring to when we've talked about the performance and risk of the market so far in this guidebook.

The S&P 500 and the Dow are not the *only* market indexes, however. Standard & Poor's and Dow Jones (the creators of the S&P 500 and Dow Industrials indexes, and owners of the trademarks) have each created dozens of indexes. Other financial outfits have also developed indexes that are now widely used to measure all different parts of the market, from big companies to small, from utilities to technology stocks.

Yet the S&P 500 is the most commonly used index

because it consists of the 500 largest publicly traded companies, while the Dow today is made up of only 30 large companies. And since the combined market value of the S&P 500 makes up about three-quarters of the value of *all* public companies traded in the U.S., this index is generally thought to provide a better gauge of what's going on with publicly traded companies in general.

Another important fact to know about the S&P 500 is that it's a "market-weighted" index. That means each company in the index makes up a piece of the index in proportion to its "market capitalization," or "market cap."

Market cap is the entire value a company would sell for at any point in time. Microsoft, for instance, is the largest company in the world. In 2000, its market exceeded $500 billion. It still has the largest market cap, even though it was worth only about $290 billion in mid-2003. It sells about $32 billion worth of goods and services each year, more than the annual production of many small countries.

Because Microsoft is the biggest company traded in the U.S., it also makes up the biggest single portion of the S&P 500. Next come GE and Pfizer. Each of these makes up between 4% and 5% of the index. Then come the fourth and fifth largest companies, accounting for smaller percentages of the overall index and so on.

Together, the S&P 500 companies make up about 75% of the value of all the publicly traded companies in the country. (And the top 50 of these companies, by the way, make up about *a third* of the U.S. market cap!) At the same time, the S&P 500 companies command most of the volume (or number and value of shares bought and sold) in the stock market.

Yet in terms of the sheer number of companies, the S&P 500 is a minority, since there are over 7,000 publicly traded companies in the U.S. today.

This is an important fact to remember because often the biggest profits can be made by investing in some of the 6,500-plus companies that are *not* in the S&P 500. (We'll come back to this idea a little later when we talk about long-term investment strategies to beat the market. But for now, let's continue to focus on the merits of investing in the S&P 500.)

You Know 'Em, You Love 'Em

Most of the companies in the S&P 500 are household names — to investors and non-investors alike. They make and sell the stuff we eat, drink, drive, work with, play with, and otherwise use everyday — from Coca Cola, Microsoft, McDonald's, and Disney, to GE, General Motors, Nabisco, and Wal-Mart.

If you bought these companies in proportion to their market cap (about 4.5% of your money going into Microsoft, a little more than 4% into GE, etc.), you would be buying the "market." And, as we've shown throughout this course, history shows that over the long term you can make pretty good money doing just that. But you'll do even better if you only buy it when it's selling at low or reasonable valuations.

Our first recommended strategy, then, is simply to "buy the market" when it's priced right. And the most *efficient* way to do that (meaning without unnecessary costs) is through an index fund.

How to Buy 500 Stocks at Once, Pay No Commission And Very Low Annual Costs

If you were to go out and try to buy at least a single share in each of the S&P 500 companies, you would have to spend tens of thousands of dollars and a lot of time on your phone or computer placing all those buy orders. You'd also be wasting a good deal of that money on commissions.

Even if you're paying a discounted rate of $7 a trade, your commission costs would be $3,500. And then you'd eventually pay another $4,000 or so years down the road when you sell.

But there's a much better way to do it. And that's through a mutual fund.

A mutual fund is an investment company that buys shares in many different public companies. When you buy shares in the mutual fund you are in effect buying pieces of all the different companies in which the mutual fund invests.

For the small investor — which is what your children will be until they reach their twenties or thirties — there are some very big advantages to sticking strictly with mutual funds.

First off, your children will save on commissions. The mutual fund's portfolio manager buys millions of dollars of a given company's shares and does so either without paying commission or at commission rates per share that are just a miniscule fraction of what you would pay.

Second, your children have financial professionals managing their investments for them — leaving your children the time they need to focus on *their* primary business, whether it's studying now or practicing medicine in the future. The fund manager and his team will do the research, they'll decide when to buy and sell individual companies within the fund, and they'll carry out the actual transactions on your children's behalf.

If you want your children to benefit from companies that rise in value over the long term, but you don't want to spend the bulk of your own time researching the stock market, why not have a group of financial professionals do the work for you? That, in effect, is what happens when you help your children invest their money in mutual funds.

Third, your children get instant "diversification" and reduce their risk by spreading their money among many different investments. After all, if you buy the S&P 500, that's far more diversified — and hence less risky — than if you bought just five, ten, or twenty stocks.

And since your children will be starting with small sums to invest — perhaps $250 or so in their first fund, this gives them instant diversification from the moment they make their first small investment (or you make it for them).

And even for an adult, buying all 500 stocks would be

extremely expensive for the average individual, so a mutual fund is a much better way to go. With a mutual fund, you can achieve that diversification without the enormous costs you would incur by buying 500 or even 50 stocks on your own.

Sifting Through Mutual Fund Mania

Because of the advantages I just mentioned, mutual funds have grown tremendously in popularity over recent years. In fact, *there are more mutual funds in the U.S. today than there are public companies!*

Mutual funds, in short, make investing in the market easy. But they don't make *beating the market* easy. If you choose a mutual fund at random, there's roughly a four-in-five chance you will underperform the market, and only a one in five chance you'll meet or beat the market.

Those aren't great odds.

But what if I told you that your children can achieve about 97% of the returns of the S&P 500 with almost absolute certainty? Well, that's exactly what they can do with some of the lower-cost index funds...

The First Rule for Successful Investing: Keep Costs Down

Index funds are created to imitate a particular index. As of today, there are over 200 index funds. More than 60 of them are modeled on the S&P 500, a few on the Wilshire 5000, around 50 on subsets of the U.S. market, more than 25 on international markets, and over 20 on the bond market.

Now remember, your children should be invested 100% in equities for the first 25 or 30 years of their investment career, since history shows that's the best way for the average person to get the highest returns in the financial markets when you have a very long-term horizon. With that in mind, then, we're going to focus on equity mutual funds. And since we're addressing the benefits of index investing right now, we're talking about equity index funds.

An equity index fund simply buys and sells stock of companies in relationship to the weighting of those companies in a particular index. An equity index fund, consequently, doesn't have to pay a research staff or a manager to make buy and sell decisions.

What's more, in the case of the S&P 500, for instance, since only about 8%-10% of the companies in that index are changed in a typical year, the trading activity is about *one-tenth* that of the typical managed funds. And that means much lower costs in the trading area too. Finally, about 2/3 of index funds are no-load funds as well, meaning you pay no sales commission when you buy and sell the fund.

The advantages to this low-cost approach to investing are tremendous. To see why, you have to understand how unnecessary expenses and sales commissions can seriously eat away at your wealth — even if you're a long-term investor who doesn't trade in and out of the market.

Prevent Profit Erosion

The first expense you may run into when buying a fund is the "load," or sales commission. This can be a front-end load or a back-end load, commissions charged when you buy or sell. Or it can be a deferred load, a sales charge that decreases the longer you hold the fund — often to zero after about 5 years or so.

The trouble with load funds is that you pay more, but don't necessarily get more. Sure, some load funds have outperformed the market spectacularly. For instance, Fidelity's Magellan, managed by the legendary Peter Lynch, beat the stock market by 10.3 percentage points a year between 1978 and 1992!

That's a phenomenal record. And it would be great if you could identify the next Peter Lynch at the beginning of his career. But that's a long-shot proposition, since the great majority of managed funds *underperform* the market. And not only do they gain less than the market, but also many charge you a relatively high commission for that doubtful privilege!

Overall, according to a study by the American Association of Individual Investors, when you take loads into account, load funds *underperform* no-load funds. So you should generally try to steer clear of load funds, and if you do invest in one, go for a deferred load fund whose sales charge decreases each year and ends up being zero after 5 years or so.

And while a load will typically range from 2% to 5%, there are other charges you also have to watch out for — charges that apply to load and no-load funds alike.

These are the expenses of a fund, and they are often expressed in terms of an "expense ratio."

Keep Expense Ratios Low

Expense ratios measure the fees fund managers charge to fund shareholders for fund management, distribution, and administration as a percentage of the fund's "total assets." Total assets is the net value of all the shares the fund holds.

So if a mutual fund has 10 million shares outstanding with a value of $50 per share, the total assets are $500 million ($50 x 10 million). And the fund management company will charge a percentage of that $500 million each year — to pay for their services, accounting and secretarial fees, the costs of mailing out prospectuses (brochures describing the funds), etc.

Industry-wide, these expense ratios average about 1.5% of total assets, a bit more for funds of stocks that are harder to buy, like international shares or small-company shares. An index fund like the **Vanguard 500 (symbol VFINX)**, by contrast, carries an expense ratio of only 0.19%.

Now, while a difference in fees of 1.31 percentage points may not sound like much, over time it can add up.

A Percent or Two a Year Can End Up Costing You $67,000 or More Over the Long Run

To keep the math simple, let's say your child invests $1,000 a year over 30 years at 13.2% compounded average annual returns. If he or she is investing in an Index fund like the Vanguard 500 (and, for the sake of simplicity, in a tax-deferred account), the net annual return will be 13.01% (13.2% minus the 0.19% expense ratio.)

At that rate of return, your child ends up with $331,993 after 30 years.

A pretty good sum. However, if you subtract 1.31% in higher expenses and end up actually getting 11.89% annual returns (13.2%-1.31%), you end up with $264,335. Not bad, but you have given up $67,658 of your profits to expenses. And that's for an average fund.

A fund with above-average expenses and a load to boot can end up taking even more of your profits... Just avoiding these pitfalls and investing in the S&P 500 can be a very effective investment strategy for your children...

When Low-cost, Low-minimum, No-loads aren't Available... Low-cost, Low-minimum, Deferred Loads Can Provide a Good Option

A final note on loads: there are a significant number of good no-load funds with low expense ratios. However, many of these require initial investment min-

---

P/Es in Brief

P/E stands for price-to-earnings ratio. A company selling at $100 a share and earning $10 per share is said to sell at a P/E of 10 (since 100 ÷ 10 = 10). A company selling at $100 a share and earning $5 per share is said to sell at a P/E of 20 (since 100 ÷ 5 = 20).

---

imums of $1,000 or more. That could unnecessarily delay making your first investment for your children.

Toward the end of this section, you'll find a list of some good no-load, low-cost, low-initial-investment-minimum funds and fund families. (A fund family is a group that manages a number of funds under their name, such as Janus or Vanguard.) At that point, we'll also talk about how to screen for mutual funds and find the ones you want for your children, and for which they can meet the investment minimums. We'll also incorporate a unique *Seeds of Wealth* strategy that will help your children reap maximum after-tax return, and *reduce* their investment minimums at the same time.

Yet sometimes you look to invest in a certain trend, idea, area, or industry for which you cannot find a low-cost, no-load fund with an affordable minimum. In that case, keep deferred-load funds in mind.

Many mutual funds, in fact, will have different share classes. For instance, Salomon Brothers (www.sbam.com; 1-888-777-0102 or 1-800-SALOMON) has many good funds with reasonable expense ratios and low investment minimums of just $250. However, all their funds are load funds. Yet, the loads differ according to class, and as a long-term investor your child can easily end up paying no load after all.

For instance, Salomon Brothers' Investors Value Fund (SAIFX) is a growth and income fund (meaning it targets a mix of growth companies and companies that pay high dividends in its portfolio). This fund has three load classes: A, B, and 2. (Don't ask why it's not A, B, and C!)

Class A charges a front-end load of 5%, class B has a deferred (and decreasing) load of a maximum 5%, and class 2 has a front-end load of 1% and a back-end load of 1%. In this case, the class B could be a good choice.

The class B charges a 5% back-end load if you sell in the first year, 4% in the second year, 3% in the third, 2% in the fourth, 1% in the fifth and 0% if you sell anytime after the 5th year. The expense ratio on the B is 1.7%, about average, but again the initial investment minimum is just $250.

In this way, then, you can increase the number of funds you can choose from. You can find good funds with even lower expense ratios and reasonable minimums. And, after 5 years or so, your child ends up having paid no load in any case.

So you can keep that idea in mind when you're screening for new funds. In the meantime, however, we'll continue to focus on low-cost no-loads with reasonable minimums, since there are enough quality ones to choose from for your children's first few funds at the very least.

So let's take a look at the kind of investment strategies we can target with mutual funds that will give us a good chance of high returns over time...

Strategy #1: Target the 500 At Low or Reasonable Valuations

Your children don't have to "beat the market," in order to turn a modest amount of savings beginning today into a 6-figure fortune by the age of 30 and a

7-figure fortune sometime in their 40s.

Once you get your children to faithfully save a signif-icant portion of their income and invest — even in the overall "market," or S&P 500 — you've won more than half the battle of helping them create a life of plenty instead of a life of financial struggle.

After all, the S&P 500 represents a section of the market, let's remember, that has produced 10.39% annual compounded returns over the last century, 12.6% over the last 67 years, 13.2% from 1950 to 2000, and 13.4% from 1970 to 2000. As the main phase of the current bear market ends — though it may be in one, two or three years — there is every reason to believe it will once again post those types of long-term returns

That's because the S&P 500 has a history of perform-ing exceptionally well after major market lows. That includes compounded average annual returns of nearly 14% in the 30 years following the market low in 1932. And it includes nearly 16% compounded annual aver-age returns for the 25-year period following the bear market of 1972-74.

So, for those who want to keep things simple — yet still invest with very good profit potential —our first recom-mended stock investing strategy is to buy the S&P 500 whenever it sells at low or reasonable valuations.

Specifically, that means you should have a preference for putting new money into the S&P 500 when...

It sells at low or reasonable price-to-earnings ratio. (A price-to-earnings ratio is commonly referred to as the "P/E." And, historically, a low or reasonable P/E for the S&P 500 is about 15 or below.)

It is selling significantly off its former high (about 30% or more)

When the companies in the S&P 500 have recently experienced a number of years of earnings declines. (In this case, it would be more likely that the market is closer to the bottom of an earnings cycle and may even be at the beginning of an earnings recovery.)

These are not infallible criteria. But they have proven to be very helpful guidelines for helping long-term investors earn compounded average annual returns in the low- to mid-teens from the S&P 500.

If you want to know more details about how these value factors have tended to produce superior returns over the long run, you can read the sidebar entitled "What Is Value Anyway?" beginning on page 213.

But it isn't necessary for you to read that sidebar, and it's certainly not necessary for your child to read it at this stage. I put it there for those parents and investors who may want a little more technical information to back-up the "value" argument.

For now, it's enough to keep in mind that the S&P 500 can be a good addition to your portfolio when it's selling at low to reasonable P/Es and when it has come down significantly from a former high point.

Now, when you do decide that the S&P 500 presents

good value for the long term, what's the best way to take advantage of that fact? Begin by making sure you keep costs low. Next, you'll find a number of very good ways to do just that...

Get the Lion's Share of the Profits with No-load, Low-expense Funds

The Vanguard 500 Index Fund (VFINX) is one of our favorite funds, and we highly recommend it to beginning investors especially. Most index funds are very hard to beat, but Vanguard's index funds are among the hardest to beat — simply because they have such a low cost.

The Vanguard 500 is Vanguard's fund that tracks the S&P 500. It has a record of capturing about 99% of the S&P 500's total return. At the same time, it's a no-load fund with a very low expense ratio — only 0.19%, about 1/8 the average ratio.

Compared to the Vanguard 500, in other words, the average fund is starting with a handicap of 1.31% in expense ratios (1.50-0.19) *plus* whatever they charge in commissions if they're load funds. If the load is 5%, for instance, over 10 years, that averages to an extra charge of 0.5% a year. The total extra cost for this fund, then, would be 1.81% annually over the Vanguard 500.

That means the average fund would have to outperform the S&P 500 by nearly 2% a year, after expenses and commissions, for its investors to do better than they would with the Vanguard 500. And this, as James P. O'Shaughnessy points out, is very hard to do.

In 1995, for instance, about 22% of actively managed

Continued on pg. 214...

Bargain Company Price Paid = $100 (Initially $10 earnings per share, with 10% annual growth rate)			Expensive Company Price Paid = $100 (Initially $5 earnings per share, with 20% annual growth rate)		
Year	Annual Earnings	Cumulative Earnings	Year	Annual Earnings	Cumulative Earnings
1	$ 11.00	$ 21.00	1	$ 6.00	$ 11.00
2	$ 12.10	$ 33.10	2	$ 7.20	$ 18.20
3	$ 13.31	$ 46.41	3	$ 8.64	$ 26.84
4	$ 14.64	$ 61.05	4	$ 10.37	$ 37.21
5	$ 16.11	$ 77.16	5	$ 12.44	$ 49.65
6	$ 17.72	**$ 94.87**	6	$ 14.93	$ 64.58
7	$ 19.49	$ 114.36	7	$ 17.92	$ 82.50
8	$ 21.44	$ 135.79	8	$ 21.50	**$ 103.99**
9	$ 23.58	$ 159.37	9	$ 25.80	$ 129.79
10	$ 25.94	$ 185.31	10	$ 30.96	$ 160.75
11	$ 28.53	$ 213.84	11	$ 37.15	$ 197.90
12	$ 31.38	$ 245.23	12	$ 44.58	$ 242.48
13	$ 34.52	$ 279.75	13	$ 53.50	$ 295.98
14	$ 37.97	$ 317.72	14	$ 64.20	$ 360.18
15	$ 41.77	$ 359.50	15	$ 77.04	$ 437.21
16	$ 45.95	$ 405.45	16	$ 92.44	$ 529.65
17	$ 50.54	$ 455.99	17	$ 110.93	$ 640.58
18	$ 55.60	$ 511.59	18	$ 133.12	$ 773.70
19	$ 61.16	$ 572.75	19	$ 159.74	$ 933.44
20	$ 67.27	$ 640.02	20	$ 191.69	$1,125.13
21	$ 74.00	$ 714.03	21	$ 230.03	$1,355.15
22	$ 81.40	$ 795.43	22	$ 276.03	$1,631.18
23	$ 89.54	$ 884.97	23	$ 331.24	$1,962.42
24	$ 98.50	$ 983.47	24	$ 397.48	$2,359.91
25	$ 108.35	$1,091.82	25	$ 476.98	$2,836.89

When we bought Bargain Company at $100, it had just earned $10 in the previous year, giving it a P/E of $10. During our first year of ownership, earnings increased 10% so we made $11 in earnings in that year. Then we made that $11 plus 10% of $11 in the second year, or $12.10. Through the second year, we had cumulative earnings of $23.10 ($11 in the first year plus $12.10 in the second).

What Is Value Anyway?

Benjamin Graham, a mentor of Warren Buffett, once wrote, "In the short run, the market is a voting machine. In the long run, it is a weighing machine."

What Mr. Graham meant is that in the short run, markets are driven by perception and emotion. So, in the late '90s (just as in the late '20s) analysts and investors were blithering about a "New Era Economy" where earnings didn't matter any more. And as long as greedy voters controlled the market, they were right. The S&P 500 soared to new heights, as did the NASDAQ — even though the NASDAQ was loaded down with companies that did nothing but lose money.

In the long run, however, earnings count. A company that consistently produces earnings *and earnings growth* increases its worth. As long-term investors, that's what we're looking for—only in the form of groups of companies held in mutual funds.

This is why the price-to-earnings ratio (or P/E) is the most common measure of value used by analysts and investors. A company that sells for $100 a share and produces $10 of income per share sells for a P/E of 10. A company that sells for $100 and produces $5 of income per share sells for a P/E of 20.

All other things being equal, you would prefer the share with a P/E of 10. To see why, let's call the company selling at a P/E of 10 "Bargain Company" and let's call the company selling at a P/E of 20 "Expensive Company." And let's assume that earnings for both companies stay flat, at $10 per share, for ten years.

In the case of Bargain Company, it would take you 10 years to make your money back from earnings (besides the resale value of your investment). In the case of Expensive Company, it would take you 20 years to make your money back just from earnings.

Likewise, if we assume 10% earnings growth per year for both companies, Bargain Company pays you back sooner — in about 6 ? years. Expensive Company pays you back in about 10 ? years.

But of course, all other things are *never* equal. It may be that earnings at Expensive Company are about to grow at twice the rate of Bargain company. Over time, then, Expensive Company may have proven to be the better bargain! The table on page 212 shows why.

---

funds beat the Vanguard 500 index fund. But less than 8% beat it by 2 percentage points or more.

Overall, in fact, Vanguard boasts that in a typical year the Vanguard 500 Index Fund beats 94% of funds on a pre-tax basis and 97% of funds on an after-tax basis. As a result of this track record, it has grown to become the largest fund in the world, with investors holding over $80 billion worth of its shares.

Continued on pg. 222…

By year six, cumulative earnings alone had nearly paid us back our initial investment.

For Expensive company, it took a little longer to recoup our investment from earnings—nearly eight years. But, by year 13, Expensive company produced more cumulative earnings than Bargain company had. By year 22, it had produced more than twice the cumulative earnings.

Expensive Company, in other words, turned out to be a "growth company" in the best sense of the word. It didn't simply grow rapidly in share price; its earnings grew rapidly over a long period of time. The result was that investors who paid a premium for the shares back when it traded for a P/E of 20 ended up doing better over the long term than investors in Bargain Company.

So where does that leave us with the S&P 500? At what P/E is it a bargain?

The answer, just as with the two companies above, really depends on *where you are in the earnings cycle.* If earnings are about to embark on a long period of strong, sustained growth, you can afford to pay a little higher P/E. If earnings are about to fall and perhaps tread water for quite a while after that... paying a high P/E will likely mean very poor returns in the long run.

The S&P 500 and Earnings

The table on the following page shows P/Es for the S&P 500 at the beginning of each year of the 20th century, as well as the total return for the year.

S&P 500: Price/Earnings Ratios and Total Returns

Year	PE Ratio	Return	Year	PE Ratio	Return	Year	PE Ratio	Return
1900	13.55	17.94%	1934	22.95	-1.81%	1968	17.66	10.65%
1901	15.53	19.44%	1935	19.39	44.71%	1969	17.81	-7.88%
1902	16.37	5.10%	1936	17.22	32.33%	1970	15.22	3.46%
1903	13.12	-13.82%	1937	16.69	-30.25%	1971	17.28	13.78%
1904	12.63	29.14%	1938	9.34	28.62%	1972	18.3	818.34%
1905	17.43	18.95%	1939	20.66	-0.97%	1973	19.04	-13.73%
1906	14.36	6.96%	1940	13.87	-9.04%	1974	12.47	-24.35%
1907	12.96	-27.10%	1941	10.21	-9.94%	1975	7.53	35.63%
1908	9.83	41.71%	1942	7.80	18.12%	1976	11.87	23.04%
1909	15.51	18.23%	1943	9.55	24.42%	1977	11.21	-6.44%
1910	13.37	-7.11%	1944	12.42	18.47%	1978	8.85	6.50%
1911	12.40	5.61%	1945	14.29	34.41%	1979	8.30	17.86%
1912	15.40	7.81%	1946	18.08	-7.43%	1980	7.43	30.44%
1913	13.36	-8.91%	1947	14.16	5.48%	1981	9.19	-4.08%
1914	12.71	-3.08%	1948	9.47	5.60%	1982	8.00	19.63%
1915	14.23	33.30%	1949	6.64	16.94%	1983	10.32	21.56%
1916	10.70	9.11%	1950	7.23	28.64%	1984	12.47	6.04%
1917	6.35	-21.31%	1951	7.19	22.37%	1985	10.05	30.15%
1918	5.21	23.34%	1952	9.71	17.17%	1986	13.78	18.09%
1919	7.99	18.17%	1953	11.06	-0.78%	1987	16.34	5.69%
1920	9.66	-16.38%	1954	9.88	49.33%	1988	15.64	16.10%
1921	8.48	13.11%	1955	13.27	30.53%	1989	12.19	30.56%
1922	25.29	25.74%	1956	12.65	6.83%	1990	14.71	-2.82%
1923	12.75	3.31%	1957	13.59	-9.76%	1991	15.21	29.22%
1924	8.94	23.91%	1958	11.73	41.29%	1992	23.30	7.33%
1925	11.15	27.02%	1959	19.58	11.64%	1993	24.31	9.77%
1926	10.12	13.23%	1960	17.84	0.40%	1994	23.05	1.35%
1927	10.88	33.73%	1961	18.94	25.99%	1995	16.86	36.59%
1928	15.73	42.94%	1962	21.20	-8.51%	1996	17.47	22.08%
1929	17.64	-7.35%	1963	17.27	22.00%	1997	20.58	32.67%
1930	13.32	-23.01%	1964	18.34	16.01%	1998	23.88	28.01%
1931	15.81	-37.99%	1965	17.90	12.12%	1999	32.34	20.67%
1932	13.31	-9.49%	1966	17.45	-9.45%	2000	33.29	-9.08%
1933	16.80	50.06%	1967	14.66	23.17%	2001	24.57	-11.54%

The table shows that the average P/E for the index over the entire 20th century (at least using beginning of year figures) is 14.2. The median P/E is 13.6. (Median is simply the midpoint; that is half the P/Es are greater than 13.6 and half are less.)

If you sort and crunch the numbers a little further (which I have), a few more interesting points arise.

If you bought the S&P 500 when it traded below the median P/E, your average return over the year would be 12.1%. If you bought it when it was above the median, your average return would have been just 9.4%. What's more, the low P/E advantage holds up over 5- and 10-year periods too.

If you bought the S&P 500 when it traded below the median P/E, your average return over the next 5 years would be 81%. If you bought it when it was above the median, your average return would have been just 56%.

For 10-year periods, if you bought the S&P 500 when it traded below the median, your average returns over the next 10 years would be 222%. Buying above the median, you'd realize just 115%.

Going by these findings, it would seem that lower P/Es tend to produce higher returns over the long run. There are some notable exceptions, however.

Exceptions Prove the Rule that Earnings Matter

If you bought the S&P 500 at the beginning of 1922, you would have been buying at a P/E of 25.3. And yet, over the next 5 years, you would have raked in 131% gains.

Likewise if you bought the S&P 500 in 1993 and 1994, you would have been buying at P/Es of 24.3 and 23.1, respectively. Yet, you would have made gains of 146% and 187% over the next 5 years, even though you bought at "expensive" levels.

Finally, at the beginning of 1946, the S&P 500 traded at 18.1 times 1945 earnings. And yet it returned a stellar 330% over the next 10 years

How is that possible?

Again, in each case, it's because of where the S&P 500 was in the earnings cycle.

Soaring demand for new inventions (such as the automobile, telephone, and radio) in the Roaring '20s, the postwar recovery in the late '40s, and the sharp decline of interest rates in the 1990s all led to earnings booms.

What's more, in all these cases, earnings or share prices or both were coming off periods of long, substantial declines. In 1922, for instance, the index was selling for less than its 1905 level. Earnings had fallen 40% the year before and finished the year below pre-WorldWarI levels.

In 1946, the index was selling for less than its 1929 value (even less than its 1927 value!) and earnings were below levels reached 20 years before.

By 1993, share prices had been doing very well,

posting nearly 13% compounded annual returns (including dividends) in the previous decade. Yet earnings were still below 1984 levels. As interest rates continued to fall, earnings skyrocketed between 1993 and 1997, and the index soared.

In all these "exceptional" instances, strong earnings recoveries pulled the market higher.

Also keep in mind that the numbers show — beyond any doubt — that it is always disastrous as a long-term investor to buy high P/Es after a prolonged period of earnings increases and substantial share price increases. When earnings correct (which they inevitably do after a long expansion), high P/E stocks soon become exposed as overvalued stocks. See 1929, the mid-'60s and late '90s.

The moral is that earnings matter over the long term. And the lower the price you can get relative to earnings, usually the better. On average, low P/Es provide significantly higher returns over 1-, 5- and 10-year periods. And the exceptions to this rule only pan out after a prolonged earnings decline is about to lead to a substantial earnings recovery.

Buying When the Market Has Corrected

Sorting and analyzing the performance number of the S&P 500 during the 20th century, another interesting pattern arises. During any given year, the market low of that year averages about 26% below the market's former high. The median yearly low, meanwhile, was about 31% below the market's former high.

That means that in half the years of the 20th century, the market traded at a discount of 31% or more to its former high. In the other half of the years, the yearly lows were less than 31% off the former high.

And here's where that matters: If you bought the S&P 500 in years where it traded at a discount of 31% or more to its former high, you would have done better, on average, than if you bought it in years when it traded at lesser discounts to its former high. And those advantages, apply to 1-year, 5-year, 10-year, and even 30 — year periods.

Buying at the steeper discount would have produced 12.1% average gains in one-year periods vs. 11.8% for the lesser discount.

For 5-year periods, you would have made 74.2% on average vs. 67.2% for lesser discounts.

For 10 years, the performance advantage is 211% vs. 146%.

And for 30 years, it's the difference between making 20.3 times your money vs. 14.5 times your money.

Again, we see that, for long-term investors especially, there are significant advantages to buying "low" — that is, trying to steer your money into the value end of the market.

These Are Value Guidelines (Not Magic Numbers)

As I said at the outset, there are no magic numbers. You shouldn't simply buy the S&P 500 (or any sector or market, for that matter) just because it's trading below a P/E of 14.4 or a discount to its former high of 31% or greater.

There will be some occasions (rare, but they do happen) when a market is 30% off its high and yet can fall another 30% to 40% or more from there. This kind of situation is most likely to happen after a massive bull market and as the economy enters a major recession.

There will be other times when the market may be a slightly low P/E but earnings are still rapidly declining. This means the low P/E of today turns into a higher P/E even if the share price doesn't move. But, again, this is more the exception than the rule.

Overall, low P/Es and significant discounts to former highs can be very useful guidelines for identifying value — *especially when they appear after there have been stagnant or declining earnings for a number of years.*

As a long-term investor, then, you should have a preference for the S&P 500 when it sells...

At low or reasonable P/Es

At a significant discount (30% or more) from its former high

After earnings have already corrected for a number of years (and therefore are likely to be bottoming out soon or already on the way to recovery)

History shows that these criteria generally present an opportunity for healthy returns over the long term. And the common sense notion of "buying low" reinforces what the stats reveal.

Unfortunately, Vanguard does have one major drawback for children who are only beginning to invest. All their funds carry relatively high minimums. For UTMA and UGMA accounts (accounts for minors), the minimum initial investment is $1,000. So, if your children already have $1,000, this could be an excellent way to start to invest their savings. And, of course, if they already have $800 or $900 in savings, when you add new savings they could also begin to invest in this fund very soon.

If, however, your children don't have that much savings already accumulated, it could take them a while to reach the $1,000 to meet Vanguard's minimum. In that case, you may want to purchase an "exchange traded" index fund, such as the Ishares S&P 500 Index Fund

(IVV) or the Standard & Poor's S&P 500 Index Fund (known as spiders, and trading under the symbol SPY).

Bite-sized Minimums Perfect for Kids

Exchange-traded funds (ETFs) as a rule have very low expense ratios. In fact, quite a few have lower expense ratios than Vanguard, the mutual fund company that used to be, hands-down, the low-cost lead. IVV's expense ratio, for instance, is just under 1/10 of one percent. That's about half Vanguard's 500 Index Fund's already-low ratio of 0.1945%.

Exchange-traded funds are also broken into shares that trade at a certain percentage of the index they track. IVV and SPY, for instance, each trade at roughly 1/10 the value of the S&P 500 index. Therefore, if the market doubles over the course of 5 years, so does your share (give or take a percentage point).

But the real benefit for your children (besides the low expense ratios) is that, with exchange-traded funds, your children don't have to wait to accumulate $1,000 in savings to buy into the fund. Instead, you can buy a single share of an ETF for a lot less than $1,000. As of this writing, for instance, IVV and SPY are priced around $100.

However, because these funds do trade on an exchange, you will have to pay a broker's commission to buy and sell them. Still, a deep discount broker like Scottrade (which charges just $7 commission on a market order) can soften the blow. For instance, if you bought $300 worth of IVV, your $7 commission would only come out to the equivalent of about 2.3% load — not too bad. And the longer you hold the fund and the more it goes up, the less that one-time commission costs you as a percentage of the investment's ultimate value.

We'll explain index shares and talk a bit more about discount brokers in a little while. For now, however, keep in mind that investing in the S&P 500 via an index fund can be a perfectly good strategy if you want to be relatively conservative.

You'll get instant diversification. And your child will own a piece of America's largest and most successful companies (and a handful of large international companies that are included in the S&P 500). What's more, you'll be able to do it without trying to predict the market, or having to invest hundreds of hours every year researching individual companies and funds.

Next, we'll talk about other, more aggressive investment strategies. But, for now, if you just want to make sure your child gets returns that are very close to the returns of the 500 largest U.S. traded companies of the next 30 years or so, investing in an index fund is the way to go.

Strategy # 2: Going for Bigger Gains By Targeting Smaller Companies

They say big things come in small packages. When it comes to stocks, that is often the case.

In *Stocks for the Long Run*, Jeremy Siegel points out that $1,000 invested in the S&P 500 in 1926 was worth about $727,000 by year-end 1992. The same $1,000 invested in the small cap companies, however, grew to $2,279,000 — creating more than triple the wealth!

During that period, he found that small cap stocks beat large cap stocks 56.71% of the time on a one-year basis, and 94.7% of the time on a 30-year basis.

How Small Is Small?

So what is a small cap stock? There are different ways to look at it. Most use dollar figures. But because the size of the U.S. market has tripled in the last 5 years, the dollar figures that define a small cap have been changing rapidly.

In *What Works on Wall Street*, James O'Shaughnessy, using 1996 figures, referred to small caps as companies with market caps under $500 million. In the wake of the soaring bull market of the late '90s, the standard definition for small caps changed. Today, the Investment Company Institute (the mutual fund industry trade association) marks $1 billion as the cutoff for small caps.

This would imply that in 1980, for instance, the cutoff for a small cap was much smaller than $500 million and in 1960 and 1940 it was much smaller still. Because of the changing dollar size of the market then, perhaps the best way to look at small caps is in "tiers."

Jeremy Siegel, for instance, calculated the better-than-3-to-1 long-term wealth creation of small caps by measuring the performance of companies in the lowest quintile (or lowest 20%) in terms of market value.

Professors Gabriel Hawawini and Donald Kleim published a widely cited paper at the Wharton School of Business that shows portfolios of stocks in the smallest quintile of the U.S. market posted about 16.2% annual returns between 1962 and 1994. That's about 5 percent-age points better on a compounded basis than the return of the S&P 500 over that period. And that's enough of an advantage to create ***nearly 6 times the wealth*** when compounded over the 32-year period.

The popular Russell 2000 small cap index, mean-while, measures the performance of the 2000 U.S.-trad-ed companies next in size *after* the largest 1000. Since the top 1000 companies cover about 80% of the U.S. equity market capitalization, the Russell fits in the bot-tom quintile (20%). But it's not the entire bottom quin-tile. After all, there are about 7,000 U.S. companies in total, and the Russell 2000 makes up the top 2000 of the smallest 6000 more or less. In total it makes up about 8% of the U.S. market cap.

As of mid-2003, the median company size of the Russell 2000 was about $444 million. The smallest company in the index had a market cap of about $117 million, while the largest reached a market value of about $1.2 billion.

As of mid-2003, this index is flat over the last 5 years (not counting dividends). The S&P 500, by contrast, is down by 18% (not counting dividends) during the same period. Going back a bit further, small caps are still the winners in recent history — confirming their long-term record of beating the big caps.

The Wilshire 1750 Small Cap Index, for instance, is another widely used small cap index. It has been around since 1980. Since then, it has posted 14.6% annual returns— about 3.4 percentage points better than the roughly 11.2% returns of the S&P 500 during that time.

So whether you're focusing on the smallest 20% or 25% or simply buying the Russell 2000 through an index fund, one thing is certain — over long periods of time, small caps tend to outperform large cap companies. And this is true not only in the U.S., but abroad too.

It's a Small Cap World

According to the University of Chicago's Center for Security Prices Research, small caps outperform even when adjusted for risk. And this advantage holds in every single country in which it was tested. Keim's and Hawawin's Wharton School study, meanwhile, showed 16 of the 17 markets it studied showed this small cap advantage.

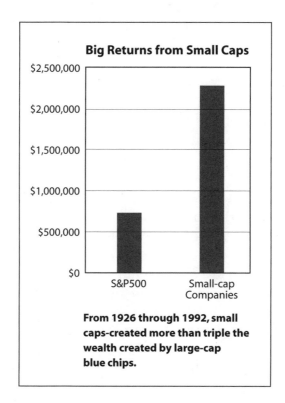

Big Returns from Small Caps

From 1926 through 1992, small caps-created more than triple the wealth created by large-cap blue chips.

The periods studied varied for each country and ranged from five to 44 years. In the U.S. the period studied was from 1951 to 1994. During that time, the S&P 500 compounded at about 11.1% while small caps grew at about an 18.4% rate. That's a 7.3 percentage-point annual advantage.

That means a single dollar invested in the S&P 500 at the beginning of that period with dividends reinvested would be worth just over $102 at the end of it. The same dollar in small caps, however, would be worth $1,688 — creating more than _**16 times the wealth!**_

In Japan and Australia, meanwhile, the "small cap premium" was even bigger. In these countries small caps posted an annual advantage of 14.4 percentage points over the broad market!

That's good to keep in mind, for when we look at opportunities in international investing a little later. But to maximize the growth of your children's investment portfolio, you can do very well focusing on U.S. small caps.

According to _Investing in Small Cap Stocks_, a book published by Bloomberg (a leading financial data firm), small caps have historically outperformed the S&P 500 by an average compounded annual return of 2 percentage points a year. That's a huge advantage. Because of compounding, over time you end with far more than 2% extra wealth. Over the course of 30 years, in fact, you can end up with a third more wealth!

For instance, if the 2% advantage holds as it has over most of the last century, and your child gets 15.2%

returns, he'd turn those few dollars a day into $460,239 by the age of 30. That's 37% more than the $335,854 he'd end up with if he got 13.2% from large caps.

Small is Beautiful

If you think about it for a moment, it only makes sense that some of the biggest profit opportunities you'll ever come across are from small companies. After all, "ground-floor" investing is about financing a great idea or business before everyone else recognizes it as a great idea or business.

Investors in IBM, for instance, made profits of about 250% between 1986 and 2000. However, investors who bought upstart Compaq when it first went public in mid-1986 had over 2,700% profits by 2000! Investors in Dell when it first went public, meanwhile, did even better — taking in profits in excess of 22,000% between 1988 and 2000!

The companies that make up the S&P 500 are, in general, excellent companies that make a lot of money. But they also have a lot of investors already and a lot of competitors trying to knock them off their perches.

For most of these S&P 500 companies (including *now* Dell and Compaq), their days of the most rapid share price growth are likely behind them. They should continue to make their investors good returns for a very long time. And they're worth investing in. They are, however, "mature" companies — and by and large no longer offer the same "explosive" potential that is offered by many smaller companies — companies that are small today, but that tomorrow may occupy a spot on the S&P 500.

So what's the price for the greater profit potential of small companies? You guessed it — it's greater risk. But, with the right mutual fund and a long-term investment horizon, you can diversify away much of that added risk.

For Long-term Investors, Small Cap Funds Can Provide Additional Returns that Far Outweigh the Increased Risk

The best way to play the small cap advantage is with a mutual fund. There are a number of reasons for this.

First, you'll save on commissions and spreads. Commissions are often a little more expensive for "OTC" (over-the-counter stocks), where most small caps trade. At the same time, the average spread on the Russell 2000 is 2.75% (compared to just 0.45% for the S&P 500). A mutual fund, however, can consolidate or even eliminate most commissions and pare-down spreads when buying in quantity.

Second, you'll be able to instantly diversify away much of the higher risk of small cap stocks. According to Jeremy Siegel, small caps have traditionally had more than twice the volatility of large caps, though much of this volatility is diversifiable.

Third, you'll save a great deal of time. Since many small caps are relatively newer companies or are not widely followed by the investing public, it's often difficult to get research on them. But for a small cap fund manager, it's his job to dig up the good and the bad on these companies.

For these reasons, a small cap fund is the way to go —
especially for investors with limited funds, such as your
children. And there's good news in that there's no
shortage of small cap funds to choose from. Because of
the success of small caps as a group, the number of small
cap funds has mushroomed — from 45 in 1985 to over
600 today.

So how do you start looking for the right small cap
fund for your child? The same way you start to look for
any kind of fund — by looking to keep commissions and
the expense ratio down.

Small Cap Index Funds Can Provide Big Returns

To find a mutual fund, you can use the "fund-screener" or "fund-finder" service of just about any financial
Internet site — ranging from Yahoo! Finance to any
online brokerage. One of the most popular sites for
finding funds is that of Morningstar, a service that specializes in rating and providing data on mutual funds.

Millions of mutual fund investors rely heavily on
Morningstar's five-star performance rating system. In
fact, according to the Vanguard Group, 85% of the new
mutual fund money flows in 1997 went into funds with
a four- or five-star rating.

This would seem to make perfect sense; success attracts
customers. The only problem with this is that a fund's performance rating has very little correlation with its future
performance. In fact, the opposite is actually true.

Studies repeatedly show that most funds that earn

five-star performance ratings do not continue to outperform the market over the next three to five years or more. In fact, a good many go on to underperform the market since the sectors they represent may no longer be "hot." But that's only natural — all things, even good investments, move in cycles.

So a better way to go is to look for <u>low-cost</u> funds that are fully invested or nearly fully invested (90% or more invested) in the kind of companies and industries you want to invest in. (After all, you don't want to buy a mutual fund where the manager is going to hold a large part of your investment as cash — you could hold cash yourself.) Then check to see that the fund has generally kept close to the performance of the fund's overall benchmark.

Let's say, for instance, the fund you're looking at is a small cap fund, and its index, the Russell 2000, has returned 15% annually over the last 10 years. In that case, a <u>low-cost</u> fund that has produced 14.5% returns will probably be a much better long-term investment than a high-cost fund that has produced 15.5% returns.

Over the long run, the performance of these two funds may even out, but the lower cost fund will leave you with a greater share of the profits. After all, relative performance, even for the best managers, is always a bit cyclical.

A good fund manager may outperform for a few years, then underperform for a few. Over the *long run*, however, the chances of the fund matching or exceeding the benchmark are far better for a low-expense ratio fund than for a high-expense ratio fund.

It's better to first identify funds that are investing in the sector you want to target — whether it's small caps, Asian stocks, technology, etc.

Then, limit your search to no-load or deferred-load funds, the sales charge of which eventually decreases to zero (since there is evidence that load funds tend to underperform no-load funds after costs are taken into account).

Then, among this group, your first screening criterion should be a low expense ratio because — all other things being roughly equal — the expense ratio is going to make a big difference in the return you get over the long term.

In fact, William Sharpe (a Nobel-prize-winning economist and developer of the Sharpe Ratio, the most widely used measure of risk-adjusted returns in the financial industry) did an extensive study on mutual fund performance a few years back. He concluded that, when looking for a mutual fund, "the first thing to look at is the expense ratio."

Once you've found your list of low-cost, small cap funds, you can choose your type of small cap fund from basically three types: a generally diversified small cap fund, a small cap growth fund, and a small cap value fund. Of these three types, you'll find they exist in both managed and indexed form.

Growth funds focus on companies that have the

potential to grow rapidly or are already growing rapidly. For small caps, this growth is often in the form of sales, not earnings, as many growth fund managers will buy stocks that are still in the early stages of their business and are not yet posting profits.

Value funds, on the other hand, tend to focus on profitable companies that are temporarily out of favor with investors and, consequently, sell at prices that are attractive relative to their earnings.

As a rule, says Christopher Graja, value funds beat growth both in the U.S. and abroad. And the same holds true for small cap funds. From 1975 to 1997, for instance, small cap growth funds returned about 15.8% annually while small cap value returned closer to 18.8%.

Still, small cap growth stocks still deserve consideration because they should be a bit more tax-efficient than small cap value funds and because relative performance is cyclical. Both styles have proven to provide returns significantly above the S&P 500 over long periods of time, and you want to diversify your investments among different types of successful investment approaches.

To get small cap value and growth stocks in your fund, then, your best bet might be to simply buy a small cap index fund. The i-Shares S&P Small Cap 600 Index Fund (IJR), for instance, tracks the S&P 600 small cap index. The i-Shares Russell 2000 Index Fund (IWM), meanwhile, tracks the Russell 2000, perhaps the most widely cited small cap index.

You will have to pay commissions on both these funds. But through outfits like Scottrade you can keep commission as low as $7-$10. And with shares of each in the range of $120 to $170, both these funds can give your children the opportunity to purchase two, three, or four shares and tap into the overall higher returns of the small cap subsector, with a mixture of value and growth. And they can help you do it while keeping the expense ratio low. (For each fund, the annual expense ratio is just 0.20%, or 1/5 of one percent).

Alternatively, you can go for a low-cost managed small cap fund that has kept pace with (and even slightly underperformed or outperformed) the Russell 2000 benchmark index.

With an actively managed fund, the manager may have the discretion to hold onto a successful company a little longer after it's grown beyond small cap limits — even if it causes "style slippage." That's in contrast to an index fund, which would typically be obliged to sell a small company soon after it soars to $1 billion or so in value. The moment the company stops meeting the "small cap" criterion, in other words, it drops out of the index — and out of an index fund's portfolio.

Two good actively managed small cap funds are Strong Small Cap Value (SSMVX) and SSgA Small Cap (SVSCX). Both are no-load funds that have kept pace with the Russell 2000. Strong's top sector is energy, while for SSgA it's technology. The expense ratios are reasonable for both, 1.70% and 1.07%, respectively, and both have minimum investments for custodial accounts of just $250.

Keep in mind, however, whether you invest in a managed or index small cap fund, you will have more ups and downs investing in a small cap fund than you would in a large cap fund. So don't forget that you're investing on behalf of your child for the *long term*. You can't predict when the dips are going to happen. So don't jump in an out. Stick with the long-term plan.

History says you'll be amply rewarded for doing so.

Strategy # 3:
Go for Maximum Long-term Profits Through Growth Investing

Many investors think growth stocks are synonymous with small caps. It's not so. Growth stocks, like value stocks, can be found in both the small and large cap category. GE, Cisco, and Microsoft, for instance, are three of the largest public companies in the world. Yet all three were considered growth stocks—right up until the market peak in 2000.

The key criterion for a growth stock is that its sales and/or earnings are growing rapidly. For small stocks and new issues especially, it is often only the sales that are growing. For large stocks, in most cases, earnings should be growing rapidly, too.

But whether it's a small or large cap growth stock, the company's rapid growth often causes the investing public to push up its price so that it is expensive relative to its earnings, sales and book value. But even though these stocks may trade at heftier multiples than the rest of the market, they are often still very good buys.

Why?   Because often their long-term growth rate soon makes the price at which you bought them appear reasonable, and then even cheap. For instance, if you buy stock of company X at $10 a share with per-share earnings of $0.25, you're paying 40 times earnings. But if earnings are growing at 42% a year, two years later the company will be posting just over $0.50 in per-share earnings, and the $10 you originally paid will now represent just under 20 times earnings. Two years after that, you'll have over $1 in per-share earnings, and the $10 you paid then represents less than 10 times earnings.

That, in a nutshell is the idea behind growth stocks you buy for the long term. If you had waited to buy this company at a P/E of 15 or 20, you may have never gotten the chance to buy it at all—because the investing public has given it a growth valuation.

Microsoft, for instance, made investors a great deal of money in the '80s and '90s, posting over 50% compounded annual returns between the time it went public in March of '86 and 2000. Yet, during most of that time, you would have a hard time buying the stock at a P/E that was "reasonable" or "cheap" by historical standards, since it averaged a P/E in excess of 30 during much of that period.

The Nifty Fifty stocks is another example. These were a group of the most sought-after, large cap, blue-chip growth stocks in the early '70s. Today, they are often cited as an example of how overvalued stocks can become. In 1972, these stocks were trading, as a group, at a P/E of 37.3 — more than twice the P/E ratio of the

Continued on pg. 241...

How to Turn Savings Bonds Paying 5% to 6% into Investments Paying 10% to 15% or More

Usually, one of the first gifts children receive is a U.S. savings bond. It's not uncommon to give these to newborns. The idea behind these bonds is great. In fact, it connects to one of our central messages in this program: have your children begin to save and invest early and let compounding work its magic over time.

Still, whenever you receive a savings bond for your children, you should cash it in as soon as you can (usually about six months after issue) and invest the proceeds in an equity mutual fund.

Why? Because, savings bonds usually pay a rate of return that is close to that of Treasury bills. (EE bonds issued after May 1997, for instance, pay 90% of the average yield of five-year Treasury bonds.) And, as we've pointed out, over the last hundred 30-year rolling periods, stocks have beaten U.S. Treasury bills and bonds 100% of the time! (They lost to _corporate_ bonds only once, and by about 1/5 of a percentage point.)

Cash 'Em In

By investing the proceeds in equity mutual funds for the long term instead, you stand a good chance of getting 10% to 15% or more in compounded annual returns. And that creates far greater wealth than the 5% to 6% returns that savings bonds typically pay.

For instance, let's say you receive a $100 EE savings bond with an equivalent yield of 4%. That means the bond was bought for $50 and should mature to its $100 face value in about 18 years.

If, however, you cash it in after six months (the minimum time you have to hold a savings bond before cashing it in), you should receive about $51 for it. Now invest that in the stock market for 17? years (six months have already gone by, remember), and instead of ending up with $100 eighteen years after receiving the bond, it's now worth $446.56 — more than four times the value it would reach as a savings bond!

And the longer we extend this scenario, the greater the difference becomes. For instance, $50 at 4% for 30 years turns into $162. But $51 invested at 13.2% for 29 ? years turns into $1,977 — *more than twelve times the value.*

There's no question about it; your children are naturally suited to be long-term investors who can most benefit from the higher risk-adjusted returns offered by the stock market. Help them do that even with their savings bonds, and you can help multiply the future value of their current savings by more than 1,200% over the next 30 years!

Note: EE bonds issued after May 1, 1997, accrue interest every month. EE bonds issued before then accrue interest every February 1st and August 1st. So, if you're cashing in a bond that originated before May 1, 1997, try to do it in these months. Otherwise, if you cash it in July, for example, you'll get the same interest as if you had cashed it in five months earlier, in February. Exceptions to this are EE bonds issued between March 1993 and April 1995, which accrue interest monthly for at least five years. (Sorry, but it's the government, and they like to complicate things!)

Also note that for any of these bonds, if you cash it in before it's five years old, you'll lose the last three months of interest. For instance, if you cash in an EE bond after 24 months, you get 21 months' worth of interest. Go ahead and do it, nonetheless. Your children are likely to be far better off.

For instance, as in the example we used above, a $100 face value bond originally bought for $50 and yielding 4% should be worth about $51 after six months. Instead, because of the penalty, you'll get about $50.50 after cashing it in after six months (getting three months interest on it instead of six months). Yet, as we demonstrated, you're still likely to multiply the long-term value of your children's savings by as much as 1,200% more than if you left the savings in low-yielding savings bonds.

For more information on savings bonds, go to www.savingsbonds.gov.

market at that time and about 2 ? times the long-term average P/E of the market. In the bear market of 1973-74, many of these stocks fell hard — some as much as 90% or more.

And, yet, according to Jeremy Siegel, if you bought these stocks in 1972 when they were selling at their peak and held through the crash, you'd be surprised by the results. By mid-1993 you would have done better on an after-tax basis than the S&P 500 did in that time (unless you were in the very lowest tax bracket, since growth stocks tend to get taxed at lower rates than regular large cap, dividend paying stocks, as explained a moment ago).

Funds that invest in growth stocks, then, imply a willingness on the part of the fund manager to pay more for certain stocks because he believes they represent the most dynamic sectors of the economy. "Aggressive growth" funds, meanwhile, use the same basic approach but ratchet to a higher level — pursuing growth opportunities in stocks that may seem *extremely* overvalued by traditional yardsticks.

Growth Stocks Led the Go-Go '90s

In the late nineties (when the S&P 500 had its best five consecutive years in history), the largest gains came from companies in the fastest growing areas of the economy. These included many companies that sold at very high valuations throughout most of this period in finance and pharmaceuticals, diverse technology industries ranging from biotechnology to telecommunications, and, of course, the Internet.

Whether an investor in stocks or mutual funds, if you had focused strictly on value (or low price to earnings, sales, and book value), you would have missed many of the best investment opportunities in the 1990s.

When buying a growth or aggressive growth fund, just remember that growth-stock investing is a highly volatile strategy, one that is likely to produce returns above the overall market in the long run, but after a lot of ups and downs along the way.

Also, keep in mind that part of a typical growth investment portfolio is likely to include some companies that ultimately won't succeed as businesses.

Not All Growth Companies Are Cut from the Same Cloth

Granted, GE and Coca-Cola are considered "growth" companies. And they are both hundred-year-old-plus companies that should be around another 100 years. They are profitable, growing businesses with a long, successful history. A company like Amazon.com, however, is also a large cap growth stock. Yet it's only been in business since 1996 and has never posted an annual profit.

In its short history, up until the spring of 2000, Amazon made a lot of people rich. In fact, within just two years of listing in May 1997, the stock shot up 1,895%! But that's largely because investors pushed the share price up due to its growing sales and vanguard position on the Internet. It was not because of growing *earnings*. On the contrary, the company's losses got bigger every year.

In 2000, the lack of earnings finally hurt the stock, and it plunged 95% from its peak. Going forward, it's a real possibility that Amazon may never make a profit and its price will not rebound. It could eventually be bought out by another company at a lower price than it trades for today. Or it could go out of business entirely.

By mid-2003, Amazon had rebounded over 500% from its lows of 2001. Yet it has yet to post a profit, and it's still down 70% from its former high.

Amazon, in other words, may be the type of growth company that made investors rich strictly from its hyped-up promise, and later from a rebound from extreme lows. Yet it's far from clear whether the company will ever make anyone any money from actual profits. And profits (or earnings) are always what matter in the long run.

So for your children, who are starting with limited funds and no or little experience, the best way to invest in growth companies is in the context of a mutual fund.

A growth fund can well hold companies like Amazon at the right time (as it's skyrocketing up) or the wrong time (as it's plunging). But a good growth fund should also hold a diversified portfolio of profitable, new large cap growth companies like Cisco; profitable, large cap, old companies like GE, Coca-Cola, Disney, and Merck; and profitable, speculative, small cap growth companies.

Among my favorite funds in the growth area is **AIM Dynamics Inv. (FIDYX).** This no-load fund has a $250 investment minimum, a reasonable expense ratio of 1.19%. The fund invests primarily in the technology, services, and health industries.

Excelsior Value and Restructuring (UMBIX), meanwhile, is a growth fund that invests in companies expected to benefit from corporate restructuring either in the form of mergers, consolidations, liquidations, spin-offs, financial restructurings, or reorganizations.

Two-thirds of the fund is roughly equally weighted between technology, financial, and services industries, followed by lesser weightings in other industries. This no-load fund has outpaced its benchmark since 1990, and it has a reasonable expense ratio of just 0.99%.

To take an index approach to growth, try the **i-Shares S&P 500/Barra Growth Index Fund (IVW)**. You can keep the commission relatively low by buying it through a deep-discount broker like Ameritrade, and the expense ratio is only 0.18%. The index this fund tracks basically consists of half of the S&P 500 with the highest price-to-book values. (Book value is basically the money you'd be left with if you paid all a company's debts and sold off all its product, buildings, patents, and other assets — tangible and non-tangible.)

Personally, in the growth area I prefer to buy a managed fund such as the ones I mentioned above. While it is true that growth stocks will tend to have higher price-to-book values than other stocks, I don't want that to be the principal criterion for my growth fund.

I'd rather pay a proven growth fund manager a reasonable fee to select growth stocks based on the truly important criteria, such as earnings growth and the long-term prospects of particular industries.

But the best time to buy growth funds is shortly after a recession, when investment in new companies once again begins to rise. That's because growth funds (which trade at higher valuations than most stocks) tend to get hit the hardest in recessions and bear markets. They also depend more on new investment to fuel their earnings growth.

Strategy # 4
Value Investing:
Buying Good Companies at Good Prices

A very different approach to growth investing is value investing. Where growth focuses often on the "hottest" companies with little regard to relative price, value investing often focuses on overlooked, neglected, or out-of-favor companies — and with a high priority on buying the stock at a good price.

At their price peaks in the early '70s, the Nifty Fifty stocks we spoke about a moment ago, for instance, were the complete opposite of a typical value stock. They sold for high prices compared to their earnings, sales, and book value. They were all extremely popular, pursued by professional and individual investors alike, and had very small yields.

Soon after many of these stocks crashed during the course of '73-'74, however, their characteristics completely changed. Suddenly, they became good candidates for purchase for a value fund manager.

A Radical Transformation
Before the bear market of the early '70s, a high-flying,

large cap company might have been selling for $50 a share
with earnings of $2 a share and paying dividends of $1 a
share. This would mean the company was trading at a P/E
of 25 with a dividend yield of 2%. It would be an expensive stock, in other words, since, historically, the average
P/E for the S&P 500 during the 20th century is in the
neighborhood of 14 to 16 (depending on whether you're
using end-of-year numbers, quarterly, or daily P/Es). The
average dividend yield has been about 4.45%.

If, however, this company fell, let's say, 70% during
the bear market (as quite a few Nifty Fifty stocks did),
and if its earnings and dividend remained unchanged in
that time, the picture would be quite different.

Now, with a share price of $15 and earnings and divi-
dends of $2 and $1 a share, it would be trading at a P/E
of just 7.5 ($15/$2 = 7.5) and yielding 6.7% ($1/$15 =
6.7%). Now, in other words, it would be a bargain!

And, indeed, with many investors having lost money
as stocks plummeted in '73 and '74, few were willing to
"buy and hold" the Nifty Fifty in late '74/early '75.
Shares of these companies — along with stocks in general in the wake of the second most severe bear market
of all time — went from being "Wall Street darlings" to
being pariahs. And their sudden lack of admirers
showed in their lingering, depressed share prices.

These stocks were transformed in a very short time from
being beloved, expensive, and fast-growing to being
shunned, cheap, and high-yielding. They went from being
ideal growth stocks to being ideal value stocks.

Buying What's Not Popular

As in the case above, value investing often involves buying out of sync with the market. Now, that doesn't mean you're going to act as a "contrarian" investor on behalf of your children. (A contrarian investor is basically someone who always tries to buy what investors don't want and sell what investors want. A common way to put it is to say contrarian investors "buy contempt" and "sell love.")

On the contrary, you may buy companies that are currently held in contempt by the investing public, but only if the fundamentals of the company are particularly strong. At the same time, you may not sell the company once the public comes to love it again.

Warren Buffet, for instance, is probably the greatest value investor of all time. He bought Coca-Cola aggressively in the late '80s and early '90s. When he made his first purchase of Coke shares, about 7% of the company, they were selling at a reasonable P/E of 15. Yet he didn't then sell his Coca-Cola shares once the public fell in love with the stock again and began to push its shares up to high valuations again.

Even when Coca-Cola rose to a P/E of 45 — three times the P/E at which Buffet first bought it —, he continued to hold the company because he believed it was still fundamentally an excellent company with excellent prospects for continued business growth in the years ahead.

Value Investing Is a Winner

The strength of value investing is confirmed by James

O'Shaughnessy in <u>What Works on Wall Street</u>. O'Shaughnessy found that from 1952 to 1994 large cap stocks with low P/Es did better than stocks with high P/Es by better than two percentage points a year. He also found that in both large cap stocks and in the "All Stocks Universe," stocks with low prices relative to book value (P/B) and low prices relative to cash flow (P/CF) also did much better than stocks in general. And he found that stocks with low prices relative to sales (P/S) did better still.

In fact, low P/S stocks in the All Stocks Universe posted a whopping 16.01% compounded annual return between 1952 and 1994 — far better than the 12.84% return for All Stocks in general. That difference of a little more than three percentage points annually compounds to a tremendous wealth gap over time.

A single $10,000 invested in All Stocks at the beginning of 1952 turned into $1,782,174 by the end of 1954, while the same $10,000 invested in low P/S stocks turned into $5,932,7373 — more than *triple* the wealth!

But, as they say in the late-night infomercials... "Wait, there's more!"

O'Shaughnessy also found that a combination of growth and value investing produced even greater results. Low P/S stocks did even better when focusing on low P/S stocks that had had among the highest share price growth rates the previous year. In other words, this group would reflect not only value, but value in a stock that was likely showing signs of business growth reflected in its rising share price.

This group of low-P/S and high-share-price momentum stocks rose on average 18.38% during the 44-year period O'Shaughnessy studied. What's more, when he updated the long-term track record of this approach in his 1996 book <u>Retire Rich,</u> the results even improved a little to 18.81% compounded annually over a 46-year period.

Not only were these the highest returns of all practical strategies in his book, they also had the highest risk-adjusted returns as well, with a Sharpe ratio of 61 — far above the Sharpe ratio of 47 logged for the All Stocks Universe during that period.

The strategy also proved amazingly consistent, beating All Stocks 77% of the time on a one-year basis. Yet, longer term, the results were even better. This value and growth strategy beat All Stocks 100% of the time for five- and ten-year periods!

The only drawback with O'Shaughnessy's approach — for our purposes — is that it involves "rebalancing" a portfolio of 50 stocks every year according to the lowest P/S, highest share-price growth criteria we discussed.

That's fine for disciplined investors in individual stocks who have hundreds of thousands of dollars. But it would be far too expensive for your children.

Fortunately, however, we don't need to rebalance each year because it's possible to tap into the same basic idea with mutual funds.

On the one hand, you can buy a value index fund that will automatically "rebalance" its portfolio every few months, since the index itself is obliged to release companies from its portfolio that no longer meet certain value criteria and replace them with companies that do.

A good value fund along these lines is the i-Shares S&P 500 Barra/Value Index Fund (IVE). This fund tracks an index that is composed of the half of the S&P 500 with the lower price-to-book value ratios. It is an exchange-traded fund, so you will have to pay a commission to buy it (as little as $7). By the same token, the minimum is very affordable, since a single share is currently worth about $65 and you can buy four or five shares for $260-$320. Finally, the fund has a *very low* expense ratio of just 0.18%.

Managed Value

Another way to play value is through a managed value fund. This way, you can employ the services of a fund manager who has the discretion to hold onto the best companies for the long term, even when they may have technically already passed out of a "value" range.

This kind of value strategy can also pay off big. After all, Warren Buffet buys good companies at good prices, but doesn't reshuffle every year. He tends to buy and hold a company for 10, 15, 20 years or more in most cases. He buys them at a good price, and because they're good businesses, he then lets them do their thing — make money for shareholders.

For Buffet, value investing is fundamentally a long-term-biased investment approach — the type of approach that is ideal for children. The idea is to buy very good companies at temporarily depressed prices and then to hold onto them to benefit from the long-term growth of the company's business.

Buffet's returns as a long-term value investor are in fact even better than you'd get by following the winning strategy in O'Shaughnessy's excellent book. Between 1965 and 1997 he posted *after-tax* returns of 23% a year! That's enough to turn your child or grandchild into a *millionaire* before his 30th birthday even if he never makes more than an average salary!

You can even invest directly with Buffet through his company Berkshire Hathaway. It's a stock, not a mutual fund. But his company owns big pieces of dozens of profitable companies, from Coca-Cola to the Washington Post, so it has no expense ratio, and you can buy it for the same online discount commission you would any other stock.

The trouble is, however, that Buffet has never "split" his shares to keep them affordable to the average investor. As a result a single share of his fund currently costs about $70,000!

A few years ago, however, he did introduce "B shares" of his company (BRKb). These represent 1/30 of an A share (BRKa), though they have voting rights equivalent to only 1/200 of an A share. But that's not much of a drawback, since you're not likely to have a big enough stake even in A shares to sway management decisions. And the way to vote in a company owned by Buffet, in any case, is to let him make the decisions — since he has such a great long-term track record.

Berkshire's B shares still go for over $2,300 as of this writing — putting them out of reach of most custodial accounts, at least in the beginning.

But even though your children likely can't invest with Warren Buffet at this point, your children are, at the very least, developing some of the habits Buffet used to get rich: discipline, patience and a long-term perspective on investing.

What's more, fortunately, there are good, no-load managed value funds with low investment minimums that let you stay with good companies longer. **SSgA Special Fund (SSSMX)** is one such fund.

This no-load fund invests in small and medium-sized companies selected for both growth and value character-istics, concentrating in the technology, health, services and financial industries. The expense ratio is 1.10%, and the minimum investment for a custodial account is $250.

Don't Confuse Price with Value

Value is not a question of price; it's a question of what you get for the price. For instance, let's say you have a $10 share with a book value of $2 per share (P/B of 5) and earnings per share of $0.50 (P/E of 20). That stock might seem cheap in terms of dollars, but it would actually offer far less value than a $40,000 share with book value of $20,000 (P/B of 2) and earn-ings per share of $4,000 (P/E of 10).

Strategy # 5:
Invest Globally — in the U.S. *and* Overseas

Shortly after World War II, the value of U.S. stocks made up nearly 90% of the value of stocks worldwide. Fifty years later, the U.S. share of the equity market was down to about a third. But the U.S.'s diminishing share of global equity values wasn't because U.S. stocks had fallen — on the contrary, the S&P 500 rose 48-fold (not including dividends) during that time. It was because many foreign economies and stock markets were just beginning to develop — and soar in value.

Here are just a few examples:

The Japanese Juggernaut

In May 1949, Japan's Nikkei (its major stock market index) stood at 176.2. Forty years later, it stood at 39,400. That means the value of the index increased about 224 times. But that's in yen. For U.S. investors, the story was even better.

During that period the value of yen increased from 360 to the dollar to about 100 to the dollar. (Fewer yen per dollar means each yen is more valuable in dollar terms.) So for U.S. investors the market soared, not 224 times in that period, but about 806 times!

That means a single investment of $10,000 was worth over $8 million 40 years later! And people who invested year after year in that market as it was going up made fortunes. Sir John Templeton, for instance, one of the best known and most successful investors of all

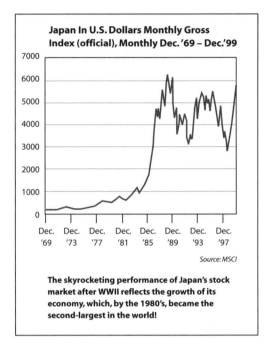

Japan In U.S. Dollars Monthly Gross Index (official), Monthly Dec. '69 – Dec.'99

Source: MSCI

The skyrocketing performance of Japan's stock market after WWII reflects the growth of its economy, which, by the 1980's, became the second-largest in the world!

time, made the bulk of his fortune investing in Japan in the 50s and 60s.

Hong Kong's Market Nearly Quintupled the U.S. Performance

Hong Kong, meanwhile, had a similar meteoric rise. According to Morgan Stanley, during the 30-year period 1970-2000, the Hang Seng's total returns (meaning including dividends) multiplied investors' capital by nearly 202 times in dollar terms.

That means a single $10,000 investment in the Hong Kong market turned into over $2 million in a generation. That's nearly five times the wealth you'd have built up if you invested the same $10,000 in the S&P 500 — during the United States' greatest 30-year stock market performance ever! (The U.S. market multiplied

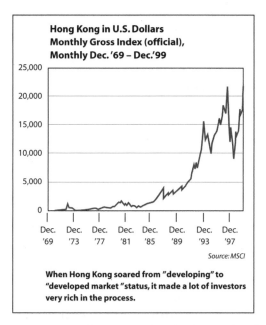

Hong Kong in U.S. Dollars
Monthly Gross Index (official),
Monthly Dec. '69 – Dec.'99

Source: MSCI

When Hong Kong soared from "developing" to "developed market "status, it made a lot of investors very rich in the process.

41.92 times on a total-returns basis from the beginning of 1970 to the beginning of 2000.)

What's more, most of the sharp rise of the Hong Kong stock market happened in a much shorter period. The Hang Seng (Hong Kong's main stock market index) stood at about 590 in September 1983. Shortly, after they fixed the value of the Hong Kong dollar to the U.S. dollar that very month, it took off. By late 1996 it was nearly 2,400.

A single $10,000 investment turned into over $400,000 just 13 years later!

From the Mid'80s to the Mid '90s, Chile Got Very, Very *Hot*

Chile saw a more dramatic medium-term rise than even Hong Kong in its heyday. Again, shortly after

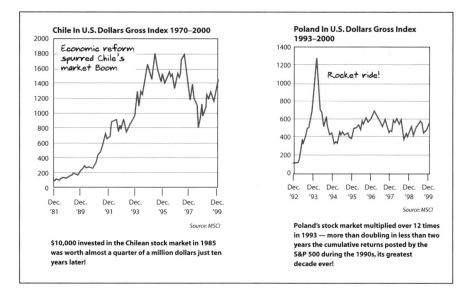

Chile In U.S. Dollars Gross Index 1970–2000

Economic reform spurred Chile's market Boom

Source: MSCI

$10,000 invested in the Chilean stock market in 1985 was worth almost a quarter of a million dollars just ten years later!

Poland In U.S. Dollars Gross Index 1993–2000

Rocket ride!

Source: MSCI

Poland's stock market multiplied over 12 times in 1993 — more than doubling in less than two years the cumulative returns posted by the S&P 500 during the 1990s, its greatest decade ever!

some very important market-oriented economic reforms were implemented, that market shot up over 2,300% in dollar terms between 1986 and 1995!

Poland's Record Two-year Spurt

But, for short-term explosive gains abroad, the prize has to go to Poland. Between 1992 and late 1994, just a few years after the fall of the Berlin Wall and in the wake of important economic reforms, Poland's minuscule stock market shot up over 1,200% in dollar terms!

There's no doubt about it. Investing abroad can pay off big.

Just be aware that — as is always the case — with higher potential rewards, you also usually get higher risks.

Some of the most explosive profits have come from "emerging markets." These are markets that are still catching up to the developed countries in the world in terms of technology, infrastructure (roads, telephones, airports, rails, sewers, etc.), and education. These include countries like Chile and Poland and until recently Hong Kong (it's now already considered a "developed" market).

Emerging Markets in U.S. Dollars
Monthly Gross Index (official) Dec. '87–Dec. '99

Massive volatility!

Dec. '87 Dec. '89 Dec. '91 Dec. '93 Dec. '95 Dec. '97 Dec. '99

Source: MSCI

The early "90s were good for emerging markets — since then, not so good.

In these stages of rapid development, these markets can provide the opportunity for explosive profits. But, as you can also see from the Poland graph, after 1993, the market gave back a good part of its gains, but has zigzagged up and down since then.

Similarly, emerging markets performed very well in the early 90s, as you can see on the chart. In the late '90s, however, most of them fell hard. Yet, as of June 2003, emerging markets came back to claim the top ten spots as the best performing markets in the world for the first six months of the year. That includes a more than 200% gain for Argentina (in US dollar terms) in the first six months of the year!

Emerging markets, then, are highly "volatile," with

returns fluctuating widely.

Even a developed market like Japan (which by 1990 hadn't only "developed," but had become the second largest economy in the world!) went into a market tailspin of more than 50% during the 1990s. And it seems to be only beginning to emerge from that slump now.

Overall, however, studies show that including diversified foreign investments in a U.S. portfolio tends to *increase* returns while *reducing* risk.

Boosting Returns While Limiting Risk

Markets of different countries and regions tend to perform in different cycles — meaning when one goes down, the other may remain flat or even go up. But as a long-term international investor, over the long term, you get the aggregate profits of both. And you end by picking up the greater long-term returns of some "riskier" investments.

Jeremy Siegel puts it this way:

"Diversification will increase investors' expected compound returns while reducing risk *even if* expected returns on foreign equities do not exceed those for U.S. stocks. In fact, a substantial portion of a dollar investors' portfolio should be placed in foreign stocks even if foreign returns are not expected to exceed those in the United States, since diversification of risk increases expected compound returns."

According to Siegel, in fact, it is "reasonable" to invest as much as one-third of your portfolio in international stocks. That figure seems reasonable to us, as well. However, if you have just one-quarter or even a fifth of your children's portfolio in international funds, you'll still get plenty of additional international diversification with the prospect for higher overall returns.

So what kind of international mutual funds?

Massive Value Abroad

Today, in 2003, the Asia Pacific region should be very interesting for any value-minded investor. After an economic crisis hit the region in the late '90s, stock markets in the area are today selling at values similar to those in the U.S. in 1933, the low-point after the crash of 1929!

These countries have developed their infrastructure significantly over the past several decades. What's more, they have a strong work ethic and, for the most

---

Globalization Has Reached
The Mutual Fund Market

U.S. "domestic" mutual funds are supposed to invest in U.S. companies. According to Vanguard Chairman John Bogle, however, about 7% of the holdings of large U.S. domestic funds are foreign shares. At the same time, about one in four mutual funds in the U.S. invest primarily in foreign companies.

Among the mutual funds that concentrate on overseas companies, there are two types. "International" mutual funds invest strictly in companies outside of the U.S., while "global" funds invest in a combination of U.S. and overseas companies.

There are over 1,200 global and international mutual funds in the U.S. today.

---

part, highly educated populations. Most of these economies, then, from Hong Kong to Thailand, Singapore, and China have laid the groundwork to continue to grow and develop rapidly; and their leading public companies should offer the prospects of very high returns for long-term investors.

A good fund to target this area is the **Strong Asia Pacific Fund (SASPX).** This no-load fund has outpaced the MSCI Pacific ex-Japan benchmark since the fund's inception in 1991. It sports a reasonable expense ratio of 1.70%, requires a minimum investment of just $250 for custodial accounts, and invests in some of the fastest growing industries in Japan, China, and SE Asia, including financial services and technology.

The SSgA International Growth Opportunities Fund (SINGX), meanwhile, is a no-load fund that targets fast-growing industries in regions from Europe to Asia and Latin America. The major industries it invests in are financial, services, and technology. The fund has a 1.10% expense ratio (very reasonable for a managed international fund) and a minimum investment of just $250 for custodial accounts.

Mixing High-Return Investment Strategies for Maximum Wealth Creation with Diversification

We have looked at five investment strategies that have historically provided high compound annual returns over the long term:

Investing in S&P 500 index funds to capture the returns of America's largest and most established companies

Investing in small cap funds to profit from the growth of some of the companies that may develop into tomorrow's industry leaders

Investing in growth funds to profit from companies with rapidly expanding sales and earnings

Investing in value funds to capture the gains of good companies selling at bargain prices

Investing in international funds to benefit from the growth of economies, industries and leading companies overseas — all the while introducing an added measure of diversification into your children's portfolio.

Incorporate all five into your children's portfolio and you can construct a low-cost, highly diversified portfolio with a high probability for high risk-adjusted returns.

For the sake of illustration, let's look at what an equally weighted portfolio in these strategies would do using historical returns.

A Fantastic Five Mutual Fund Portfolio

For small caps, we'll use 16.2%, the compounded average annual returns realized by U.S. small caps during the 32-year period (1962 and 1994) covered by the Wharton study.

For the growth portion of our portfolio, we'll use 16.99%, the compounded average annual return for MSCI USA Growth Index from its inception at the beginning of 1975 until the beginning of 2000.

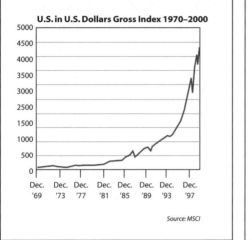

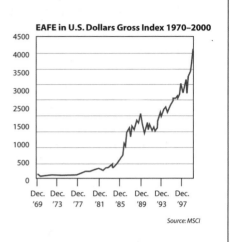

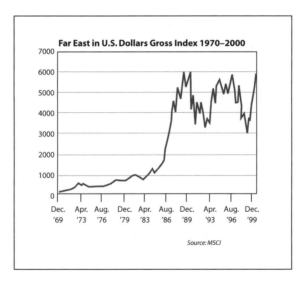

EAFE stands for Europe, Australasia and the Far East, representing largely developed European and Asian markets. This index largely performed in sync with the U.S. from the beginning of 1970 to the beginning of 2000. During that same time, The Far East Index has posted about 14.2% compounded annual returns, out-performing the U.S. by about 1% annually. And that's even taking into account the Asian Crisis and Japan's bear market of the '90s. Compounding the one percentage point advantage would have given you nearly an extra $125,000 on an initial $10,000 investment. That is, $10,000 invested in the S&P 500 in 1970 would have turned into $412,470 by 2000. The same amount invested in the MSCI Far East markets would have turned into $537,011. It pays to diversify internationally.

Fund Category:	Growth	Value	Intl. cap	Small	Large cap	Total Return
Historical Gross Return	16.99%	16.98%	14.61%	16.21%	13.20%	15.60%
Example Fund	Invesco Dynamics (FIDYX)	SsgA Special Fund (SSSMX)	Strong Asia Pacific Fund	i-Shares Russell 2000 Index Fund (IWM)	i-Shares S&P 500 Index Fund (IVV)	
Expense Ratio*	1.03%	1.10%	1.70%	0.20%	0.09%	
Return Net of Expenses	15.96%	15.88%	12.91%	16.01%	13.11%	14.77%

* All funds are no-load, except for i-Shares, which can be bought for a commission as low as $7, just as you would buy a stock through an online discount brokerage.

For value, we'll plug in 16.98%, the return of the MSCI USA Value Index from its launch in 1975 until 2000.

For the international portion of our portfolio, we'll target markets like Asia, which are selling at bargain valuations by historical standards, and so offer higher long-term growth potential. Consequently, for our international portion, we'll use 14.61%, the compounded average annual return for the MSCI Far East index between 1970 and 2000. (It outperformed the U.S. during that period — even after the lost decade of the '90s in Japan and the crash of the Asian Tigers in 1997!)

Using high-return funds with low costs, our net returns might look something like the chart above.

Past results are no guarantee of future performance, but these are strategies that have consistently proven to produce high returns over long periods of time. The point is, it gives you an idea of how your children can invest with low costs and, beginning with little capital, with a good probability for high long-term returns.

Under this scenario, at 14.77%, your child builds a net worth of $429,269 by the age of 30. And it's achieved with a diverse group of high-return styles that are somewhat counter-cyclical to each other for added safety.

Taxing Matters

The only costs that can eat away at a portion of your children's investment returns that we haven't discussed so far are taxes. We've avoided the issue until now because talking taxes can be about as appealing as a trip to the dentist.

Still, even in the area of taxes, your children have great advantages over ordinary investors!

On the one hand, your children will be long-term investors and so won't be incurring capital gains taxes as often as short-term-focused investors. Plus, a good part of the funds they'll target (such as small cap and growth) are the types of funds that typically generate no or very low tax liabilities. And, finally, for about the first 15 years or so of your children's lives, they are in a _no-tax or ultra low-tax income bracket_, meaning they can even reinvest dividends tax-free over long periods — even before they open their first IRA.

In this section, we'll explain these advantages and discuss strategies they can use to continue to invest in a highly tax-efficient manner, even as they grow up and enter higher tax brackets.

Before we get into children's unique tax advantages, however, let's briefly discuss the impact taxes can have on the average adult because taxes can take quite a bite out of your financial life...

The Tax Bite

Taxes are the biggest single cost for millions of Americans. When you combine what you pay in federal and state income taxes, sales taxes, excise taxes, and property taxes, you can easily shell out more than a third of your income each year to governments of one form or another. And that's if you're simply an average earner with household income of about $80,000 or so for a family of four. If you're in a higher tax bracket, meanwhile, you could pay as much as half or more of your income in taxes.

But, of course, you don't pay taxes only on money you earn from your job, you also pay taxes on money you earn from investments. Over the long term, these taxes can take a significant bite out of the amount of money you accumulate through investments.

The One-Two

Investments are taxed in two ways.

First, your realized capital gains are taxed. In fact, even if you invest in an S&P 500-index fund, there will be realized capital gains. That's because the index is rebalanced every year, and that creates long-term capital gains, which are currently taxed at 20% for most taxpayers.

However, for the S&P 500, capital gains taxes are minimal. Between 1998 and 2000, a little less than 10% of the index was rebalanced every year.

In effect, then, perhaps 10% of your capital gains are taxed at 20%, meaning you give up 2% of your capital gains to taxes every year. And if we look at the S&P 500 between 1970 and 2000, we see that capital gains made up three-quarters of total return. So only 1.5% of your total return is eaten up by capital gains on a year basis (75% x 2% = 1.5%).

But now we come to dividends, and that's a bigger tax bite.

Dividends are taxed at your income tax rate. And, again, between 1970 and 2000 about a quarter of the total return of that index came in the form of dividends. That means if you're in the 28% tax bracket, 28% of a quarter of your returns go to the government. Or 7% of your total return is paid out in income taxes incurred by dividends (28% x 25% = 7%).

In total, then, between 1970 and 2000, about 8.5% (7% + 1.5%) of your yearly total return *is not reinvested*. It goes to capital gains and income taxes instead. And that can take a big chunk out of the amount of wealth you ultimately accumulate.

Taxes and the Loss of Compounding Can Cost You More than a Third of Your Accumulated Wealth

Let's see how it works using simple numbers.

If you made a single $10,000 investment in the S&P

500 in a <u>tax-sheltered account</u> at the beginning of 1970, thirty years later you'd have $433,753.

Not bad. You averaged 13.4% compounded annual returns and multiplied your original investment more than 43-fold over the course of 30 years.

But what happens if you're in the 28% tax bracket and you make the same investment at the same time in a <u>non-tax-sheltered account</u>?

Instead of $433,753, you end up with $314,260.

Even though taxes took a yearly bite of about 8.5% of your total gains, the loss of compounding resulted in your ending up with $119,473 less than you would have accumulated if you had invested in a tax-sheltered account.

Still Building Great Wealth

Now, granted, you don't want to give up a quarter or so of your wealth if you can help it. But even after that tax hit, the net result was to reduce yearly compounded annual returns from 13.4% to about 12.2%.

And if your child averages 12.2% after-tax returns, going by our average income assumptions, he will still amass a nest egg of $289,466 by the age of 30!

Over a quarter-million dollars *after-taxes*!

That's still pretty good.

But the fact is, your children can do even better.

First, because they'll be investing in a diversified basket of the kinds of mutual funds that have proven to produce higher returns than the S&P 500.

And also because your children are naturally <u>tax-efficient</u> investors.

Let me show you what I mean...

Natural Tax-Deferred Investing

Your children are naturally "tax-efficient investors" for a number of reasons. In a nutshell, it's because they are just beginning to build wealth, and their annual realized capital gains and dividends should fall under the "floor" for capital gains and income taxes for much of their young lives. Then, from their middle teens through college, they are in very low tax brackets — which means that most, if not all, of the money they use to fund their investments is also income tax free.

These tax advantages can give your children a nice edge in building significant wealth by the time they begin to raise families of their own.

No-Tax and Low-Tax Brackets

For the first 15 years or so of your children's lives, in most cases you can do absolutely nothing and your children can still earn 100% tax-free income and have their investments grow 100% tax-deferred.

On the one hand, they get tax-free income because allowances, gifts, and household chores money falls under the $11,000 annual gift exclusion and is not taxable. Then, even when they do start to earn formal income from a job, they benefit from the fact that a dependent does not have to file or pay taxes with less than $4,700 in formal "earned income" in the IRS sense of the word. And for the first 15 years, in our income assumptions, your child is steadily building wealth without ever coming even close to that figure.

Next, even when your children reach high school age and begin to have formal earned income above $4,700, their income taxes are very small. After the $4,700 standard deduction, for instance, the income tax on $5,200 in formal earned income would be about $50. On $7,800 in earned income, it would be about $465 a year.

What's more, with certain deductions it's quite possible they could pay zero income taxes during those years. For instance, there is currently discussion by both major parties to make all or part of college tuition tax-deductible. Such a move would eliminate your child's small income tax burden during that period and save him about $1,000 over the four years.

Tots Can Grow Their Capital
Tax-Deferred Even without an IRA

As far as capital gains and taxes on dividends are concerned, your children should have none to pay for probably the first 10 to 15 years of this program. That's because federal tax law says that people with no declared income can receive dividends and capital gains up to $750 each year tax-free.

Since we're investing with a bias toward funds that pay little or no dividends and that minimize realized net capital gains, it's reasonable to assume only about 1/5 of our gains in any given year should be in the form of taxable dividends or net realized capital gains. (After all, only 26% of the total returns of the not-particularly-tax-efficient S&P 500 has been in the form of taxable dividends over the last 50 years.)

With our table on page 45 as a guide, then, taxes wouldn't likely be incurred until the age of 16-17, when your child realizes just over $3,500 in gains and perhaps just over $750 in taxable gains.

What's more, between the ages of 17 and 21, the amount of taxable income that he or she makes above the $4,700 standard deduction should be just a few thousand dollars, with that portion being taxed at the absolute lowest rate (10% as of this writing).

And even after the age of 22, when your children begin to earn significant income and their investment nest eggs begin to grow by a significant amount each year, the tax impact on the growth of their wealth can remain minimal. They simply have to take maximum advantage of tax-deferred vehicles while putting non-sheltered capital in growth-oriented, tax-efficient funds.

Finally, concerning tax-deferred funds, they should begin to invest in them the moment they have earned income. In fact, they should begin doing it the moment they have formal jobs with earned income — even if they don't have to pay or file income taxes because they make under $4,701 a year.

By doing this, they can do even more than achieve financial security by the time they begin to raise families of their own.

In the course of just three years, for instance, between 15 and 17, they can even plant the seeds for multimillion-dollar retirement nest eggs — even if they never after that put another dollar in a retirement account!

How to Create a Multimillion Dollar Retirement In Three Years

If your child puts $3,000 a year into a Roth IRA at the ages of 15, 16 and 17, he can build a multimillion-dollar retirement — even if he never invests another dime towards retirement.

Compound those investments tax-free at 13.2%, and by the age of 65, that total of $9,000 invested will be worth over $4.4 million! What's more because he grew that wealth in a Roth IRA, when he begins to withdraw that money, he can do it totally tax-free!

Or he/she could officially retire early at 59 ? with that money worth about $2.2 million at that point. And, if your child switches his/her funds into bonds or dividend-paying stocks or both yielding an average of 6% a year, he could pay himself $132,000 tax-free (or equivalent to over $200,000 in taxable terms, given today's tax rates) — and without eating away at the $2.2 million in principal!

And remember, this is just from the $9,000 invested in a Roth IRA between the ages of 15 and 17. It doesn't count the other investments during your child's lifetime.

The point is simply that by investing early, not only can your child begin to acquire significant wealth in his/her early 30s, a portion of that wealth can be enjoyed during your child's 30s, 40s and onward — and still never worry about consuming the retirement nest egg.

After all, what would be the point of beginning to acquire wealth by the age of 30 if you can't touch _any of it_ until the age of 60 or 65?

The point of *Seeds of Wealth* is to help your children create wealth they and their own families can put to good use while they're still young. They should never have to spend all of their wealth or even most of it. But they can begin to put a portion of it to good use once they're in their 30s or so, even while they continue to grow richer.

The ability to fund a multimillion-dollar retirement in just three years is another illustration of the power of investing early. However, your children can and should take advantage of tax-deferred vehicles for far longer than that.

In fact, from the moment they make formal "earned income" in the IRS sense of the word, they should begin to fund a Roth IRA. It can greatly add to the wealth they build up over the course of their lives while still leaving them with plenty of investment funds they can access in their 30s and onward — long before retirement.

Before we take a look at how that works, let's first clear up the difference between two different kinds of income.

Allowances, Household Chores Money, and Holiday Money Are "Gift Income" and Not Taxable up to $11,000 per Year

When we speak of saving money, we refer to all the

money your children receive from birth until the moment they get their first formal job as "income." For the purposes of taxes, however, this is not taxable income.

Children living at home don't pay any taxes on their allowance, holiday, and chore money, etc. Since it's money you paid taxes on and you're not deducting it, all that falls under the "gift exclusion," which allows you to give up to $11,000 a year to a person without his or her having to pay taxes on that money.

What's more, when your children turn 15 or so and start to work at formal jobs and make "earned income" from an employer, they still don't have to pay federal income taxes on the first $4,700 they make in "earned income." In fact, they don't even have to file an income tax return if they make less than $4,701 in "earned income."

So, if your 15-year-old child makes $4,700 at a job and at the same time picks up an extra $500 or $1,000 in allowance, gift money, etc., he or she still doesn't have to file a tax return because that extra money isn't "earned income" for him. It's money gifted by you or by others. You or your child's uncle, etc. didn't deduct the money you gave your child for birthdays and holidays or as an allowance.

In this way, then, your child could receive money totaling $5,200 as a high school senior or $7,800 as a college senior (as in our assumptions) and pay no income taxes nor have to file!

The Zero Tax Bracket

For instance, if your high school senior receives $4,700 in "earned income," $250 in dividends and capital gains, and $250 in gifts, his or her total money received, is $5,200. And for our savings purposes, living at home, your child will save half that, $2,600.

Yet for tax purposes, his or her earned income is still under the standard deduction so he owes no income taxes on that. As for unearned income (capital gains, etc.), you can make $750 tax-free if you have no earned income. If you have earned income, that threshold is lower; but if it doesn't exceed $250 in this case, he or she still doesn't owe taxes on it. As for the allowances, chores, and gift money... they're just gifts! As such, they fall under the $11,000 annual exclusion for gifts.

The net result is your child doesn't have to pay income taxes or file a return!

How Your Teenage Children Can Use Roth IRAs To Create Greater Wealth

At 15 years old, your child shouldn't even be thinking about retirement. (In fact, if he gets into a career that's right for him, he probably won't even think about retirement when he's 65!)

Still, even though your children are 50 years away from official retirement age, they should immediately begin to fund a Roth IRA the moment they have "earned income" in the IRS sense of the word. The Roth IRA is one of the greatest wealth-building tools available to them.

Here's why...

Roths Offer Two Big Benefits
for Your Teenage Children

The investments held in both traditional and Roth IRAs grow tax-deferred (meaning you pay no taxes on the dividends or capital gains while the capital is still in the IRA). The difference is the tax treatment of dollars going into the IRA and coming out of the IRA.

With a traditional IRA, you deduct the amount you put into the IRA from your current income taxes, currently up to a maximum of $3,000 for an individual. Then when you pull the money out (which you can begin to do once you reach 59 ?), you pay income taxes on it. It's treated as earned income at that point, and you're taxed according to how much you take out and what tax bracket you fall into.

With a Roth, however, you use after-tax dollars in the beginning and pull it out tax-free at the end.

So let's compare the two as they apply to your children.

How to Pick Up an Extra $150,000+ in Profits
From a Single $3,000 Investment

Let's say your child is a 17-year-old high school senior and has $700 in gift income (household chores money and holiday and graduation gifts, etc.) plus $6,300 in earned income from a formal job. For the purposes of saving, he has $7,000 in total income and will save half of that, or $3,500.

For the purposes of taxes, however, he has only

$6,300 in earned income. And not all of that is taxable. After the $4,700 standard deduction, he has taxable income of just $1,600. In the 10% marginal tax bracket, that means he owes $160 in taxes.

If he wants to save that $160, he can put the $3,000 of his savings into a <u>traditional</u> IRA. That single invest-ment compounded at 13.2% tax-deferred will turn into approximately $667,000 once he turns 59$\frac{1}{2}$.

Now, to keep the comparison simple, let's say he decides to withdraw the entire amount at that point. His marginal tax rate will be 35%. And that means that after all deductions *he could well have to pay over $200,000 in taxes* at that time!

On the other hand, if he put that original $3,000 into a Roth account, he would lose the initial $160 in tax sav-ings, *but he would be able to withdraw the entire $667,000 tax-free!*

But let's remember that the Roth he originally gave up $160 in tax savings he would have gotten with a tra-ditional IRA. To be completely fair in the comparison, then, let's weigh that opportunity cost. Let's compound the $160 at 13.2% over 42$\frac{1}{2}$ years. Once we do that, we see your child *still* is much better off with a Roth IRA.

The $160 comes out to an additional $31,088 — far short of the $200,000 or so he would have paid in taxes when withdrawing the money under a traditional IRA.

Once Your Children Begin Working as Teenagers, They'll Be in the Lowest Effective Tax Brackets of Their Lives...

That's Why Roths Are the Way to Go

It can get a little complicated, but let me make this one point clear:

If you have a tax rate now that is lower than the tax rate you're likely to have when you finally withdraw your IRA funds, as a rule of thumb, you're almost certainly better off with a Roth. And since your children are likely to have extremely low — and perhaps even zero — income tax rates when in high school and even in college, the Roth is definitely the way to go during these years.

In the example above, it meant your child netted almost $170,000 more on a single investment. On many such investments over a number of years, it can literally help him build millions of dollars of additional wealth.

But there's another great advantage to the Roth: your child can access some of the money in his IRA account sooner — long before he turns 59.

Money You Can Touch

Under a traditional IRA, you can't touch the money in that account until the age of 59. There are only a few exceptions.

You can withdraw money without penalty in a traditional IRA (though you will pay income tax) to cover medical expenses that exceed 7.5% of income. You can also withdraw funds penalty-free to cover college expenses, and you can take out up to $10,000 without penalty to buy, build, or rebuild a first home for yourself or your child.

Other than that, there are a few other rare limited exemptions. But if it's not for one of these reasons, you'll have to pay at least a 10% penalty plus the income tax if you withdraw your money from a traditional IRA account before $59^{1/2}$.

With a Roth IRA, however, your child can take advantage of all the special exemptions without penalty *and without income taxes* (because he or she used after-tax income in the first place to fund the Roth IRA).

What's more, five years after having made his or her first contribution to a Roth IRA, your child ***can also take out his original investments*** penalty-free and income-tax-free!

He or she can't take out gains, but can take out the money put in so far, and can do it free and clear. That's because the original investments were made with after-tax dollars in the first place.

This can give your child greater compounded growth of his or her investments and greater access to a portion of his or her tax-deferred funds at the same time.

How to Pull $30,000 out of a Roth IRA — Tax- and Penalty-free at the Age of 30

So let's say your child has put $5,000 a year into an

IRA from the age of 15 to 30. (We're using $5,000 because the maximum IRA contribution is scheduled to go up to $5,000 in 2008 and then adjust with inflation every year after that.)

At 30, your child decides to buy a house. He or she can take out $10,000 from the IRA for the first home purchase. *Then, he or she can take out an additional $80,000* ($5,000 x 16 years), which represents the capital put in.

Much of this money went in nearly tax-free or with low after-tax rates since your child was in no-tax or low-tax brackets when many of the original investments were made. It then grew tax-deferred and was withdrawn tax-free!

In addition, if your child continues to fund the IRA and at age 35 wants another $25,000, he or she can take it out free and clear, since it all represents original capital (new money put into the IRA within the previous five years, in this case).

The Roth IRA, then, helps your children build maximum wealth by shifting any income tax liability to their lowest income tax-rate years *and* by letting the investments compound tax-free. And it also gives them the ability to access the capital they put in throughout life, once the initial five-year period has passed.

How Your Child Can Make Three-Quarters of a Million Dollars And Not Pay a Penny in Taxes

As a final example, imagine a child who receives $7,000 a year during the ages of 15, 16, and 17. $1,300 of that each year is in the form of non-taxable gifts (household chore money, etc.) and $4,700 in earned income.

He or she saves $3,500 a year (income for saving purposes is $7,000). Only $4,700 is earned income each year so no taxes are paid on that income because it's within the standard deduction.

We'll assume this is happening this year, in 2002-04, so the maximum permissible IRA contribution is just $3,000 each year.

Each year $500 of your child's savings go into non-sheltered investments and $3,000 goes into a Roth IRA. As we showed earlier, those three years of $3,000 annual Roth investments then grow tax-free, and at retirement your child also withdraws the entire $4.4 million tax-free.

No income taxes at any time…. That's a great deal!

And, remember, your child will be saving more than $3,000 a year. As we showed in this example, he or she can also have some of his or her investments in non-sheltered accounts. So that will be available anytime, with normal tax consequences.

To maximize the returns on the non-sheltered investments, your child simply has to steer them into the kind of funds whose gains mostly come from long-term capital appreciation. Those would include growth funds, small cap funds, and many international funds — many of the kind of investments we said your children should target anyway because they traditionally produce high returns over the long run.

In this way, even though the investments are not in a tax-sheltered account, they're compounding at a rate that is as close to tax-free as possible — while your child's sheltered investments are, indeed, compounding tax-free.

So even though much of the money your children have in tax-deferred accounts won't be accessible until 59 1/2, your children will still have a good deal of money they can access any time in their 30's, 40's and beyond from the non-sheltered accounts. They'll simply pay the long-term capital gains rate when they sell portions of those investments.

And five years after their first Roth contribution, they will also have a significant amount of money they can access from their Roth IRAs without paying any penalty or taxes at all!

How to Open a Custodial Investment Account

If your child is a toddler or pre-teen, he or she may be a few years away from having earned income. And that means eligibility for a Roth IRA. If that's the case, the thing to do for now is to open a custodial investment account for your child.

There are two primary types of investment account for children — UGMAs and UTMAs. A UGMA account allows you to easily give gifts or transfer assets to your children under the Uniform Gift to Minors Act. Most states have also enacted a Universal Transfer to Minors Act (UTMA), which either supplements UGMA or replaces it.

Under the rules of UGMA and UTMA, a custodial account is created by an adult (the "donor") on behalf of a minor (usually, but not necessarily, the donor's child or grandchild). Gifts or transfers into the account are irrevocable, but the account is administered by an adult custodian (in this case, you, the parent) until the minor reaches the *age of majority*.

The age of majority is when control of the assets in the account must pass from the custodian to the (former) minor and ranges by state law from the ages of 18 to 21.

Though these accounts are designed to receive assets transferred by a donor to the minor, there is no reason why you can't put the child's own money from allowances, chores money, holiday gifts, etc. into the account. These are all "gifts" in any case. But, besides that, you can also put non-gift income earned by the child into the account.

Many wealthy adults use UGMA and UTMA accounts to reduce their estate tax liability by gifting up to $10,000 a year to various children and grandchildren. In that way they take money they presumably would have bequeathed to these same children out of their own estate, and it is not subject to tax at their passing.

Yet, for the purposes of your children as investors of their own money, a UGMA or UTMA account gives your child no special tax advantages. But, then again, they don't really need them, since they already have so many natural tax advantages for reasons explained in the previous section.

Easy to Do

To open an UGMA or UTMA investment account doesn't require a lawyer, and is a very simple process.

If you are investing directly with a mutual fund company, simply request a custodial account application. You'll fill out primarily identification details (name, social security numbers) for yourself and your child for whom the account is being opened.

Many fund companies, in fact, do not even have a separate form for UGMAs and UTMAs. On the same application that you would use to open an investment account for yourself, you simply check off "custodial" where it asks you to indicate type of account.

Not all mutual fund companies offer custodial accounts, but the great majority do. All the fund companies mentioned in this guidebook do. What's more, for some mutual fund companies, the investment minimum for a custodial account is often the same as the investment minimum for IRAs, which is usually a far lower minimum than for regular accounts.

If you want to set up a custodial account with a brokerage, the process is very much the same. With an UTMA account on Ameritrade, for instance, you can buy exchange-traded index shares, though you'll have to pay $11 commission per trade. Scottrade's commissions, however, are just $7 for any customer, including custodial accounts.

Still, once your children have savings in the thousands, you may want to set up an account with a brokerage like E-Trade. They have an enormous "fund supermarket," where you can choose among thousands of funds, including hundreds for which you won't have to pay a commission or transaction fee of any kind.

Don't Pay a Load on a No-Load

But don't use Scottrade or Ameritrade to buy no-load funds that are not part of their no-fee offers. You can end up paying as much as $29 to buy a fund that would cost you zero commission to buy directly from the mutual fund company.

Since your children are starting out with limited capital, then, it's advisable to just open custodial accounts directly with the mutual fund companies themselves. Over a number of years, you may end up with four or five accounts for each child. But as your children will be long-term investors, keeping records should not be more complicated than looking at the accounts as they come in and then filing them.

What's more, a number of these mutual fund companies have various, good no-load funds of different kinds that you can choose from with relatively low investment minimums ($250 to $500) for custodial accounts. In this way, then, your child could end up owning five or six funds in just two or three accounts. (More on low-investment minimum mutual funds and fund families toward the end of this section.)

Once your child reaches high school age or so and gets to the point of earning and saving a few thousand dollars a year, that may be the point where it makes the most sense to have a low-cost online brokerage account as well. At that point, you can take advantage of centralized purchases of certain no-load/no-transaction-fee funds and low-commission/low-expense-ratio exchange-traded funds. Still, at the same time, you will probably also maintain certain accounts directly with mutual fund companies.

There is no charge to open a custodial account with an online brokerage firm or directly with a mutual fund company — as long you meet the initial investment minimum. Some fund companies, however, will charge a yearly fee of $10 or so if you do not maintain a certain balance.

But most mutual fund companies that have $250 or $500 minimums are targeting the small, and even beginning, investor. And they do not charge a yearly maintenance fee, regardless of the balance. Look at the fine print on the application form or call the 800 number and put the question directly to a representative of the company.

A final note: once your children make their first investments, make sure they see the account statements once a month or so. They'll receive positive reinforcement as they see their wealth growing after socking away just a few dollars here and there. And even when the account dips in value (which will certainly happen), over the long run they should learn a valuable lesson that staying with a good investment pays off in the long run.

How to Research Mutual Funds for Your Children

All the funds mentioned in this guidebook have been carefully chosen. They are all no-load, low-expense ratio funds that have kept close to, equaled, or sur-passed their benchmark indexes. The exception to this is in the area of loads, since the exchange traded funds (ETFs) do entail a commission.

Nonetheless, ETFs can be bought for commission as low as $7, their minimums are generally lower than even the lowest investment minimum of a mutual fund (since you can buy a single share of an ETF). And their expense ratios are usually very low.

Most importantly, all the funds mentioned in this guidebook target the aggressive investment strategies we spoke of that can help your children make the most of their tremendous advantages as young investors — most notably, their ultra-long-term investment horizons.

However, it may be months before you buy your first mutual fund for your children. And you will consistent-ly buy new funds over time as their savings accumulate. With this in mind, then, you'll want to be able to look for small cap, growth, value, international, large cap, or other types of mutual funds on your own.

In this section, we'll tell you how you can do that quickly and efficiently.

Use Online Mutual Fund Screening Services

There are basically five steps you can use to narrow down your list of mutual funds.

First decide on what objective or sector you want to target, whether it's small caps, Asian stocks, technology, etc.

Second, limit your search to no-load or deferred-load funds whose sales charges decrease to zero after five years or so (since there is evidence that load funds tend to under-perform no-load funds after costs).

Third, once you've narrowed it down to this group, your next screening criterion should be a low expense ratio because — all other things being roughly equal — the expense ratio is going to make a big difference in the return you get over the long term.

Fourth, look at performance. Don't focus on 4-star or 5-star funds. According to John Bogle of Vanguard, studies show that most mutual funds that get very high ratings in a given year go on to *underperform* the market in subsequent years. Instead, it's much better to look for funds that are investing in areas you want to invest in, that have no loads and low expense ratios, and that have kept close to their benchmark as far back as their history goes. "Close" means they can have equaled or exceeded or even underper-formed their benchmark by a percentage point or two over the fund's history. Remember, per-formance is cyclical. And while a particular fund may now fall a little short of the long-term per-formance of its benchmark, if it's true to its objective and has a low-expense ratio, it has a better chance of outperforming its benchmark from here on out than a fund that gives away much of its returns to expenses.

Fifth, among the group you've narrowed it

down to so far, look for funds with custodial account investment minimums that you can meet with your children's funds. If there are none, consider an exchange-traded index fund.

You can buy a single share of an ETF, currently for as low as $45 to $100 (depending on the fund, though share prices will vary). Try not to invest, however, until your child has $250 or so accumulated in savings — in order to keep commissions reasonable as a percentage of the investment.

This way you can choose among low-minimum funds like those offered by the Strong Group and Monetta, as well as among ETFs (while reducing the percentage cost of the commission when buying an ETF).

Recommended Screening Services

There are dozens of free mutual fund screening services on the Internet. Perhaps the most well known is Morningstar, a 17-year-old mutual fund rating service. Just go to www.morningstar.com and click on "funds."

Besides Morningstar, Yahoo! also has a decent fund-screening site. It's at http://screen.yahoo.com/funds.html. Setting the criteria for the kind of funds you're looking for is very straightforward.

You can also access the mutual fund site at Charles Schwabb without having to have an account at the brokerage firm. Simply go to www.schwabb.com and go the mutual funds section.

But the best free mutual fund screening service I've come across is E-Trade's. At this site, you can set more criteria than with any other site.

E-Trade Has an Excellent Fund-Screening Site

At E-Trade's Mutual Fund Center, you can search by fund category (growth, small cap, international, etc.), by fund family (Strong, Vanguard, Janus, etc.), by expense ratio, investment minimum, by load or no-load, by management strategy (index, tax-efficient, emerging markets, etc.), and more.

This is a great tool. You can quickly hone in on the kind of funds that meet your need and then get a quick synopsis of each — from performance, to portfolio holdings, to management philosophy and more.

Then, when you've narrowed it down to two or three, you can download the prospectuses for each — and dig a little deeper into the methods and strategies of the fund, if you so choose.

What's more, E-Trade offers hundreds of funds in their fund supermarket that have no-load and no transaction fee. This is important because if a no-load fund doesn't have an agreement with a brokerage, you'll pay a commission to buy that fund from that brokerage.

If that's the case with a no-load fund you want — it happens even with E-Trade — just look up the fund company on the web and download an application and open an account directly with the fund. Or call them and have them send you a prospectus and UGMA/UTMA custodial account application. Alternatively, look up the fund in the short list of no-load, low-expense-ratio, low-minimum investment fund families on page 296.

You can use E-Trade's excellent fund-screening service

without having an E-Trade account. Simply go to https://us.etrade.com/e/t/home, then click on the "Mutual Funds & ETFs" tab.

The Fourth Box

We've talked about the "two-box system," a primary tool for helping your children steadily create wealth over time. Those two boxes are the "temporary savings" (or spending) box and the "permanent savings" box, from which they generate investment capital.

We also discussed an optional third box your children may use from time to time. This is the "special purchase fund" box and it is to be funded _strictly out of temporary savings_ (never permanent savings). And its purpose is to help your children save up for larger-cost items they may want to buy — whether it be a skateboard, bicycle or video game.

Now we introduce an optional fourth box. It is a box for charity.

"Give and You Shall Receive"

By encouraging your children to regularly put aside a small portion of their income for charity from an early age, you can accomplish two very worthy goals. One, you can help your children help others in need. Two, you can help your children help themselves.

As we discussed at the beginning of this guidebook, the benefits of getting your children to save and invest a significant portion of their income from a very early age include more than just wealth.

Continued on pg. 299…

Selected No-Load Funds with Low Investment Minimums and Low-Expense Ratios

AGGRESSIVE GROWTH	Expense Ratio	UGMA/ UTMA minimum	Topsectors/ Industries
AIM Dynamics (FIDYX)	1.19%	$250	tech, services, health
Strong Discovery (STDIX)	1.40%	$250	tech, services, energy
Trans America, Premier Focus (TPAGX)	1.36%	$250	tech, financial, retail
Monetta (MONTX)	1.43%	$250	tech, services, ind. cyclicals
Janus Olympus (JAOLX)	1.03%	$500	tech, services, health
Federated Kaufman Fund (KAUFX)	1.95%	$500	tech, services, financial, health

VALUE	Expense Ratio	UGMA/ UTMA minimum	Top sectors/ Industries
Trans America Premier Core Equity (TPVIX)	1.20%	$250	Services, tech, health
SSgA Special (SSSMX)	1.10%	$250	Services, financial, tech
Janus Contrarian Fund (JSVAX)	0.98%	$500	Services, ind. cyclicals, energy
Excelsior Value & Restructuring (UMBIX)	0.99%	$500	Tech, financial, services

Selected No-Load Funds with Low Investment Minimums and Low Expense-Ratios (Continued)

SMALL CAP	Expense Ratio	UGMA/ UTMA minimum	Top sectors/ Industries	
Monetta Select Technology (MSCEX)	3.23%	$250	Tech, services, industrial cyclicals	
Strong Small Cap Value (SSMVX)	1.40%	$250	Energy, industrial cyclicals, services	
SSgA Small Cap (SVSCX)	1.04%	$250	tech, services, financial, ind. cyclicals	
INTERNATIONAL	**Expense Ratio**	**UGMA/ UTMA minimum**	**Top sectors/ Industries**	**Countries/ Regions**
SSgA International Growth Opportunity (SINGX)	1.10%	$250	Financial, services, tech, health	Eur.,Asia, Latin America
Strong Asia Pacific Japan,(SASPX)	1.70%	$250	Financial services, tech, ind. cyclicals	Japan, China, SE Asia
TECHNOLOGY	**Expense Ratio**	**UGMA/UTMA minimum**	**Top sectors/ Industries**	
AIM Dynamics (FIDYX)	1.19%	$250	Computers, communications, video, electric, oceanography, office and factory animation, robotics	

SELECT EXCHANGE-TRADED INDEX FUNDS
Select i-Shares

i-Shares Trust S&P 500 Index (IVV)	0.09%	America's 500 largest cos., equaling 77% of total U.S. market cap
i-Shares S&P 500/Barra Growth Index Fund (IVW)	0.18%	Highest price/book (P/B) of S&P 500 making up half the index cap
i-Shares S&P 500/Barra Value Index Fund (IVE)	0.18%	50% lowest price/book (P/B) of S&P 500, making up half the index cap
i-Shares S&P Midcap 400 Index Fund (IJH)	0.20%	Includes cos. from $1 to $5 billion market cap; total cap of index = 6% of U.S. market
i-Shares S&P Midcap 400/Barra Growth Index Fund (IJT)	0.25%	Highest price/book (P/B) of S&P Midcap 400, making up half the index cap
i-Shares S&P Midcap 400/Barra Value Index Fund (IJS)	0.25%	Lowest price/book (P/B) of S&P 500, making up half the index cap
i-Shares S&P Small Cap 600 (IJR)	0.20%	General small cap fund, with index market cap equal to 2.5% of overall U.S. market
i-Shares Russell 2000 Index Fund (IWM)	0.20%	General small cap fund, with index market cap equal to 6.5% of overall U.S. market
i-Shares Europe 350 Index Fund (IEV)	0.60%	350 leading European cos. in 12 major Western European markets
i-Shares Dow Jones U.S. Total Market Index Fund (IYY)	0.20%	Approximating total U.S. market; equals 95% of total U.S. market cap
i-Shares Dow Jones U.S. Consumer Cyclical Index Fund (IYL)	0.60%	Over a dozen industries that tend to do well during expanding economies, including airlines, auto mfrs., toy mfrs., advertising cos., and others

---

SELECT EXCHANGE-TRADED INDEX FUNDS (continued)
Select i-Shares

i-Shares Dow Jones U.S. Consumer Non-Cyclical Index Fund (IYK)	0.60%	Ten "defensive" industries that tend to maintain value better than other industries during downturns in the economic cycle. These include food, distillers and brewers, tobacco and agriculture, and others.
i-Shares Dow Jones U.S. Energy Sector Index Fund (IYE)	0.60%	99.8% oil and gas companies
i-Shares Dow Jones U.S. Financial Sector Index Fund (IYF)	0.60%	42% specialty finance cos. (like brokers and insurers) and 35% banks
i-Shares Dow Jones U.S. Healthcare Index Fund (IYH)	0.60%	78% pharmaceuticals and biotech
i-Shares Dow Jones U.S. Technology Index Fund (IYW)	0.60%	70% computer hardware and equipment, 30% software
i-Shares Dow Jones U.S. Telecomm Index Fund (IYZ)	0.60%	86% fixed line communications companies
i-Shares Dow Jones U.S. Utilities Index Fund (IDU)	0.60%	92% electric utilities
i-Shares Dow Jones U.S. Real Estate Index Fund (IYR)	0.60%	Hotels, resorts, and real estate investment trusts (REITs)

SELECT EXCHANGE-TRADED INDEX FUNDS (continued)
Select Spiders

Standard & Poor's Depository Receipts (SPY)	0.1967%	S&P 500 Index Fund, represents 77% of total U.S. stock market
Diamonds Trust Series I (DIA) (also known as "Diamonds)	0.18%	Index Fund tracking the 30 stocks making up the Dow Jones Industrial Average
NASDAQ 100 Index Tracking Stock (QQQ)	0.18%	NASDAQ's 100 largest companies, 76% technology
The Consumer Services Select Sector SPDR Fund (XLV)	0.56%	Entertainment and publishing, prepared foods, medical services, lodging, and gaming
The Consumer Staples Select Sector SPDR Fund (XLP)	0.57%	Cosmetic and personal care, pharmaceuticals, soft drinks, tobacco' and food products
The Cyclical/Transportation Select Sector SPDR Fund (XLY)	0.56%	Building materials, retailers, appliances, housewares, air transportation, automotive mfg., shipping and trucking
The Energy Select Sector SPDR Fund (XLE)	0.56%	Crude oil and natural gas, drilling and exploration, other energy-related services
The Financial Select Sector SPDR Fund (XLF)	0.57%	Financial services firms from investment management to commercial and business banking
The Industrial Select Sector SPDR Fund (XLI)	0.56%	Industrial products, incl. Electrical equipment, construction equipment, waste mgt. services, and industrial machinery products
The Technology Select Sector SPDR Fund (XLK)	0.58%	Defense, telecom equipment, microcomputer components, integrated computer circuits, and process monitoring systems
The Utilities Select Sector SPDR Fund (XLU)	0.56%	The Utilities Select Sector Index includes communication services, electrical power providers, and natural gas distributors.

| **Affordable Fund Families** | |
| (Contact Information for Fund Families That Offer No-Load, Low-Expense Ratio Funds with Low Investment Minimums) | |

Wells Fargo Investments PO Box 2936 Milwaukee, WI 53201 www.estrong.com 1-800-359-3329 1-414-359-1400	$250 UGMA/UTMA min. direct and through certain fund supermarkets
Monetta Funds 1776-A S. Naperville Rd. Wheaton, IL 60187 www.monetta.com 1-800-666-3882 1-630-462-9800	$250 UGMA/UTMA min. direct and through certain fund supermarkets
TransAmerica PO Box 9232 Boston, MA 02205-0232 www.transamerica.com 1-800-892-7587	$250 UGMA/UTMA min. direct and through certain fund supermarkets
Invesco Funds Group, Inc. PO Box 173706 Denver, CO 80217 www.invesco.com 1-800-675-1705 1-303-930-2700	$250 UGMA/UTMA min. direct and through fund supermarkets
SSgA Funds (State Street Global Advisors) PO Box 8317 Boston, MA 02266 www.ssgafunds.com 1-800-647-7327	$250 Custodial IRA min., $500 Education IRA min., $1,000 regular UGMA/UTMA accts.

Affordable Fund Families	
Janus PO Box 173375 Denver, CO 80217 www.janus.com 1-800-975-9932 1-303-336-7777	$500 UGMA/UTMA min. direct and through certain fund supermarkets
Excelsior Funds C/o Chase Global Funds Services PO Box 2798 Boston, MA 02208 www.excelsiorfunds.com 1-800-446-1012	$500 UGMA/UTMA min. direct and through certain fund supermarkets.
The Kaufmann Fund, Inc. 140 E. 45th St., 43rd Floor NY, NY 10017 www.kaufmann.com 1-800-261-0555 1-212-922-0123	$500 UGMA/UTMA min. direct and through fund supermarkets
Van Wagoner Funds, Inc. PO Box 1628 Milwaukee, WI 53201-1628 www.vanwagoner.com 1-800-228-2121	$500 UGMA/UTMA min. direct and through fund supermarkets
The Vanguard Group PO Box 1110 Valley Forge, PA 19482-1110 www.vanguard.com 1-888-285-4563 1-610-669-1000	$1,000 UGMA/UTMA min., $500 Education IRA min.
The Vanguard Group Viper Funds www.vanguard.com 1-866-499-8473	Single share minimum below $100, purchase through online brokerage for commission as low as $7

Affordable Fund Families

Salomon Funds C/O PCFPC PO Box 9764 Providence, RI 02940 http://www.citigroupam.com/pub/ pageserv/aboutsbam 1-888-777-0102	$250 UGMA/UTMA minimum direct and through certain fund super-markets. Salomon doesn't have no-loads, but it does have B shares with low expense ratios and deferred loads that decrease to zero after six years
i-Shares C/o SEI Investments Distributions Co. One Freedom Valley Dr. Oaks, PA 19456 www.ishares.com 1-800-474-2737	Single share min. — currently as low as $100-$200, purchase through online brokerage for commission as low as $8
S&P Spider Index Funds C/o ALPS Mutual Fund Services, Inc. 370 17th St., Suite 3100 Denver Co. 80202 www.spdrindex.com 1-800-843-2639	Single share min. — currently as low as $100-$200, purchase through online brokerage for commission as low as $8

How to Buy Exchange Traded Funds (ETFs)

As discussed, exchange-traded index funds (ETFs) are available only through brokers (unless you want to buy 50,000 shares!), so you must pay a brokerage commission to buy and sell them. On Ameritrade currently you'll pay $11, on Scottrade, $7.

Index shares can trade at small premiums and discounts to their net asset value, while a mutual fund will always trade at exactly net asset value (NAV). Yet that difference can be in your favor as much as it can be against you, and, in any case, it's usually far less than a single percentage point difference. Because of arbitrage (where large traders and investors buy and sell similar securities based on price discrepancies), this difference is not likely to diverge any more than that for any sustained period of time.

Contact information: Scottrade is at www.scottrade.com, tel. 1-800-619-7283. E-Trade is at www.etrade.com, tel. 1-800-786-2575. Ameritrade is at www.ameritrade.com, 1-800-669-3900.

Your children will likely gain a first-hand experience of the discipline required to build wealth. They're likely to be more responsible with wealth once they acquire it — and far less likely to squander it, as so many "newly rich and famous" unfortunately do. The act of charity perhaps can also help reinforce these good habits.

What's more, the habit of giving can be a small reminder that we are responsible for more than just the pursuit of our own happiness. And that again may pay off in personal ways for your children, since it would seem that people are often happiest when they have a balanced perspective — when they take care of and invest in themselves, but also look outward and do for others as well.

So How Much?

The act of giving — and the decision of to whom and how much — is, of course, a completely personal one. Yet if you decide to encourage your children to regularly set aside a portion of their income for charity, here are a few examples of how it might work.

"Tithing" is the age-old tradition of giving 10% of your income to charity. For most middle class families today, such an amount would be out of the question. But then again, as we stated early on, our children start off with 100% disposable income.

If you and they decided on a 10% figure, then each dollar in income might be divvied up as follows: 45% permanent savings, 45% temporary savings (or "spending"), and 10% to charity. Any "special purchase fund" would be funded strictly from the 45% in temporary savings.

In this case, going by our average income guidelines at 13.2% compounded annual returns, instead of acquiring a fortune of $335,854 by the age of 30, your children would acquire a fortune of $302,269.

That's still a very significant sum. And they'd have achieved over a quarter-million dollar mark while having contributed roughly $30,000 to causes they believe in — and all by the age of 30!

Alternatively, you and your children may decide that they'll give 5% of their income away — and perhaps they'll contribute a bit to their community in the form of volunteer work as well. In that case, the permanent savings might remain the same, and the income might be allocated as follows: 50% permanent savings, 45% temporary savings, and 5% charity (again with any special purchase funds funded strictly out of temporary savings).

In this case, at 13.2% returns, they achieve the full $335,854 by the age of 30 — while at the same time having contributed their own time to helping others _and_ having given away roughly $15,000 to charities of their choosing.

How to Involve Your Children
In the Investment Process

If you have children under the age of five, you'll take care of investing any and all cash gifts they receive. From the age of five, however, your children will be handling their own savings, with your supervision.

But when is the time to include your children in the investment process?

You can do that from the time they're old enough to read.

When your children are five or six years old, shortly after they give you their first batch of accumulated savings to invest ($250 or so), you can show them the mutual funds you bought for them with that money.

When they're very young, you can do that simply by showing them their account statements. They don't have to read the complicated stuff. All you have to show them is their name and the dollar amount of the worth of their investments.

As Your Children Grow, Let Their Involvement Grow

When your children are 8, 9, or a little older, you should also get physical copies of the prospectuses your children own. Either download them from the brokerage company's or mutual fund company's website and print them out or request a prospectus be sent to you by mail.

When your have the prospectus in hand, you can turn to the section that shows the companies the fund has in its portfolio, and you can point out to your children some of the companies they own — especially companies they might know.

But I would advise against buying a single company that your children know and like just to get their interest piqued. That's not diversified enough.

Instead, why not buy a fund like the S&P 500/Barra Growth Index Fund, which holds Coke and Microsoft and Disney and a bunch of other companies your children know and whose products they use.

Again, show them their account statements, show them the part of the prospectuses that lists company holdings and show them that they own that company. Take the Coke bottle out of the fridge and tell them they own a piece of the company that makes that.

What's more, to bring it home to them all the more, you can call Coke's, Disney's and Microsoft's Investor Relations offices and order a prospectus of each company. Or download the prospectuses from the companies' respective websites.

Then show your children the company prospectuses — not the financial reports if they're tots or pre-teens, but the pictures of the bottling plants, movie studios, company trucks, etc. This way, they can hold in their hands — and visualize — part of what they actually own.

From Short-term Consumers to Long-term Investors

You'll be amazed at how this experience will gradually transform their attitudes toward money as they grow up. They'll understand that successful businesses aren't just things that are run by other people — they themselves will own pieces of hundreds of successful businesses. And they will be steadily and surely building wealth because of it.

Once your children are teenagers, whenever you collect a few hundred dollars of their permanent savings to invest, have them sit down with you and see how you select their mutual funds.

You can include them just at the tail end of this process — once you've decided which mutual fund to buy or add money to. Just show them how you screened for and selected the fund. Then you can even have them click the "place order" button if you're doing it on the Internet, or you can have them put the check in the envelope, seal it, and put it in the mailbox if you're doing it by post.

Once they've done this a few times, they'll likely want to pick a mutual fund themselves...

From Trust Beneficiary to Independent Young Investor

When your teenage children indicate a desire to help make the decisions of where to invest their own money, you can have them sit with you during the screening process and "assist" you. Soon after that, if they want to "lead" the process, let them — as long as they understand that it's a "custodial" account, so you have to approve the particular purchase.

Once they've decided on a fund, have them justify their decision to you.

Have them show you what the fund's performance has been relative to its benchmark, what the expense ratio is, whether it's a load or no-load fund, which companies make up the biggest three or four holdings in the portfolio, and what industries or sectors the fund is primarily investing in.

Then have them tell you why they think it's a good buy at this time, and ask them if there is another fund that can target the same goals they seek, but have lower costs or the same costs but a better track record.

When they can answer these questions to your satisfaction, they're ready to lead the investment process — with your supervision.

By the time they leave home and are living on their own, they will already have had supervised experience in picking their own investments. And they'll be ready to make investment decisions — and continue to grow their wealth — completely on their own.

Where to Put Your Children's New Money

When you begin to invest your children's savings for them, you can start out by setting yourself at least a five-fund goal, $250 each in growth, value, small cap, international, and large cap U.S.

Now as we've pointed out, it's usually a very bad idea to try to "time" the market. You want to invest your children's money in $250 increments or so, as it becomes available. You don't want to hold on to it and wait "for the right moment," since that requires predictive powers humans simply don't have and since the evidence is overwhelmingly clear that you're likely to make less money with a timing approach to the markets.

Nonetheless, even though you're not trying to time the market, you will have to choose which category of fund to buy first, second, third, fourth and fifth. The answer to this question, in a nutshell, is to put the new

money in the fund category that offers the best value —
or is most depressed — at the moment.

So, for instance, in late 2000, that's Asia. Buy Asia
first. Six months later, your child has another $250.
Let's say the S&P 500 is still selling for around twice its
historical P/E average and about a third its historical
yield, so you go for a value fund instead since those
stocks, by definition are selling at *relatively* reasonable
multiples.

A year later you have another $250, and by now you
find tech has finally corrected and is now selling for a
third of its former high. You put $250 in a tech fund as
part of your growth objective. Nine months later you
have another $250, and by now the S&P 500 has correct-
ed, so you put your $250 there. A year after that, the
entire market seems to be beginning a new bull cycle,
and you put your next $250 in small caps.

Obviously this example is ultra-simplified. But the
point is that you first target your five funds. Then, as the
money becomes available, you buy them one by one in
the order that offers the best value at the moment.

A good way to determine the how cheap certain
funds are by investment objective is to go to BARRA's
website at www.barra.com. BARRA is the partner with
Standard and Poor's in creating various growth and
value indexes.

At this website you can see a summary of the valuation ratios of their different indexes. In this way you can
compare the price-to-sales, price-to-earnings, price-to-
book, and price-to-cash flow for nine different invest-

ment objectives. These include the S&P 500, the S&P Midcap 400, and the S&P Small Cap 600 — plus the S&P/BARRA growth and value versions of each of those indices.

At the same time you can see the return on equity posted by each of these indices, the median market cap, the yield, and five-year growth rate.

To see these comparisons, go to www.barra.com, then click on "research and indices," then click on "fundamentals."

To get an idea of the value of the relative international market values, go to Standard and Poor's Global website. The address is www.spglobal.com. Then click on "current stats," then "emerging market stats." You'll be able to see how countries and regions are selling — in dollar terms — versus their 1984 and 1988 values.

Focus on the regions, since you want diversification among different countries in your international fund. These regional indices include Latin America, Asia, Europe, Eastern Europe and the Middle East, and Africa.

Keep in mind that in both cases — for U.S. funds and international —you'll be looking at the valuations of these particular industries. If you're buying a managed fund in small caps, for instance, the actual P/S and P/E valuations, etc. will differ.

But this gives you a good starting point, and you can get a more precise idea of the actual valuations for the specific funds you're thinking of investing in with each fund's prospectus.

Adding to the Five Funds

Once you've built up a five-fund portfolio in this way, you can add to each fund as new savings become available from your children. Again, for exchange-traded funds (ETFs), you'll have to pay commission each time you buy a new share of the funds.

That's why it's best to stick with open-end no-load and deferred load funds (with sales charges decreasing to zero) whenever possible, since you can add money to these funds without charge.

For open-end, no-load mutual funds, in fact, while each particular fund may have an investment minimum of $250 to $500 or so, most of these funds allow you to add to existing holdings in these funds — at no charge — in increments of as little as $50 to $100.

When to Sell

As we have stated repeatedly, your children are going to be long-term investors. That's because you incur the fewest taxes and costs as a long-term investor _and_ you tend to get the maximum benefit of compounding when you buy good investments and hold them for the long term.

That's why they should be 100% in equity mutual funds — because their time horizons allow them to go for the higher returns with less risk than that faced by a short-term investor. It's also why your children shouldn't be so quick, as a short-term investor might, to sell an investment that's underperforming.

In fact, for a moment let's talk about selling and diversification strategies for short-term investors. This will help us understand how your children's selling strategies will differ from that of most adult investors.

Risk-control Strategies for Short-term Investors and Investors in the Wealth Preservation Stage

The average market cycle since World War II — from peak to trough to peak — is about 2¹⁄₂ years. So if your time horizon is shorter than this period, you're a short-term investor and should take steps to limit any potential short-term loss of the value of your investments. In fact, to be conservative, you can take steps to limit your potential downside if you're going to need your money within ten years or less.

This would include putting a portion of your portfolio into debt securities with a maturity equal to or less than your time horizon. Also, you can sell your equity investments whenever they hit a predetermined "trailing stop."

A trailing stop is a self-imposed system whereby you commit to selling any security if and when it falls by a certain percentage from its high since you've owned it. So, for instance, if you buy a stock at $100, the moment you buy it your trailing stop is $75. If it falls to $75, you sell — no matter what.

A trailing stop is a safety valve. It's a point where you say, "I must have been wrong on this investment, and I'm not going to hold onto it _hoping_ it will come back."

A trailing stop will rise to "trail" the price of your

investment, but it should never be adjusted downward. The key to using a trailing stop successfully is to stick to the discipline.

So if your $100 stock goes up to $110, your trailing stop is now $77.50 (75% of $110 = $77.50); when the stock goes up to $200, your trailing stop is $150, etc. In this way, a trailing stop helps you lock in gains while limiting potential losses.

In addition if you want to be very protective of your money, you can also use an initial stop loss that is tighter than the trailing stop. So for instance, if you buy this same stock for $100, your initial stop loss might be at $90, instead of $75. As the stock begins to rise in value, however, you use a maximum 25% trailing stop.

So the stock rises to $100; your stop is still $90. Even though that's less than 25%, it represents the initial maximum 10% loss you were willing to incur on the initial investment. Once the stock gets to $120, your trailing stop is still $90, but now that stop is indeed 25% off the high. And now for every dollar your stock goes up, the trailing stop goes with it — so that your trailing stop at $125 is $93.75, then at $150 it's $120, and so on.

In short, the trailing stop can be a very effective strategy for active investors and for investors who are in the wealth preservation phase of their investment careers. That's because it helps you limit the maximum potential loss on any given investment — but can also help you ride your winners for long-term gains.

Exactly what trailing stop you pick depends on your level of risk tolerance. In general, 20% might be used, as the average standard deviation of an S&P 500 stock in the 20th century was 18.5%; a 20% drop would indicate a move outside of the normal movement of the stock and could hint trouble. Or you might use 40%, if you're willing to take a little more risk (volatility). That's a little more than twice the standard deviation of the market and so would cover more than 95% of the normal range of stock fluctuations. You could deem any downward move beyond that as very much a cause for concern.

A Different Risk-control Approach for Long-term Investors Like Your Children

As concerns your children's portfolios, you should sell a fund for one of only two reasons: because the reason you bought it changed or because it has trailed its benchmark by 25% or more for a period of a year. (As we'll explain in a moment, trailing the benchmark is not the same as trailing the high price since you've owned the investment.)

Let's look at the first reason first.

Something drastic happens that completely goes against the reason you bought the fund in the first place. For instance lets say you bought an energy sector fund as a growth U.S. large cap investment. The fund is 95% oil and gas companies, and all of a sudden some company perfects an electric car and the fuel cell, and the price of gas drops by half.

Other than such an extreme situation, however, sell the fund only if it trails its benchmark by 25% or more for more than a year. Now, that does not mean sell the fund if it drops in value by 25% or more in a give year. You are targeting high-return investment strategies for the long run. And in the short run, these can be very volatile. So you can certainly expect that at certain times, these fund classes (small cap, growth, etc.), will go through significant dips.

You want to stick with the strategy through its ups and downs because they have proven, over the long run, to have more dramatic ups than downs and because over the long run they produce high compounded average annual returns.

So if small caps fall out of investors' favor, or if their business environment gets tough for a while, it's likely your particular small cap fund will fall with its group. (Small caps, for instance, tend to suffer more than large caps in a tight credit environment.)

If it's an index fund, it should fall a tiny bit more than the index it tracks (because of fund expenses). If it's a managed fund, it may fall less or more, depending on the particular portfolio of the fund.

But whether in a rising or falling market, your managed fund can't be expected to outperform its benchmark index every year. You have to give it some leeway to underperform sometimes so that it has the opportunity to outperform sometimes.

But significant underperformance over a sustained period of time is a sign you're probably better off switching to another fund in the same group. That warning bell should ring if your fund underperforms its index by 25% over the course of a year.

In this case, you've given your fund ample time to correct whatever poor investment decisions it has made — and simply return close to the performance of its fund class

So if your small cap fund has the Russell 2000 as a benchmark and the Russell 2000 returns 20% over a one-year period, but your fund only returns 14%, sell it and switch to a small cap index fund or a low-cost, no-load, well performing managed small-cap fund.

You can find out how a fund is doing against its benchmark by checking its latest quarterly statement. Or you can use the fund-screener at E-Trade or Morningstar or the chart quote system on Yahoo! or similar service.

APPENDIX

Smart Money Tips
For Young Grownups

The Seeds Take Root

You are to be congratulated again. You're doing a great service for your kids. You're helping them achieve competence — and abundance — in one very important, practical area of their lives.

You now have the tools you need to help your children begin to build wealth and develop responsible money habits that will serve them well their entire lives. Whether your children are newborns or of grammar-school or high-school age, or a combination thereof, you can put them on a path to lifelong financial security starting today.

Manage the savings and investments for your preschoolers. Then have your school-age children follow the *Seeds of Wealth* program from the time they're old enough to count, and by the time they're old enough to *need* money... they'll have more than they need.

See to it your children always take care of their permanent savings first and foremost — and that they save for purchases from temporary savings only. Provide them with enough opportunities to earn a few dollars around the house.

Cash in your children's savings bonds and any other low-yield investments they may have. These don't make the most of some of your children's great assets as young investors — their youth, ultra-long-term investment horizon, and ability to go for the highest-return equity investments. And then invest the proceeds — along with their permanent savings on a regular basis — in strategies that have proven to produce high returns over the long term.

Let your children see their financial statements from the time they're old enough to read. They don't have to read the complicated stuff — just their own names and the dollar figure that shows them how their wealth is growing over time.

As they become young teens, make sure your children understand the difference between good and bad debt, and with a portion of their permanent savings, help them take advantage of Roth IRAs from the moment they have formal "earned income."

Let them see the prospectuses of the mutual funds they own. Look at the top three or four holdings of the fund and get prospectuses of those very companies. Then let your children take a closer look at some of the companies they own through their mutual funds. Let them understand that they are true owners of these companies.

In short, your children's wealth and understanding of money matters will grow simultaneously and naturally over time. They will acquire the kind of knowledge that can only be gained through experience. And they will build their own fortunes themselves.

No one will have given wealth to your children. You'll guide them while they're at home. But they're the ones who will make it happen through their own work, savings, and investment in their own futures.

Leaving the Nest

By the time your children leave for college — and certainly when they begin careers of their own — they will make all their decisions for themselves. That's why it's important to help them develop good habits now so that they have the knowledge and discipline to make the right choices as adults.

In this section we will address the first major financial decisions your children will have to make as young adults. These are the selection and financing of college, the purchase of homes (both their own residences and as investment properties), and the purchase of their own cars.

We've already looked at these issues briefly in the context of good and bad debt. Here we'll show exactly why a college education and home ownership are great investments and how to make them even better investments. And we'll talk about ways your children can finance good cars that meet their budgets and don't eat into their permanent savings.

We'll begin by looking at ways your children get a quality college education for less, since this is a subject for which you may already be planning and investing...

Appendix A:
College-bound

Common sense and the official income statistics show that for most people a college education is a great advantage.

On the one hand, college grads make on average about 75% more than people with only a high school diploma. And as we pointed out on page 78, that can lead to over an extra million dollars in income over a working career. Investing a portion of that extra income, meanwhile, can lead to millions of dollars of extra wealth.

On the other hand, the ability to go to college is a great privilege because it's usually the only time in an adult's life (before retirement, anyhow) when he or she can devote the bulk of his or her time and energy toward learning and acquiring new skills.

Perhaps the most important thing you can do, then, to help your children get the most out of their college education (and even primary and secondary education) is help them understand the value of the opportunity they have

After all, most people like to learn, but few like to sit in a classroom. So if you're child isn't focused, he can end up wasting a great deal of time, money and opportunity. And you could end up spending tens of thousands of dollars primarily to finance a four-year party.

A college education, in short, should be treated like the major investment it is. Help them understand the tremendous long-term benefits it can produce. And encourage them to enter the investment with specific personal or professional goals and assess their own progress every semester to see to it that they're moving toward the realization of their own goals.

Paying the Tab

Once your children are ready for college (meaning they're ready to make the most of it), the next challenge is to pay for this investment.

My first suggestion in this regard would be to consider having your child pay for a good portion of his college education — perhaps a third to two-thirds.

Toward that end you can have him create a special savings fund out of his temporary savings from the time he's a teenager. If we go by our teenage income assumptions and from the age of 13 through 17 your child puts 50% of every dollar he receives into permanent savings, 40% into temporary savings, and 10% into a college fund, he/she will have a good head-start.

Even at a 4.5% money market return, he'll have roughly $1,900 for college by the time he's ready to enter his freshmen year. The rest of his portion he can finance through college loans (as we'll discuss in a moment) and from the income he'll make while in college, no matter how modest.

But don't let him pay his portion with the investment nest egg he's built up so far. That nest egg is only now beginning to reach "critical mass," an idea I'll speak about in a moment. The fact is, he can pay for a good portion of his college and continue to grow his wealth at the same time.

Before I explain how, let me offer the reason your

child could be better off by letting him pay for a good portion of his own tuition and expenses in the first place.

Financing Your Child's College Education

By paying for a good part of his own college, and some of that with college loans, your child will be making his first large-scale *financed* investment — one that should pay off for him his entire life. With so much of his own money at stake, he should also be a bit more motivated to make the most of that money and use the time well.

What's more, he'll also have another major accomplishment to be proud of — another important confidence booster in the best way. He's not developing practical self-confidence simply from pep talks, but because he is achieving major long-term goals from an early age.

First, he'll be developing his own capabilities through a lifelong commitment to learning. Second, he'll consistently continue to build wealth through a long-term commitment to savings and investment. Third, he's furthering his education and his wealth by financing a good part of his own college education.

So how can he afford it? Especially _without_ cashing in his investments so far? With a little planning and work, it shouldn't be very difficult at all.

Take Advantage of the Many
Resources That Are Out There

Let's say, for instance, that you and your spouse are prepared to pay for half your child's tuition and costs.

The portion that he is responsible for, then, can come from a variety of sources.

These include part-time jobs, work-study programs, grants, scholarships, and school loans the child will begin to pay off once he or she has graduated. (There's a whole science to digging up little academic and financial scholarships; a day at the library could pay off in tens of thousands of dollars of savings.)

At the age of 18, 19, 20, or 21 *your child should not touch the wealth he/she has accumulated in the Seeds of Wealth program in order to pay for college.* In most cases, it will be only now that the child will have begun to acquire significant financial assets (between $30,000 and $40,000 most likely), and it's at this point that the investment money reaches "critical mass."

At the Point of Critical Mass, Even Average Market Returns Increase Your Children's Wealth By Tens of Thousands of Dollars Every Year

Let me stray from college financing particulars for a moment to explain why it's not necessary to crack open your child's investment nest egg to cover college tuition and costs — even if it's a relatively costly college.

There are two principal reasons. One, he can finance his portion of college without cracking that egg. Two, his investment assets are only just beginning to reach "critical mass" at this point. Let me explain.

If you get the long-term market average of 13.2% in the financial markets, that means you're doubling your money about once every 5½ years. And that means the really big payoffs begin to come down the road, once you've begun to acquire enough wealth to actually make a difference in your life.

If you start with a single thousand-dollar investment, you double your money every five years. Start with a single thousand dollar investment, and it won't make that big a difference for a while.

At the end of five years, you have $2,000. Then five years later you have $4,000. Five years after that, $8,000, then $16,000, then $32,000.

$32,000 in 30 years from a single $1,000 investment. Not bad, but it's probably not enough to dramatically change your life.

But now look at what happens in the next five years: it doubles to $64,000. You've made as much money in five years, as you made in the previous thirty. Five years later it doubles to $128,000 and you've made as much in five years as you did in the previous 35 years.

Then it doubles to over a quarter million, half million, million and more.

At a certain point, the money has reached "critical mass," meaning its growth in value every few years now has a significant impact on your life.

Exactly where it reaches critical mass for you depends on your lifestyle. In the survey we cited on page 5, over half the respondents said they'd feel wealthy even if they had less than $500,000 in total assets, while only 8% said it takes more than $1 million to qualify as rich.

But whatever your children's critical mass point might be, at a certain point in time the five- or six- or even seven-year doubling of their money makes a huge difference in their financial security and their ability to afford things.

By the time you're doubling from $256,000 to $512,000 and beyond, you're now making more each year in passive income than many people earn working at their full-time jobs.

Get the long-term average annual market return of 13.2% on $256,000, for instance, and you're making $33,792 in passive income. That's about 12% *more* than the $30,305 in average income for high school graduates in 1999.

Get the same returns from a "critical mass" of $512,000 and now you're making over $67,500 a year — about 27% more than the average income of all full-time working college grads.

And that's *without* having to go into an office, punch a clock or do anything but follow your savings and investment program.

Help Your Children Reach the
Million-dollar Mark Seven Years Earlier

With the *Seeds of Wealth* program, your children average less than a dollar a day in savings through the age of 12, then about four dollars a day through the teenage years. At the long-term market rate of return of 13.2%, that turns into $32,141 by the end of his 17th year — just as he's about to begin college.

At a 13.2% rate of return, it takes about 5^1/$_2$ years for your child to double his or her money. But because new capital is being invested as he/she goes along, even at this rate of return money doubles about once every five years. This means at this rate your child will have over $268,000 by the age of 30. And it can double and then double again within ten years of that, making your child a millionaire by the age of 40, simply from investing modest amounts at average market returns *over the long term*.

But this won't happen if he or she takes out the $32,141 to pay for college. Instead, for the purposes of personal wealth accumulation, your child will have to start all over again.

And at 13.2% returns starting all over again at the age of 22 (once graduated from college), even with the relatively high 15% and 10% *Seeds of Wealth* savings rates, it will now take your child until the age of 47 to become a millionaire.

Granted, that's still pretty good. Your child will still be far better off than the average person simply because of the savings and investment habits picked up through *Seeds of Wealth*. But why put off achieving that kind of wealth for seven years if you can help it? Especially, when your child can easily work college loan payments into his/her budget.

It's better to have your child pay for some college tuition and expenses, partly from the previous college fund, partly from a one-day-a week part-time job, and partly from scrounging up some funding through scholarships and aid. Then you pay for some and have your child finance the rest with low-interest-rate school loans.

Once graduated, he or she can begin to pay back, say, an 8% school loan over 10 years, get tax deductions on the interest, and keep the capital in long-term investments in a stock market that's averaged 13.2% from 1950 to 2000.

But the wealth built up with Seeds of Wealth is not to be spent on college.

Finance your child's college education separately and treat it as seriously as you would any extremely important investment decision.

You can help make sure your child is serious about college mostly by communicating about the purpose and relevance of education as he/she is growing up. By letting your child understand the career and monetary advantages and also by having him or her save up for, pay for, and finance a good portion of college education through past, current, and future income.

But I suggest college education should *not* be paid for by your children's accumulated investments and certainly not at the expense of the ongoing savings and investment schedule (10% in the college years).

This will help your child continue to develop good financial habits. At the same time it will help assure your child in a college education and thus has the best chance for education to serve him or her well in the long run.

Still, college does have to be paid for. So let's briefly

look at ways you can plan and prepare so that your child can go to the best school he or she is qualified for and interested in, almost regardless of your level of income...

Eleven Ways to Slash College Costs

#1: Get Advanced Placement credits in high school: Students can knock as much as an entire year off their required course loads. At current rates that saves about $8,500 at the average public school and about *three times* that at a private school! This is especially true for students who belong to a high school baccalaureate program, where the curriculum is designed so that many of the courses are applicable toward college credit at many colleges and universities. Most students, moreover — not only the valedictorians — should be able to eliminate the need for at least two to four courses. For instance, students who speak, read, and write a foreign language well can earn up to six credits at most good schools and eliminate the foreign language requirement. This alone would save at least $1,000 at the average public school and perhaps twice that at a good private school.

#2: Your child can take up to half his credits at low-cost, local public colleges even while getting a degree from a more expensive school: Simply check with the degree-issuing school beforehand on course-specific and university-specific credit transfers they will allow. Instead of paying $60,000 in tuition for a degree from a top private college, you can get the same sheepskin for as little as $35,000 to $40,000 this way — and that's even before financial aid further reduces that number.

#3: Finish school in three years instead of four: This can help you save on room and board. With some schools, you can also save on tuition by cramming more courses into a semester and by taking courses in the off-sessions, which are sometimes cheaper than regular sessions. This move can easily knock $15,000 in tuition and room and board off a $60,000 4-year tab.

#4: Finish college and grad school in five years instead of six: If your child plans on getting undergraduate and graduate degrees in the same school in the same discipline, check with a department counselor early on. He or she may be able to take advanced undergraduate courses that apply toward a master's degree as well as take other steps to complete the two degrees in five years instead of the usual six. Since graduate-level courses are usually more expensive than undergraduate courses, this approach can reduce total undergraduate and graduate education costs by as much as 20%, saving you over $20,000 at many top-level schools.

#5: Take advantage of all merit scholarships and grants, academic, sports or civic: Federal grants, such as the Pell Grant, are generally limited to families with very low incomes. State educational grants, however, often are not tied to family income. Even a partial sports scholarship, meanwhile, can save you thousands of dollars a year in tuition. Academically, a B+ high-school average with 1200 SATs can garner very generous college-specific, merit-based awards at a college in the 75th percentile. Often overlooked is that exceptional community service can also help you achieve additional financial awards. Eagle scouts, for instance, are eligible for free admission to U.S. military academies as

long as the scouts meet minimum academic require-
ments. They can also apply for Eagle Scout scholarships
to other universities of $4,000, $8,000, or $48,000 over a
four-year period. (See www.bsa.com.) The ROTC
(Reserve Officers Training Corps) also offers scholarships
in exchange for service in the corps after graduation.

**#6: Your child can enroll in work-study/co-op study
programs:** There are currently over 300 universities with
large co-op programs.   These include American
University in Washington, DC; Drexel University,
Philadelphia; Georgia Institute of Technology, Atlanta,
Purdue University, West Lafayette, and Northeast
University, Boston. At Northeast U, to take one example, three-quarters of the students participate in these
kinds of programs, earning an average of $9,300 a year.
They also gain valuable work experience in their chosen
fields, and they earn credits at the same time that they
earn money.

**#7: Study at least one year close to home to save on
room and board:** The average annual cost of room and
board at a four-year public college in 2000 is $3,510,
according to The College Board. The average room and
board cost for private universities is $16,332!
Eliminating a room-and-board cost for a year can save
between $3,500 and $16,000 — just for starters. That's
because you will also save an additional thousand dollars or more in round-trip travel expenses at the beginning of the school year, end of the school year, and at
major holidays.

**#8: Take advantage of interest-free installment plans
to pay tuition over 10-12 months:** Keeping your money
in 6% six-month Treasury bills while paying in this fashion can save you as much as $300 a year in instances

where you're paying $10,000 a year in college tuition and costs.

#9: Take advantage of low-rate, tax-advantaged college loans: The federal government Perkins Loans program offers undergraduate students loans of up to $3,000 a year. Another federal educational loan program, Stafford Loans, comes in two varieties. The first is needs-based; it has the government pay your interest for you while you are in school, and you can borrow up to approximately $18,000 over four years. With the second kind you incur interest from the moment each loan installment is disbursed, but any family can qualify regardless of income levels, and you can borrow up to about $35,000 over four years. P.L.U.S. loans are government-sponsored loans to parents of undergraduate students. These loans are based strictly on the family's credit rating, and you can borrow up to the cost of attendance (tuition, room and board, fees, and books) minus financial aid. All these loan programs include interest rates that are very competitive, they usually permit the borrower to pay back the loans over ten years after graduation, and the interest paid on the loans is tax-deductible.

#10: Use Education Tax Credits: Tax credits are better than deductions. Deductions reduce your taxable income directly and reduce your tax bill indirectly. Tax credits reduce the taxes you owe dollar for dollar. A married couple filing jointly with up to $80,000 in adjusted gross income can use the Hope Credit to save up to $1,500 for the first two years of college of each child. With, a Lifetime Learning Credit, they can save up to $1,000 a year. You can't take both credits at once. But you can save up to $6,000 on tuition for your child over four years with these two credits.

#11: If Your Child Is Going to a Private School, Get Him or Her to Share an Off-Campus Apartment and Save Over $29,000: The following table shows the average annual costs for tuition and room and board in 2000 for four-year public and private universities:

TYPE OF SCHOOL	TUITION	ROOM & BOARD	TOTAL
4-year public	$4,960	$3,510	$8,470
4-year private	$6,209	$16,332	$22,541
Source: The College Board			

From the above table, you can see that room and board make up over 72% of combined tuition and room and board costs at private schools. Even in the ritziest college towns, however, you should have no problem finding a 2-room apartment for $1,000 or even less. With a $500 monthly rent bill and another $500 for food and utilities, your child would spend $9,000 over a nine-month school year. That's enough to save him over $7,300 a year, or in excess of $29,000 over the full four-year tab at an average private school.

How to Get a $90,000 Education for $17,750 Even if You Don't Qualify for Financial Aid

As we just saw, the four-year cost at a typical private college can run in excess of $65,000. Yet your child can get the same quality education — or even better — for far less.

For instance, The Student Guide Series America's 100 Best College Buys lists universities around the country that have above-average academic programs and below-average costs. All the colleges profiled in the guide have entering freshmen classes with SAT and high school grade point averages above the national averages, yet tuition and boarding costs below the national averages for private and public schools.

Among the "best buys" listed in the current edition are such well known schools as Rutgers, The University of Florida, Brigham Young, Auburn, James Madison, Baylor, and Texas A&M. The average costs of tuition and room and board for these seven schools, for instance, was less than $9,000 total for in-state students.

You may find a few of these best buys in your own state, and if your children want to attend one that's out of state, they can qualify as in-state residents for the purposes of lower tuition after establishing residency in that state for one year.

What's more, The Student's Guide also identifies which of these schools are particularly highly rated (academically and by *employers*) in specific fields — from engineering to English literature to business. (*U.S. News and World Report* and other national magazines also do similar yearly rankings of cost and quality.) Target one of these "Better Buy" schools in the particular disciplines your children are most interested in, and you can save tens of thousands of dollars.

But that's only for starters...

Also use the cost-slashing techniques we just listed, and you can reduce the cost of your children's education even more — without sacrificing quality. And that's even if you don't qualify for significant financial aid, and even if your child doesn't graduate at the very top of his high school class.

For example, let's look at a "Best College Buy" type school where tuition costs $4,000 a year ($2,000 a semester), and room and board cost $4,500 a year ($2,250 a semester). We'll estimate the cost of books, travel, and related costs at an additional $1,500 a year (or $750 a semester). The total for four years, then, would be $40,000. Let's see how we can knock $22,250 off that cost:

Strategy	Save
Get one semester's worth of Advanced Placement Credits	$ 5,000
Reduce tuition costs by just 10% in scholarships and grants	$ 4,000
Take three semesters' worth of credits at a qualified state or community college (whose credits are transferable to a degree-issuing school) while living at home with parents at tuition cost of $1,500 a semester (vs. cost of $4,250 a semester in tuition, room, and board for a degree-issuing school)	$ 8,250
Hope Education Tax Credits (first two years only)	$ 3,000
Lifetime Learning Credit (You can't take it in the same year as the Hope Credit for the same student. After that, however, you can get up to $1,000 in year from this credit.)	$ 2,000
Total Savings:	$22,250

By taking advantage of various programs and strategies available, you've reduced the total costs by 56%, saving you $22,250. Your total college costs are now $17,750 for the full four years — even while getting a degree that is equivalent to that issued by a typical private school that otherwise might be prohibitively expensive.

So let's take a hypothetical look at how that bill can be handled without undue strain by you and your child.

Paying the College Bill

We've used current dollar figures so far. So let's add inflation into the picture.

Let's assume for the moment that you have a newborn and that we will experience a 4% annual inflation rate (the average from 1950 to 2000) between now and the time your child is ready for college. At that rate, instead of coming up with roughly $17,500 for the four years of college, you and your child will have to come up with about $34,000.

You've agreed to pay half of out-of-pocket costs of your child's tuition. So in this case that means you and your spouse will be responsible for $17,000.

Putting just $500 a year into an Education IRA or tax-deferred college savings plan netting just 9% tax-deferred from the time your child's a baby would more than pay for your $17,000 portion.

If, on the other hand, you haven't started saving and your child is already a teenager, you can still make up for lost time by putting more money into a tax-deferred college savings plan.

Invest $2,600 a year in a tax-deferred plan from the time your child is 13 through 19, and if you get just 9% annual returns, you can still pay for the full $17,000 without having to borrow a dime.

How to Fund a $17,000 Share Of the Education Bill Example 1: Starting Early ($500 a Year Into a College Education Savings Plan)	
Age	End of Year Balances, at 9%
1	$ 545
2	$ 1,139
3	$ 1,787
4	$ 2,492
5	$ 3,262
6	$ 4,100
7	$ 5,014
8	$ 6,011
9	$ 7,096
10	$ 8,280
11	$ 9,570
12	$10,977
13	$12,510
14	$14,180
15	$16,002
16	$17,987
17	$20,151
*End-of-year figures	

How to Fund a $17,000 Share of the Education Bill Example 2: Late Start ($2,600 a Year into a College Education Savings Plan)	
Age	End-of-Year balances at 9%
13	$ 2,834
14	$ 5,923
15	$ 9,290
16	$ 12,960
17	$ 16,961
* End-of-year figures	

If you started earlier, all you'd need is $500 a year in a tax-deferred college education savings plan. But this is to illustrate that even if you start late, with the right planning, you can still pay for a high-quality education without too much strain.

How Your Child Can Handle His Portion of the Education Bill

Continuing with our premise, if your child is an infant today, after inflation he or she will have to come up with $17,000 to cover his half of the education bill when he/she is ready for college.

As we stated earlier, at today's wage rates it's reasonable to assume that your child can earn between $5,400 and $6,300 a year even during the college years. If we inflate earnings over the next 17 years, just as we have inflated costs in our example, your child will be able to make over $9,000 a year during the college years.

But just to put our suppositions to a stress test, we won't inflate his earnings. We'll keep them between $5,400 and $6,300 during the college years — even though we've increased our college costs by almost 100%. To keep things simple, let's assume an average of $5,700 a year (which is, in fact, the average in our income assumptions for the college years).

As we discussed earlier, your child saves 10% of that income, even in college. That means there is $5,130 to contribute towards college expenses ($5700 — $570). Since, in our example, the $17,000 for which your child is responsible already includes room, board, books and supplies, we don't have to make any allowances for that out of his/her income.

Let's, however, suppose an average of $3,130 a year is spent on movies, the occasional beer, and a trip to Fort Lauderdale for Spring Break. That means there is

$2,000 to contribute to college tuition and costs each year from current income. Over four years, that's $8,000 your child contributes out of current income.

If, as we suggested earlier, 10% of his or her income from the age of 13 through 17 has been saved in a money market fund paying just 4%, your child will have already saved $1,900 for college. This leaves him or her with only $7,100 that he has to be borrowed during the college years to make up the difference.

Through Stafford loans, a relatively low-interest-rate loan can be had (semester by semester, as needed). If your family income permits him to qualify for a subsidized Stafford loan, you can avoid incurring any interest buildup in the balance due until *after* graduation. Only at that point, does the clock start ticking on the interest and regular payments are due. (page 327.)

At 8% interest, a $7,100, 10-year loan would result in monthly payments of about $88 a month. After savings from tax deductions, the net cost of the loan is more likely to average about $80 a month. (The IRS allows you to deduct up to $2,000 a year in school loan interest charges.)

That's a reasonable, very manageable amount to pay for an education and degree from a prestigious university. And all the while your child will have done it without having to interrupt the growth of his/her investments.

In fact, given continued long-term market returns of 13.2%, the $32,141 in investments not touched when college began will now have grown considerably. Combined with the 10% savings added while in college, upon graduation your child's nest egg will be $55,973.

At an age when your child is just beginning a working career, investments have already achieved "critical mass." With continued regular contributions, that amount should exceed a quarter of a million dollars by the age of 30, then more than a million dollars by the age of 40... and so on until it reaches into the millions — probably before the first gray hair shows up!

Take Advantage of Education IRAs and College Savings Programs That Offer Stock Market Returns

"Guaranteed Tuition" programs are gaining in popularity all over the country today. But programs whose rate of return is tied to inflation, rather than to the stock market are not necessarily your best option when you have 10 or 15 years before your child is due to enroll.

These inflation-indexed programs usually have you invest a percentage of the cost of a four-year education now; and, by the time your child goes to college, that percentage of his or her education at any state school within the state will be paid for.

But when you look at the stock market over 15-year rolling periods going back to World War II, you'll find an average gross return (10.9% per year) that's far above the average annual inflation rate of 4.3% for 15-year rolling periods over the same time.

What's more, during that time, the stock market beats inflation over 15-year rolling periods 93% of the time. Even over 10 year periods, stocks win 73% of the time.

These facts suggest that if you have 10 to 15 years before your child enters college, you have about a 73% to 93% chance of doing better with a diversified basket of stocks than you would with a prepaid college education program.

If, on the other hand, you use Education IRAs, you can have a good portion of those investments grow tax-deferred, and you can withdraw the funds without paying tax, too.

In addition to Education IRAs, you can also use a new "529" college savings program (based on the IRS section that created tax-deferred college savings programs), many of which allow you to get returns of the overall stock market. And stock market returns (for 10- and 15-year periods, especially) are likely to be considerably higher than the inflation rate.

California's Golden State ScholarShare Trust, for example, gives you various different options for investing these funds. One is an "Age-Based Asset Allocation Option," which shifts more of the portfolio toward bonds and bills, the closer your child gets to college age.

Another is the 100% Equity Option, which invests 100% of holdings in both domestic and international stocks — giving you the opportunity for higher gains (with higher risk).

What's more, the funds can be used to pay for higher education expenses (tuition, room and board, and books, and supplies) at any qualified post-secondary school throughout the U.S. (and even some outside the U.S.), including vocational schools.

Also, a great added benefit of this program (and others like it) is that the funds not only grow tax-deferred on state and federal levels, but also when you withdraw them to pay for the education, the gains are taxed at the beneficiary's rate! And since that is almost certain to be far less than your rate, the tax savings are increased considerably.

Finally, some programs (such as the NY Saves Program) have another benefit in that the funds accumulated are not considered when calculating eligibility for financial aid programs from that state. And most of these programs do not affect your eligibility to claim the Hope or Lifetime Learning tax credit, either.

For more details on these particular programs, go to www.scholarshare.com. and www.nysaves.org. You can also type in "college savings program" in any Internet search engine and find information on many more.

Make sure to read the program descriptions and ask questions, however, as each program is unique.

The Skinny on Education IRAs

By and large, education IRAs are good deals. The major drawback, however, is that you cannot take a Hope or Lifetime Learning Credit in the year you withdraw funds from an Education IRA. However, you not only get tax-deferred growth, but also tax-free withdrawal at the end — plus near-complete flexibility of investment options. Here's a quick look at the pros and cons of Education IRA:

PROS:

You can contribute up to $2,000 per year per child.

Earnings in the account grow tax-free until withdrawn or distributed.

You don't pay taxes on withdrawals for qualified education expenses, including tuition, fees, books, supplies, equipment, and, in some cases, room and board.

You can transfer the assets to another child if the first child chooses not to continue his/her education.

Money in an IRA need not be used before the child reaches age 30, so an Education IRA can help pay for post-graduate education like medical or law school.

You get full flexibility of investments, meaning you're not restricted to choosing among a small group of mutual funds.

CONS:

You cannot claim a Hope or Lifetime Learning Credit in the year you make an Education IRA withdrawal.

No contributions can be made to an Education IRA on behalf of a beneficiary if any amount is contributed during the tax year to a qualified state tuition program on behalf of the same beneficiary.

The limit of $2,000 a year is per child. That means, for instance, that a parent and grandparent cannot each contribute $2,000 per year for a given child.

Money not used for education expenses or transferred to a sibling is subject to a 10% penalty and taxed at the ordinary rate.

In summary, if you invest enough to fund a four-year education with an Education IRA, it could end up costing you $5,000 for that child in potential tax savings via forfeited Hope and Lifetime Learning Credits.

On the other hand, college savings programs grow tax-deferred but they're taxed at the beneficiary's income tax rate when withdrawn. If you withdraw $10,000 in gains from a college savings program over four years, for instance, you might accumulate, say, $1,500 (probably less) in taxes on those gains.

That means for an Education IRA to be a better deal than a college savings program in this case, the IRA would have to outperform the college savings program by about $3,500 to make up for the net cost of losing the Hope and Lifetime Learning Credits.

Couples making up to $104,000 in adjusted gross income can file for the Hope and Lifetime Credits. So unless you expect you'll make too much to qualify for the Hope and Lifetime Learning Credits when your child goes to college, your best bet is probably to find a college savings program that lets you invest in the stock market for higher returns.

This way, though you will pay taxes on withdrawal, it will at least be at a relatively low rate (your child's tax rate). Plus, you should be able to target the same kind of higher returns you can go after with an Education IRA. And you won't lose up to $5,000 in Hope and Lifetime Learning credits.

More Money-saving Strategies for College

Send Your Children to College for Free

Full-time employees at most colleges and universities get to send their children to class at that institution for free. What's more, most of these schools also have arrangements with a handful of "sister schools," whereby your child can have a choice of schools he can attend tuition-free. These highly valuable benefits usually apply not only to the faculty, but also administration, maintenance workers, security workers, and others.

If you or your spouse is thinking of changing jobs, or if one of you is currently not working and thinking of beginning a new job, this could be a great strategy for you. If working in a university atmosphere might appeal to you, and especially if you have a few children coming into the college years soon, this could save you well into the six-figures!

Check with the human resources departments of your local universities and colleges and find out if free education for employees and their dependents is part of their benefits packages.

Get a Prestige Master's Degree while Saving Big Money

Here's another strategy for getting a quality education and opportunity-boosting degrees for less.

According to <u>America's Best 100 College Buys</u>, "A top graduate from a small, inexpensive but high-quality college will have a much better chance of getting accepted into the best graduate schools than will a student who is just average at a big but lower-quality university or an expensive private school. Class rank has much more to do with getting into graduate school than the cost or the so-called prestige value of an expensive college."

This means that if your child can excel at a good lower-cost university at the undergraduate level, he may be able to get a master's degree from one of the best universities in the country. This will allow him to save a considerable amount of money while still getting the prestige of a "marquee" academic degree. And if he gets his undergraduate degree at a quality institution while living with his parents, he can save even more.

A friend of mine, for instance, got her undergraduate fine arts degree from a perfectly good but not widely known Catholic college in New York. Her room and board costs were zero, since she lived at home with her parents during her college years. She went on to excel in her studies and was admitted to Yale University's graduate school.

This enabled her to save toward the cost of graduate school while she was an undergraduate. Then, with a financial aid package consisting of loans and grants, she was able to pay the rest. Today she is the department head for set design at a major university.

The strategy is to use free room and board in college and then to take advantage of low-cost tuition at a good local university or college. (That means living with mom and dad for another few years.) In other words, if your child excels at a good "Best Buy" college, he or she can position him/herself for admission at the graduate level to some of the best universities in the country.

In short, you can save a great deal on the cost of a quality university education. And you don't have to crack the investment nest egg to do it.

For More Information on Getting
A Quality Education for Less...

To begin researching private and public scholarships, read **America's Best College Scholarships** (Annual Series), John Culler & Sons, Camden, SC.

For the best college deals, in general, and by discipline, read **America's 100 Best College Buys** (Annual Series), John Culler & Sons, Camden, SC.

For information on Advanced Placement Programs, scholarships, financial aid, preparing for the SAT and more, check out **The College Board**, 45 Columbus Ave., NY, NY 10023-6992, tel. (212) 713-8000; website: http://www.collegeboard.org/.

For extensive information on full- and partial athletic scholarships, check out **College Athletic Scholarships, A Guide for High School Athletes**, Baca Sports Books, Hurricane, WV.

To determine eligibility for federal educational loans and aid programs, get the **Free Application for Federal Student Aid (FAFSA)**; tel. (800) 433-3243; website: http://www.fafsa.ed.gov/

For wide-ranging general information on subjects ranging from accreditation to educational standards to financial aid, go to the **Department of Education** website at http://www.ed.gov

For the tax benefits and rules of **Education IRAs** and state-sponsored tuition programs, go to www.irs.ustreas.gov, and download IRS Publication 970.

For a free work-study guide, write away for **A College Guide to Co-op Education**, published by the National Commission for Co-op Education, 360 Huntington Ave., Boston, MA 02115.

For information on college savings plans nationwide, go to www.collegesavings.org.

Appendix B:

How Real Estate Can Be a Smart Investment For Young Adults

In a short while from now, you'll begin to invest your children's accumulated savings in mutual funds in their own names. So home ownership will not be their first serious wealth-building experience as the way it is for most people.

But even though your children will be building wealth through long-term investments in mutual funds from a very early age, you'll be doing them a favor if you also let them understand — from their teen years on — that owning your own home is also a very good deal.

What's more, investing in real estate apart from your own home can be an excellent, very profitable investment *outside of the financial markets.* In other words, once your children are young adults and have accumulated substantial capital from their long-term investments in the stock market, real estate can provide them a low-risk way to continue to go for high returns while further diversifying by spreading risk among different asset classes.

In this section we'll look at real estate in two ways. First, we'll look at the financial advantages of owning your own home versus renting, and we'll see how that ownership can provide returns equaling or even surpassing those offered by a bull market. Next, we'll look at how your children can make sizable gains by investing in real estate besides their own homes.

Home Sweet Home

Besides the pride of owning your own little piece of the rock, owning your own home is also a very profitable move when you buy the house at a fair value and live in it long enough.

What's "long enough?" Well, real estate, like stocks, is likely to pay off the most the longer you have it. Real estate, after all, is very much like any other market in that it will also have its ups and downs. But over the medium to long run — 5, 10, 15 years, or more — it can pay off big.

Let's take a look at a couple of real-life examples to see what I mean...

344

**If You Stay Put, Owning Your Own
Home Is Almost Always a Good Deal**

The World War II generation built up their retirement nest eggs largely through home equity. My parents, for instance, bought their first home in 1955. It was a Victorian with four stories including basement and attic. (And with eight kids in the family, we used every floor.)

The house was located on a fifth-of-an-acre corner lot in a suburb 40 minutes from Manhattan. They bought it for $11,000 and 15 years later were forced to sell it to the village under "eminent domain" laws. They got $28,500 for it.

That was equivalent to a 6.5% annual appreciation on the value of the house. But the payoff of the investment was much bigger. Why? Because they put only $2,000 down on the original investment. When they sold the house, then, they paid off the roughly $7,000 in outstanding mortgage, which left them with $21,500.

Let's say they netted $20,000 after costs, since they didn't use a real estate agent. That means their profit was $18,000 — or 900% after fifteen years. Not bad — and they got to live in the investment, too!

What's more, a similarly positive result occurred with their next house.

When Borrowing Money Helps You Make Money — with Relatively Low Risk — That's "Good" Debt

After selling their first house, my parents bought a nicer, slightly bigger home on a quarter acre lot in the same town, across the street from a state park. This house cost about $47,000 in 1970. In 1985, they sold it for $220,000. Fifteen years later, the house sold for $500,000.

While the first house appreciated by about 6.5% annually from

1955 to 1970, this house appreciated by about 10.8% annually from 1970 to 1985, then by about 5.6% a year from 1985 to 2000. But because the purchasers in each case had "leverage" (or borrowed money) working for them, their actual returns were much greater.

How to Leverage Appreciation of 10.8% into 21.3% Returns

The fact that 99% of the people who buy homes in this country do it with a mortgage is a big part of what makes it such a good deal for them. After all, getting just 4%-5% on an investment is not that exciting, but when you can leverage it into 10%-15% annual returns over the long run and live in the house to boot, that's a combination that's very hard to beat.

For instance, let's say that in the second home my parents put down a $10,000 down payment (a little more than 20% of the $47,000 purchase price). Fifteen years later, about 76% of the original loan would still be outstanding.

That meant my father had to pay off about $28,000 when he sold the house. And when he sold for $220,000, let's say he paid another $12,000 in commissions and closing costs. (There were no agents involved.) His total costs on closing, then, were $40,000, netting him $180,000 free and clear.

And what was his original down payment?

Just ten thousand dollars!

While his first investment multiplied 10 times in 15 years, this one multiplied 18 times in 15 years! That's an average annual compounded rate of return of 21.3% — Warren-Buffet-like returns!

You Can Get Warren-Buffet-Like Returns on Your Own Home

Warren Buffet, the greatest stock market investor who ever lived, reportedly has averaged about 23% a year over a 32-year period as an investor. That's a phenomenal return.

Most people realize that he's an old-fashioned "value-investor," buying companies he believes will steadily make money over the long term. But few people realize that this risk-adverse, conservative investor also uses leverage for low-risk investments. A similar principle is at work with real estate investing.

Even with Other Costs Thrown In, Long-term Home Ownership Is a Profitable Proposition

Now, of course, during the 15 years my parents owned the second house they paid property taxes and a great deal in mortgage interest. In fact, combined, these two items cost approximately $52,000 during that time — more than the original cost of the house!

(We're using average property tax ratios, which are 1.1% of the market value of a house, according to the Department of Census. At the same time, we're increasing the market value by 10.8% year, just as occurred, and accordingly reassessing the taxes upward every five years.)

Sounds like a deal killer. But those costs can be mostly ignored.

Why?

Because we as a family lived in the house! In other words $52,000 in mortgage interest and property taxes over a 15-year (180-month) period, works out to about $290 a month. That's pretty reasonable (even back then) for a large house to accommodate ten immediate family members, a dog, some cats, and armies of friends...

Now, technically the equity part of the monthly payments is not a cost because you get it back. In fact, you get it back plus appreciation. And you even get it back with that appreciation *multiplied* by the leverage we talked about earlier.

So while the market value of the house appreciated nearly 11% a year, the value of my parents' original equity investment in that house appreciated at nearly twice that rate. That's because of the "leverage" provided by the mortgage. (That's why we talked of borrowing to buy a home as one of the very few examples of "good debt.")

What's more, the costs of that mortgage, and even of the property taxes, paid for themselves. They simply took the place of what would have been a necessary expense anyhow — rent.

But monthly payments are something you have to come up with every month — so let's add the equity in (even though it's technically not a cost), just to fully show what a great deal owning your own home can be.

Scrutinize All the Costs and Home Ownership Still Pays Off Big over the Long Term

The total monthly payments on that $37,000 mortgage at 8.25% (the average 30-year fixed mortgage in effect in 1985) including average property taxes that go up with the value of the house would have been about $340 a month.

As the saying goes, you've got to live somewhere! And for $340 it would have been nearly impossible to find a place to rent for the same price that was nearly as nice. And at the end of it all, my dad wouldn't have walked away with $180,000 free and clear!

Even if you consider that as a homeowner you will have maintenance expenses that you wouldn't have as a renter, it still almost always works out very much in your favor if you're a long-term owner.

For instance, if my parents averaged $100 a month in repairs during those 15 years, that adds up to $18,000. We can then take into effect by calculating the "opportunity costs" and seeing what $100 a month invested in the stock market would have gotten at that time.

Between 1970 and 1985 the stock market delivered compound annual returns of about 10.3%. But because my parents would have been making steady small investments rather than a lump-sum $18,000 investment at the beginning, near the '72-'74 bear market, they actually would have averaged even better returns.

The result is $100 a month in a tax-deferred investment account would have brought them about $60,000 before taxes. But that's not all.

By renting instead of buying (again, assuming they could find something suitable to rent to accommodate ten people for about $340 in the seventies and early-to-mid-eighties), they also would have been able to save the $10,000 down payment and put that in the stock market instead. They also would have saved closing costs. At 5% of purchase price, that would mean they would have had roughly another $2,500 to put into the stock market....

Combining the down payment and closing costs, a lump-sum investment of $12,500 in 1970 would have grown to about $60,000 in 1985.

To keep things simple, we'll use today's long-term capital gains rates and assume average dividend yield. This means this total of $120,000 they could have accumulated by saving a little money as renters and investing in the market instead would be reduced by about $30,000 by taxes. They would have netted, then, $90,000 as renters investing their house-ownership savings in the stock market.

That's about *half* what they actually netted as home-owners!

If Your Home Appreciates Just 3-4% a Year, You Can Still Get Double-digit Annual Returns on Your Investment

Granted, this last example involved a period that saw skyrocketing home values. But even if you bought that same house (or any other house) in 1985 for $220,000 and it appreciated at the average market rates between 1985 and 2000, you would still end up with a great value.

According to the Department of Housing and Urban Development (HUD), home prices appreciated 4% annually between 1985 and 2000 (and that includes the real estate slump of the late '80s and the S&L crisis of the early '90s). That means a home you bought for $220,000 in 1985, you would now sell for about $390,000 in 2000. That's a $170,000 profit above the original purchase price.

So let's say you put down 20% down on a $220,000 house in 1985. That's a $44,000 down payment. The value of the house has appreciated $170,000, *plus* you've picked up an roughly additional $45,000 in equity while paying down the mortgage over those 15 years.

The result is you walk away with $215,000 total. Let's say you buy and sell without an agent, so we'll figure in $10,000 in closing costs when you bought the house and $20,000 in closing costs when you sell.

The result is roughly the equivalent of walking away with $185,000 in equity from an original investment of just $44,000.

That's a net profit of 320%, or 10% a year — and that's after a relatively *mediocre* 15-year real estate performance period!

And the profits are free of capital gains taxes. And that means to walk away with the same long-term capital gains in the stock market would require a profit before taxes of 422% after 15 years — or 11.6% compounded annually!

Real estate, like any other market, goes through its ups and downs. But if you can get your monthly mortgage, interest, and maintenance costs within 20% of what you'd be spending on rent anyway, and if you're prepared to own your home for the long haul (at least five years, preferably longer), it is almost always an *excellent* deal.

But to make it all work, there are certain guidelines you have to follow.

Buy a Home You Can Afford

The first guideline you have to follow to make sure your home purchase pays off is to stay in the house at least three to five years, preferably longer. You can't have the kind of job where you're transferred every three or four years and expect to have a good chance of making money by buying and selling your own homes. Chances are the closing costs and commissions will eat up any profits.

The second major guideline is you have to buy right. And that means two things.

First, you have to buy at or below the market. (I'll talk about how you can make sure you do this every time in a moment when I touch on real estate as a business investment.)

The second point to "buying right" is simply buying a house you can afford. And there are two criteria to measure that.

Criterion number one is to make sure your monthly payments (including mortgage, and pro-rated property taxes and maintenance bills) are not more than 20% above what you would pay to rent and live a similar lifestyle. Criterion number two is to make sure these same payments do not exceed 35% of your income.

The 20-35 Rule for Home Ownership

Keep your home purchase within the 20-35 margins and live in a home for at least 5 years, and the chances of your making good returns on your home are very good indeed.

To see how it works, consider the lending guidelines of banks. They generally are unwilling to give you a mortgage if your total monthly debt payments (including the mortgage, property taxes, and all personal debt) will exceed 36-41% of your gross income.

Now, since your child will have gone through the *Seeds of Wealth* program, hopefully there will not be any credit card or consumer debt at all. The only debt will likely come from the purchase of a first home, car payments (again, in line with income), and perhaps school loan payments.

Let's take a look at how these ratios might work.

How to Buy Right

Let's say your child is married, and the couple has just had their first child. Together they make $5,000 a month and could rent an apartment to accommodate their small family in a good section of town for $900 a month.

Instead of paying rent, however, the couple decides

to buy a home for $134,400 (the average price for an existing home in 2000, according to HUD).

They put down 20% and take out a $107,000 30-year 8.25% fixed mortgage. Monthly payments of principal and interest come out to $811 a month. According to the government, average property taxes are 1.1% of the value of a home, which in this case would be $1,462 a year, or $122 a month. At the same time, government figures estimate the average monthly maintenance and repair bills for homeowners to be $54. We'll raise that maintenance figure to $67, in order to round our total monthly payments up to $1,000 a month ($803 + $122 + $67=$1,000).

For a home-owning family of three, taxable income should look something like this: subtract $8,250 in exemptions and $7,200 in standard deductions, about $9,000 in mortgage interest... and take a credit of a couple hundred dollars for child care, and your tax bill will be about $5,000 a year — or about $415 a month.

Now, add $300 a month in car payments, $200 in student loans, and $500 in savings (10% of income); and their monthly debt, mortgage, property taxes, home maintenance payments, and share of federal taxes make up only 50% of their total income, leaving them $2,500 after federal taxes to cover utilities, food, state taxes, gas, insurance, etc. (What's more, in a few years, when the student loan is paid off, that percentage will drop to 48%, assuming their income doesn't go up.)

Everything's fine here, except for one problem. They're spending 11% more on mortgage and maintenance than they would have spent as renters. So wouldn't they be better off if they were just renting?

Not a chance. Because, as time goes on, for long-term owners this "excess" disappears and even turns into a savings.

For Long-term Owners, Home Ownership Beats Renting by a Mile

According to the Census Department's American Housing Survey, rent has increased by an average annual rate of about 4.9% over the last 30 years. If the same is true going forward, an apartment worth $900 today 15 years from now would be going for $1,844. And the average rent over that period would be $1,348. Total rent paid would be about $242,000.

For homeowners with a fixed-rate mortgage, however, monthly costs are fixed. They can go down if interest rates go down and you refinance. But with a fixed rate loan, they can't go up.

As homeowners, your total payments over 15 years — including mortgage payments, property taxes, and maintenance of $67 a month — are $175,000. However, approximately $114,000 of this was mortgage interest. And if we assume an average marginal tax rate of 28% over the next 15 years, that means we got about $32,000 of that mortgage interest back as tax deductions.

Our total home ownership cost, then, was $143,000 — about $99,000 less than it would have cost to rent ($242,000 in rent costs over 15 years minus $143,000 in net mortgage, property tax, and maintenance costs for homeowners).

That works out to average savings of $550 a month!

And don't forget: at the same time, we've amortized our loan (or reduced what we owe) by $25,000, while our house has appreciated by about $140,000 (assuming housing prices increase in line with rental price increases.) That's $165,000 in equity gains on top of $99,000 in housing payments we saved (compared to rent) over the last 15 years...

That's a great deal! When you buy your house in the right way, mortgages pay off big. There's no question about it.

Summing Up the Benefits of Home Ownership

A house you buy for your own long-term residence is usually a very good investment for all the reasons I cited and because it offers some diversification against investments in the financial markets.

Just make sure you intend on living in the house at least 5 years (preferably longer) and you buy one in line with your income. As long as your monthly payments are within about 20% of what you would have paid for rent and within 35% of your income, you won't have to worry about sacrificing your ongoing savings to meet your payments. And the investment will likely turn out to be a very good one — even when you weigh the opportunity costs.

And speaking of opportunity costs, they're important, but they're also a bit overdone sometimes. After all, when we measured opportunity costs above, we assumed you would have put all the money you didn't use to buy a house into the stock market if you rented instead of bought. It assumes you would have invested the $10,000 down payment and the $2,500 in closing costs and the $100 in monthly maintenance bills...

But the truth is, a good chunk of that might have gone to nights out on the town, extra vacations and new shoes. You almost certainly would have ended up with less invested — perhaps much less — than in the renter's scenario.

That's why people used to talk about one of the benefits of owning a home being that it creates "forced savings." It still is one of the benefits. But if you buy right, the extra you pay in mortgage payments versus rent shouldn't be much of an *additional* bite out of your monthly income at all.

You'll simply convert the bulk of what you would have paid in rent into mortgage payments, and you'll build equity along the way. And your monthly payments as a homeowner will stay the same.

In fact, given enough time, your monthly payments may even drop 80-90% or more (once you pay off the mortgage and have only property taxes and maintenance to pay). Your rent, meanwhile, would have gone only one way — up.

Teaching Your Children about Home Ownership

Leverage, opportunity costs, property taxes, deductibility of interest, capital gains taxes, and amortization are too complicated for small children. While your kids are tots and young teens, when the subject comes up, just let them know that when they're going to

Continued on pg. 359...

The Power of Leverage in Home Ownership

According to the U.S. Department of Commerce, the average price for existing homes in the U.S. was $23,000 in 1970. By 2000, it had risen to $134,400. And that's even after the real estate slump of the late '80s and the S&L-related real estate of the early '90s. That represents a compound annual average return of 6.1% over that time. When you can get leverage of 5 to 1 (meaning you put down 20% and borrow the rest), annual returns of 6% tax-free can result in some very nice profits over time.

If your mortgage payments (after income-tax breaks on mortgage interest and property taxes) roughly cover what you would have spent on rent, getting 6% on a dollar you paid only 20 cents to control results in a big payoff.

After thirty years, every dollar of down payment is now worth $28.72, for a compounded annual return of 11.8%

And, remember, this compounds tax-free, and you can take the profit tax-free - up to $500,000 for a married couple filing jointly. Depending on your tax bracket, then, these 11.8% compounded annual returns can be the equivalent of pre-tax 13% — plus returns in the stock market.

Take into effect all opportunity costs - closing costs when you bought the house compounded at market returns, commissions and closing costs at face value when you sell… and you've still got a great deal.

In fact, when the real estate market is going well, you can get returns that compete with best raging bull markets. And when the real estate market is simply doing average long-term numbers, you can still make double-digit annual gains overall.

And all the while — don't forget — you get to own and live in the house, but you can't live in a stock certificate!

live in one place for a long time, home ownership is a very good idea. And it's one of the only reasons they should ever take on debt.

Then when they're juniors or seniors in high school, you can begin to explain the detailed advantages of long-term home ownership to them, using the very same examples we just provided.

When your children reach their mid- to late 20s, they'll have the basic knowledge to make good home purchase decisions. And because they'll have continued saving and investing in the stock market all along, they should also have by that time enough capital in stocks so that a move into real estate would be wise diversification at that point.

Buying Real Estate as a Business Investment

Investing in real estate other than your own home can be a great move for all the reasons that buying your own home can be a great deal. The only major difference is that the money you spend on interest, property taxes, and maintenance do not take the place of what you would have paid in rent, since you wouldn't be living in this property — you'd be renting it out.

But, if you buy right, the income you receive in rent should cover your monthly payments and a little bit more. The end result is you get monthly net investment income plus tax-deferred appreciation of the value of the house (leveraged by a factor of two or three because of the mortgage), *plus* increasing equity in the house as you pay down the mortgage.

For these, reasons, once again you can turn a 4-5% increase in the value of an investment property into a 10-15% annual return — even more. Here's a quick example to show how it works...

Real Estate Can Offer Net Rental Income
Plus Tax-Deferred Capital Appreciation

Let's say you buy a two-bedroom home for $100,000. You do your own research and buy direct, so you have no brokerage costs. You put $20,000 down and borrow $80,000 at 8% fixed over 30 years. You pay $5,000 in closing costs, so your total initial investment is $25,000.

You have good credit, and you've put 20% down, so there's no mortgage insurance; and we'll assume property taxes equal 1.1% of the value of the house (in line with the national average). Your total monthly payments, then, including principal, interest, and taxes are $684.

We'll further assume that monthly maintenance costs average $66 a month (or nearly $800 a year), again in line with national averages. Your total cost to own the house, then, is $750.

Rent the two-bedroom home out for just $850 a month and you get $100 in net income every month — or $1,200 a year in income after expenses.

On your initial investment of $25,000, that works out to a "dividend" of just 4.8% a year. Not bad — but let's see where the real profits come into the picture...

Appreciation Again

Let this house appreciate by just 4% a year, and at the end of 10 years, it's worth $148,000. You've also amortized, or paid down, some of the original $80,000 mortgage so there is now only about $70,000 due on the loan. So now you sell the house for $148,000.

You pay the bank the $70,000 you owe them, and even if you incur $10,000 in commissions and closing costs, you walk away with $68,000. Since your original investment was $25,000, you have a cumulative capital gains of 172% in ten years — or a compounded average annual return of about 10.5% a year.

Now add in the 4.8% you made every year from the rent, and your total yearly returns were 15.3%. What's more, capital gains formed the bulk of those returns, so they grew completely tax-deferred. What's more, all or a portion of the yearly taxable income you would make in rent could be offset by taking tax deductions for expenses you incur associated with your maintaining the rental property.

In other words, besides being a low-risk, high-return investment it is also a highly tax-efficient one. But there is another big benefit to buying rental property at the right price and owning rental property for the long term...

Your Rental Income Goes Up While
Your Debt Payments Stay the Same

Let's bring inflation back into the picture and see how this affects your investment. If rental prices go up on average 4% a year, at the end of 10 years you will now be getting approximately $1,250 a month in rent. Because you have a fixed-rate mortgage, however, your monthly principal and interest charges do not rise a single dime. The only portion of your monthly bill that might go up would be the maintenance and property taxes.

In year one, our monthly payments were $750. This was made up of $592 in principal and interest, $92 in property taxes, and $66 in maintenance. If we increase those two by 4% a year, 10 years later maintenance averages about $98 a month, and property taxes average about $135. Yet principal and interest stay at $592.

The result is that instead of monthly total payments of $750, we now spend about $825 a month. Yet your rental has gone up to $1,250.

In other words, instead of keeping almost 12% of the monthly payments you would receive (100/850=11.8%), you now keep over a third (425/1250=34%). And the longer you held this particular property, the more your net income would go up.

For instance, after 30 years your principal and interest payments would be zero. If maintenance and property taxes increased by 4% compounded yearly over that time, they would now cost $510 monthly, combined. Yet if rent went up by the same 4%, you would now receive just over $2,750 in monthly income.

That means you would net $2,240 after expenses every month, or 81% of the rental payment is yours — even while the value of the house continues to appreciate and you now have 100% equity in the property.

Buy Below Market

Real estate, like stocks, will go through ups and downs. Yet also like stocks, real estate tends to produce positive net returns over the long run. And with the low-risk leverage provided by a mortgage, you can turn 4-5% annual appreciation in the value of the investment property you buy into gains of 10-15% or more.

If you try to "time" the real estate market, however, you're likely to do far worse than even if you try to time the stock market. That's because real estate has high transaction costs.

When buying a property, then, look for a combination of growth and value. Signs of growth include rising real estate prices nationally and — on a local level — they include rising employment, increasing rental rates, and decreasing vacancies.

Another positive is if you find increasing test scores at the local public schools. You can get that information by calling the local school board.

Identifying value, meanwhile, is basically a three-step process.

How to Find a Great Real Estate Value

First, select two or three neighborhoods where you would be interested in investing because of the growth characteristics we just discussed. Then go to your local tax collector's office or connect to their database on the Internet and find out what the last dozen homes in each of those neighborhoods has sold for.

You can do this at no cost since it is public information. You can find out the selling price history of each particular home since it was constructed, the square footage, the current yearly property taxes, the number of bedrooms, whether there is a garage, the type of heating, and other details.

With this information, you can come up with an estimate for price persquare foot of structure and per square foot of property in each neighborhood or subdivision you're looking at.

Then stake out the newspapers for homes offered by owner with asking prices at or below the going market rate. It may take a while, but with patience and spending perhaps 10 minutes a day reviewing the real estate section in the local paper, you're bound to find a few properties in this range.

After you've examined a particular property or properties you're interested in, your goal is to purchase at 10% to 15% below the current market price.

Jimmy Rogers, a highly successful and well known stock market investor, has said that his success in investing has been because he waits to find values to the point that it's like seeing a pile of cash in the corner and all he has to do is walk over and pick it up.

You're using the same research-based, value-oriented, and patient approach to real estate investing.

The result is that if the local real estate market turns

flat or even declines for a while after your purchase, you have an added cushion, since you bought at a good price. Plus, it will make it easier to get financing, since your loan against appraised value will be a lower percentage than if you paid the market value or above. And finally, when the market eventually recovers and begins to rise again, when you eventually sell, your profits will be that much greater.

Assuring Positive Cash Flow

At the same time that you're doing your research, you should also speak to a few local mortgage lenders. You'll get an idea of how much of a loan you can qualify for and at what rate. Then, take the yearly property taxes and divide by 12. Then budget 1% of the value of the house for yearly maintenance and divide that by 12.

Add these costs together, and you'll have a very good idea of what your total monthly payments and costs will be.

At the same time, review the rental market. See what one-, two- and three-bedroom homes are renting for in the areas you're thinking of buying. Discount that rate by 5% again to give you added cushion. So, if a 1000 square-foot home with two bedrooms is renting for $900, project income from the same two-bedroom property of $855.

With these pieces of information, you can move to close on a deal only when the rental income will meet or exceed your total monthly payments.

And even if your rental income just covers your payments and costs, over time your rental income should increase more than your costs. That's because the biggest part of your monthly costs — principal and interest — are fixed, while rent can easily average an annual increase of 4% or more per year. (Nationally, as we stated, it has increased 4.9% a year since 1970.)

And again even if your net cash flow is zero, you can still get 10-15% tax-deferred returns on your initial investment (down payment and closing costs) because of leverage. After all, a $100,000 home that increases by 5% in a given year represents a 20% gross gain for you if your initial investment was $25,000.

At the same time, those gains will be enhanced by the fact that you'll be paying down your mortgage and owe less than the initial loan when you sell the property and pay off the remaining balance of the loan.

How Your Children Can Invest in Real Estate as Minors

If you're a real estate investor or would like to buy investment property, your children can invest in real estate with you through a Family Limited Partnership (FLP) that you, the parent, control. An FLP allows you to gift up to $10,000 a year in appreciated property to family members. But you don't have to "gift" your child anything to have him invest along with you.

If you're making a $25,000 initial investment on a property and your child has $250 in savings, he can give you the $250, and you can give him 1% of the property. A year later, let's say, if he has another $250 he wants to invest in real estate, you can give him another 1%.

In this case, he would now receive 2% of the net rental income and 2% of the net capital gains when you sell the property. What's more, his share of the gains would be taxed at his lower tax rate.

For more information on FLPs, you should talk to an accountant who specializes in real estate.

Appendix C:

Cars and Kids

As we stated in the section on good and bad debt, the one type of loan that is not an investment and yet represents a reasonable cause for taking on some debt is a car loan. Since cars are a necessary item for most people, a car loan can be a prudent debt as long as the car is "bought right" and the loan is a good deal.

In this section we're going to talk about how your children can buy their first and subsequent cars "right" and how they can see to it they get a good deal on the financing.

To Own or Not to Own

The first thing for a young adult to determine when he's considering buying his first car is whether, in fact, he *really does need a car at this point.* After all, not everybody needs a car.

If your child lives in a city, or if your child is thinking of going to college in a city, he may find a car to be more trouble than it's worth. It's hard to find parking, traffic is horrendous, vandalism and theft are more common than in other areas, and insurance is more expensive. It might make sense just to take mass transit.

I know city dwellers, in fact, who have long since graduated from college who have found it more economical (and fun, since they're constantly driving new and different models) to rent a car on the occasions once or twice a month when they actually need one. They rent the cars with an American Express card, which automatically picks up collision (and the balance of which has to be paid off in entirety each month), and they save the cost of insurance, too — not to mention parking, repairs, and maintenance.

But let's assume your child does need a car. There are now three primary aspects he should consider in order to make the car purchase a financially sound move.

How much of a car can he handle financially? How can he get a good value on a car in his price range? How can he get good financing?

Let's begin by looking at value.

Bigger than a Skateboard

The best thing your child can do to help him buy his first car is to begin a special purchase fund just for the car from about the time he gets his first driver's permit — at the age of 15 or 16 or so. The idea is the same as when we discussed how he might save up for a skateboard when younger.

And, as with the skateboard, the fund for the car is to be strictly financed from temporary savings and *not to encroach at all on permanent savings*.

Going by our income guidelines, then, if your child sets aside 10% of income for an eventual car purchase from the age of 15, by the time he/she is 18, he/she will have just over $1,550 for a down payment. (That's assuming a 4% annual return on the car savings from a money market fund.)

When 18 years old, your child can buy a $4,000 car by financing the rest. At 8% over five years, for instance, the monthly payments on the $2450 needed to be borrowed would be about $80 a month.

Today, by the way, $4,000 is around the average retail market value of a 7 year-old Saturn and a 5year-old Ford Escort. Not luxury, but they both have good reliability ratings, and neither is bad for a kid's first car.

The big expense, of course, will be gas and insurance. If we assume driving 10,000 miles a year and getting 25 mpg, your child's car will use 400 gallons of gas a year. If we assume an average price of $1.50 a gallon, that's $600 a year — or $50 a month — in gas.

Insurance, meanwhile, for someone so young — even just the minimum coverage required — can run $900 a year if he/she has a clean driving record. Throw in an average of $50 a month for maintenance, and his/her total annual car bill will be just over $3,000 a year. ($960 in car payments + $600 in gas + $900 insurance + $600 maintenance = $3,060.)

And that simply means that to afford that, your child will have to earns more than the $5,400 income for an 18year-old that we use in our projections. But that shouldn't be too hard to do. If he/she averages just two 8-hour shifts a week at a job paying $10 an hour or 20 hours a week at a job paying just $8 an hour, that results in annual income of $8,320 a year.

So, your child's college budget might look something like this:

Income	$8,320
Taxes	$ 600
Permanent Savings (10% during the college years)	$ 832
Contributions to college tuition from current income	$3,000
Total Car payments and expenses	$3,060
Surplus	$828

Now, granted, $828 isn't a huge surplus. But the problem isn't the savings. That's only a little more than $800; it's the fact that he/she decided to take on a big expense by purchasing a car.

If he/she works just 4 or 5 more hours a week and averages $200 in weekly income instead of $160, income goes up to $10,400 and the surplus rises to just over $2,300 (after increased taxes and putting $1,040 in permanent savings).

The point is, without discipline it's easy to choose a car *instead of saving*. But that's one of the worse things to occur for a financial future. By committing to permanent savings early on and by using techniques like special purchase funds, your child can learn to buy what is affordable — and work to afford what he or she really wants to buy!

In short, even while your child is in college, there are things that can be done to make a reliable car affordable, without cracking the investment nest egg — and without taking on an unreasonable amount of debt.

But let's look at the car purchasing process in a little more detail and we'll see how your child can buy a more recent, little more expensive car once he/she graduates from college — without great financial strain.

How Much of a Car Do You Need?
How Much of a Car Do You Want?

Let's say your child has just graduated from college and gotten a job that pays the average salary for a college grad in that age group, $2,327 a month. So your child should ask two questions:

First, what's the least expensive car that will suit my needs?

Second, what's the *most* expensive car I can responsibly afford?

The car that is bought can be anywhere in this range. As long as it doesn't exceed what is responsibly affordable, the purchase of the car will never interfere with continuing to steadily build wealth through regular savings and investment.

Now, if he or she just wants transportation, that means may mean being able to get a car he or she is happy with for strictly the cash on hand from temporary savings. If that's the case, great.

If, however, there is need for a car that will require a loan, that's fine too — as long as the car is bought at a good price and as long as the loan payments do not make up too big a portion of income.

How Much Car Is Too Much Car for Your Child's Income

As a guideline, a car loan payment should be no more than 5% of gross income for a single person and no more than and 8% of gross household income for a two-car family.

What's more, these 5 and 8% guidelines should be considered maximums. In other words, if your child suddenly doubles his/her income, that doesn't mean that twice as much should be spent on a car. But this, in fact, is what happens with many newly wealthy people.

When their income goes up, their expenditures go up *dollar for dollar*! And by the time their peak earning days are over, many of them are struggling to get by — when in fact they should be wealthier at that point than ever before.

But let's get back to the car. And as we do that, we'll just speak in the second person from this point on since if your child is old enough to drive soon, he's old enough to read this section. Plus, the tips on getting a good deal on cars here can be put to good use by anyone.

Determining the Kind of Car You Want and Need

You decide that since your job requires you to travel a bit locally, you need something reliable and presentable. But you're not going to overdo the appearance part. After all, you're interested in getting value and building wealth, not trying to act the big shot, so there's no need to try to impress people with your car — especially if you'd have to spend your *future wealth* (i.e., savings) to do it.

So now you ask yourself, what's the maximum amount you can responsibly afford? And that means how much of a down payment can you come up with and how big a monthly car payment can you handle without trouble?

You now do the math and figure you can manage a hundred-dollar-a-month car payment. You calculate a little more, and you see that means you can swing roughly a $5,000 loan at 8% payable over 5 years.

Scrape together a $2,000 down payment, and you're in the market for a car in the $7,000 range...

But how do you get the down payment?

Leave the Nest Egg Alone!

Now, you're in your early twenties, let's say. And at this point in your life, you have $50,000-$60,000 or so in your investment account because you've been following the *Seeds of Wealth* program since you were a kid. But <u>*under no circumstances are you to touch that nest egg!*</u> The wealth you're building up is not to be blown on a hotrod in your 20s.

Let your wealth grow until you're at least 30 completely untouched (preferably a little longer). Why? Well, for one reason, because your investments are only now beginning to reach "critical mass," as we spoke about before. And also because, frankly, when you're single, you generally don't *need* to spend a great deal of money to lead an interesting and fun life.

However, if and when you begin to raise a family at some point, *then* your financial *needs* will go up considerably. And at that point, it's especially helpful to have built up a store of wealth — part of which you can spend, and part of which you can add to with continued new savings and continue to grow into even greater wealth.

So for now, though, keep in mind that the wealth you've built up through investments will not be a source for a down payment for your car.

And that means your down payment will have to come out of the special purchase fund you've put aside for the car over the previous few years, out of current temporary savings, or a combination of the two.

If this seems unreasonable, consider that most college grads have no savings or investments of any kind at that point. So you're way ahead of the ball game compared to most, at the very least.

Of course, you'll be putting 15% of your income into permanent savings at the same time. But this shouldn't be seen as a huge disadvantage, either. After all, you'll find that other people *who are making 15% less than you* manage to scrape together down payments for their cars.

So you can put money aside for a car down payment — even if you *didn't* start a car purchase fund early on, and even while continuing to save 15% of your income strictly for long-term investment purposes.

If you're a little short on your car down payment at graduation time, then, maybe instead of getting your own place right away, you'll stay home with your folks for four months (if they'll let you) while working full time. The money you save on rent and utilities over three months can give you another $1,500 to $2,000 toward the down payment.

If, on the other hand, you are determined to get out on your own immediately, then maybe you'll take on a weekend job for a couple of months just to get the down payment together.

If you've got an urgent need or desire for it, then you've got to take urgent measures — *But never touch your permanent savings!*

With planning, however, you should hardly ever face these kinds of "crunch" times. It's a question of deciding what you want to do with your discretionary income, and using the same discipline you use with your permanent savings to make the large purchases you want out of your temporary savings.

In any case, you've now got the downpayment, so let's shop for the car. Because not all $7,000 cars are created equal.

How to Get a Good Value on a Car

You don't need to be a mechanic to buy a car at a good price. You need to know the market, and you need to know how to get the opinions of mechanics and other car experts on any car you're thinking of buying.

When buying a new car, for instance, nothing beats a little research on the Internet. Just type in "Car Buying Guides," and you should find at least a half-dozen free services that will tell you the dealer costs on every make and model, as well as their costs on all options — from special tires to CD players.

Just keep in mind that manufacturers and dealers know the public has gotten wise to them on this score, and they've begun to pad the "dealer's invoice price." One of the techniques they use, for instance, is to ship to the dealer at a higher invoice cost and then rebate 2 to 5% of the cost of the car back to the dealer once he's sold it.

As a consumer, that provides you with a higher base price to work with while the dealer ends up not actually paying more for the car. These kick-backs go under the name "special dealer incentives," "hold-backs," and other similar terms. Fortunately, a few of the car sites above do a pretty good job tracking these and also post them on their sites.

(One site that I find very impressive — for both new and used cars — is Edmund's. The address for the website is www.edmunds.com. Another good site providing the same basic service is cars.com at www.cars.com.)

Of course, your object isn't to bleed the dealer. He has to make a living. But you want a fair or a little better market price. And knowing, even approximately, the true dealer invoice (net of the price padding) can help make sure you never pay above the average market value for a new car and should actually help you pay 5 to 10% below the average market value in most cases.

Once you know the true costs, you can then figure in competitive mark-ups in the industry, which usually range between 3 to 5 percent. You've now identified the car you want at a price you're willing to pay, and at a price that the competitive guys actually sell their cars at.

Let Someone Else Pay for the Depreciation
(Nearly New Offers Much Better Value than New)

We've touched on buying a new car because if you have no consumer debt, are keeping to your savings program, have the money for a new car, and have your heart set on one, go ahead.

You're taking care of business financially. So if a new car is your pleasure and within your means, you've certainly earned it. Just be aware, however, that the best way to get a great deal on a new car is *not* to buy one at all.

You'll do much better with a "like-new" car that's just a year or two old, or even a few months old. Why? Because the moment you drive a new car off the lot, it depreciates (or loses value) by 15-20%.

You can own a very nice late-model car and save up to 40% by buying one that's 1 or 2 years old. At that point, you're not paying for the initial depreciation, and you can end up with something that still runs great, has very few miles, is still mostly covered by the original factory warranty, and looks brand new.

For instance, in 1999, a 4-door Ford Escort LX had a list price of over $11,100 brand new. But in that same year I was able to buy a 1997 4-door Ford Escort LX in excellent condition that looks and runs like new for just $5,900 — saving me over 45%.

So let's go back to our example above and see how we can pick a like-new car for $7,000 or even less.

How to Get a Good Deal on Used Wheels
(Without Getting an Earful from a Salesman)

If you want to make sure you're getting a fair deal on any major purchase, you have to know the market value of the item you're buying. When it comes to used cars, the best way to do that is to get a copy of the *N.A.D.A.* (National Automobile Dealers Association) *Official Used Car Guide.*

You can get a pocket "consumer edition" of the N.A.D.A. guide at your local bookstore for about $10. In it you'll find price information on over 40 makes and hundreds of models of used domestic and foreign cars going back 10 years. At the same time, you'll find price information on about two dozen makes and hundreds of models of U.S. and foreign sports utility vehicles and pick-ups.

With this little book, you need never overpay for an automobile again. And chances are you'll save hundreds if not thousands of dollars on each and every car you buy.

The book gives values for different conditions, "high retail," "average retail," and "low retail." High retail is basically for cars in flawless condition and with mileage that falls within an "acceptable mileage" range of about 10,000-12,000 per age year. Average retail is for cars in clean condition without glaring defects that also fall within the acceptable mileage range. Low retail is generally the "fixer-upper" category and includes cars that have wear and tear to the extent that you wouldn't be likely to find them on a dealer's lot. Mechanically, however, they should be in safe running condition and be able to pass inspection.

Narrow Your Choices

Now, just because the N.A.D.A. guide covers just about every car that's out there doesn't mean you're going to be considering just about every car that's out there. The very first thing you do, as a matter of fact, before even consulting the N.A.D.A. guide, is to look at your copy of the *Consumer Reports Buying Guide* (also about $10 at your local bookstore).

Consumer Reports comes out with a new one of these guides every year. You'll be able to check out the reliability ratings of hundreds of domestic and foreign cars, usually going back about seven years. Plus, you can use these guides to do your homework before other major purchases as well, from refrigerators to stereos.

Also, it's usually a good idea to consult more than one source. On the web, you can go to www.cartalk.com for all sorts of information on cars — including warnings about recalls — as well as helpful links.

You should also go to the bookstore or auto parts store and pick up one or two automotive magazines. Look for one of the special issues in which they do a comprehensive reliability and performance rating of all the major makes and models of cars out there.

Find three or four models that you like that are well rated in both *Consumer Reports* and your automotive magazine. Find the respective model years that correspond to your $7,000 car budget and start to watch the classifieds (either on the Internet or in the actual "paper" paper).

How to Get a "High Retail" Value
for Average Retail or Less

Let's say, for instance, you want a 2-seater convertible. (*Seeds of Wealth* is about learning to build wealth over time, but it's not about being a stick in the mud. If $7,000 is your car budget and you can pick up a fun car that fits your needs, absolutely do it.)

There aren't a whole lot of 2-seater convertibles to choose from. And the good ones can be pricey. So to fit one within your budget, you're going to have to go back a few years. But you've always liked the Mazda Miata MX-5 since way back when. And you know from Consumer Reports (and probably stuff you've heard, too) that Mazdas have excellent reliability records and, if well cared for, can go 150,000 to 200,000 miles with no problem.

So you look in the N.A.D.A. book and you see a '91 model is valued at $5,600 for "low retail," $6,875 for "average retail," and $8,625 for "high retail." This is right in your range, but you also want to be aware of values just above your price range so you can be on the lookout for special bargains. Along these lines, you note the '92 model has a low retail of $7,200 and medium and high retail values of $8,600 and $10,525, respectively.

Any more recent year is out of your range, but it's possible you could get lucky on a '92, so you'll keep an eye out ...

Now, you've also thought about an Alfa Romeo Spider 4, but you have to go all the way back to 1989 to find a model of that car with a "low retail" value of

$6,200. Furthermore, when you look in the automotive magazine, you see the Alfa Romeo Spider has a below-average reliability record in the U.S. You decide you don't want to risk spending $6,000 on a bucket of trouble, so you rule out the Alfa Romeo Spider. (Maybe you'll get a later model Alfa Romeo five or ten years down the road, when you can afford to allocate a little extra maintenance money into your budget.)

You do a little further research, though, and you find an '89 2-door Toyota Celica convertible has a low retail of $5,150, an average retail of $6,375, and a high retail of $8,075. So you put that on your watch list. And you also find the Geo Metro from 1993 is also rated highly by Consumer Reports and that was the last year they made a 2-door convertible version of that model. Today, the low, mid, and high retail values of that car are $3,000, $4,200 and $5,100, respectively.

I could go on, but you get the idea. The point is to qualify the car you want by type, reliability, and price — then begin to look out for deals in those categories.

Your goal is to buy a "high-retail" quality car for "average retail" or less, or a car that falls between "high" and "average" at or below the "low retail" range. Now, this might sound difficult. But the fact is, because you're so well prepared, you'll be amazed at how *easy* it actually is.

After all, you will be one of the very few truly informed used-car buyers in the market at the moment. Most *sellers* don't even have a very good idea of the market value of their cars. Buyers, even less.

By doing this, you'll see a lot of overpriced cars listed in the papers — cars that you'll never have to waste a minute on. You'll also see a few that are in the market range. And then, suddenly, you'll find one or two absolute deals.

And if you have two or three models you're watching the paper for every day, you should be able to find an excellent value within a week, or two at the most.

How to Buy an $8,300 Car for $5,900

Take, for instance, the '97 Escort I bought in 1999. At that time, we needed a clean, dependable second car. I ended up buying this car with 47,000 miles, immaculate inside and out and in excellent running condition. This car had low, average and high retail values of $7,275, $8,575 and $10,300 at that time.

The miles were high for the year, but the car was in excellent shape mechanically and in terms of the interior and body. What's more, when I called the insurance company to get a quote, they were prepared to insure it up to $8,300.

I paid only $5,900. The car has run beautifully, and I had to do almost no negotiating.

I had my eye on a couple of models including the Escort. I waited till I saw a great deal in the paper. Then I called, asked a few questions on the phone (any problems with engine or body, had it been in an accident?), went to look at the car to make sure it was what they said it was, and then bought it, _after arranging for a one-day guarantee_.

The Non-Mechanic's Safety Net, the One-Day Guarantee

I happened to buy this particular car from a luxury car dealership. Now, this is a great car, and I'm very happy with it. But even though it's an "LX" model, the '97 Escort LX is no luxury car. It's a nice, clean, well running sedan. That's all. But that's what I was looking for, and that's what I got — at a great price.

And the fact that it *isn't* really a luxury car is probably why I got such a great deal on it in the first place. The luxury car dealer probably picked up this car in a trade. And since it didn't really fit in with his inventory, he was just happy to get rid of it at a price that was minimally acceptable to him.

Yet, after checking out the car and taking it for a spin, I arranged with the salesperson to let me take it to my mechanic. Since it was late in the day, we decided to simply put in the contract that I could return the car within 24 hours for any reason whatsoever. That gave me time to bring it to my mechanic the next day. It passed his inspection with flying colors and the deal remained done.

When buying from a private party, you can do the same thing. Rather than put it in a formal "contract," however, just ask if you can leave your car and keys with the seller while you run the car you might buy over to your mechanic. If you schedule it ahead of time, it should take an hour tops. But it could save you a lot of money, time, and frustration by keeping you from buying a car with problems that are hidden from a non-mechanic.

You've Found the Right Car at a Great Price; Now Get the Right Financing

Once you've spotted the car you want, you've got to get the financing to buy it. The best way to do that is the same way you found the car — know the value of the commodity you're looking for (money, in this case)... and shop around.

The biggest mistake on financing is automatically to have the dealer finance you. Cars and cash are two separate things entirely, and it's very rare that the same place is going to have a great deal on both.

It's possible that they may, but to avoid wasting time and to make sure you get a good deal, the best thing to do is not even mention financing when checking out and negotiating for the car itself.

Before you go out to any dealership or see a car sold by a private party, get an idea from your bank, credit union or other likely lender what kind of loan they're willing to make to you against the type of car or cars you're thinking of buying. They should be able to give you a firm quote on the rate — so that you know your worst-case interest rate the moment you begin to check out cars for sale.

Still, don't let the dealer mix financing in with the price of the car. Keep them separate. Negotiate for a price you're willing to pay, given the interest rate you've already secured from the bank or credit union. Then, after you've agreed on the price of the car, if the dealer also makes a better financing offer than you have so far, fine — take him up on it.

But if you mix and match the two, you'll come out the loser. "No-money-down" and "Super-low APR" deals are all based on your paying full sticker price, or very close to it. And that turns out to be not much of a deal at all because, in the case of new cars, you should never pay sticker price. And in the case of used cars, it will likely be a sticker price that is jacked up to accommodate the "low-rate financing."

Beware Hidden Finance Charges

Two final points on the subject of car financing: make sure to take loan initiation fees and other costs into account when comparing loans. And also be aware of the possibility of "dealer markups" on your loan. This is when dealers offer you a certain loan at a certain rate, but then sell that loan to a finance company, and add on 1 or 2 percentage points in financing charges (above what you agreed to) to cover their "processing" the loan. So make sure you get all charges spelled out.

By the same token, if the loan offer is a competitive one and you've made sure there's no funny stuff going on, you don't have to run yourself ragged. There's not much point running all over town, postponing and possibly losing good deals on cars just because you're trying to shave a quarter or half point off the interest rate on a modest car loan. After all, the difference between the payment on a 60-month, $5,000 loan at 7.5% vs. 8% is only $2 a month ($105 versus $103) — or $120 over the course of five years.

Of course, if you can get that $120 in your favor, take it. Just realize that's all it is. That way, you won't spend $120 in gas and time, and lose another couple hundred more in missed opportunity just to save $120.

See the monthly loan payments chart below to figure out and compare the difference in costs two competing loan offers will cost you. Or use an online "auto-loan calculator" like the one you'll find at cartalk.com.

How to Figure Your Monthly Payments on Any Loan

The table below will tell you what your monthly pay-

How to Figure Your Monthly Payments on a Loan					
Interest Rate	5 years	10 years	15 years	20 years	25 years	30 years
4.50%	18.64	10.37	7.65	6.33	5.56	5.07
4.75%	18.76	10.49	7.78	6.47	5.71	5.22
5.00%	18.87	10.61	7.91	6.60	5.85	5.37
5.25%	18.99	10.73	8.04	6.74	6.00	5.53
5.50%	19.10	10.86	8.18	6.88	6.15	5.68
5.75%	19.22	10.98	8.31	7.03	6.30	5.84
6.00%	19.33	11.11	8.44	7.17	6.45	6.00
6.25%	19.45	11.23	8.58	7.31	6.60	6.16
6.50%	19.57	11.36	8.72	7.46	6.76	6.33
6.75%	19.68	11.49	8.85	7.61	6.91	6.49
7.00%	19.80	11.62	8.99	7.76	7.07	6.66
7.25%	19.92	11.75	9.13	7.91	7.23	6.83
7.50%	20.04	11.88	9.28	8.06	7.39	7.00
7.75%	20.16	12.01	9.42	8.21	7.56	7.17
8.00%	20.28	12.14	9.56	8.37	7.72	7.34
8.25%	20.40	12.27	9.71	8.53	7.89	7.52
8.50%	20.52	12.40	9.85	8.68	8.06	7.69
8.75%	20.64	12.54	10.00	8.84	8.23	7.87
9.00%	20.72	12.67	10.15	9.00	8.40	8.05
9.25%	20.88	12.81	10.30	9.16	8.57	8.23
9.50%	21.00	12.94	10.45	9.33	8.74	8.41
9.75%	21.12	13.08	10.60	9.49	8.92	8.60
10.00%	21.25	13.22	10.75	9.66	9.09	8.78
10.25%	21.37	13.35	10.90	9.82	9.26	8.96
10.50%	21.49	13.49	11.05	9.98	9.44	9.15

ments of principal and interest will be for any given loan. You can use this for mortgages, as well as car loans and student loans.

To figure your monthly loan payment, find the number that intersects with your interest rate and the term of the loan. Then multiply that number by the *number of thousands* of your loan amount. This will give you a pretty accurate estimate of your monthly payments of principal and interest (P&I).

For instance, if you take out a $100,000 mortgage for 30 years at 8.5% interest, you'll find your monthly payment of P&I will be $769 (7.69 x 100). If, on the other hand, you take out a $5,000 car loan, payable over 5 years at 7%, your monthly payment will be $99 (19.8 x 5).

Just remember, this includes fees and points only if they are part of the loan amount. Otherwise, those costs are to be considered *in addition* to your monthly costs.

Also, in the case of mortgages, you'll have to add property taxes to the monthly bill. While they're not actually part of the loan, it's common practice to include them in the mortgage bill. According to the U.S. Census Department, annual property taxes average about 1.1% of the value of a home. So, if you're considering buying a home with a market value of $100,000, you can estimate property taxes to be about $1,100 a year or just under $100 a month.

Finally, if you're putting less than 20% down on a house, you may also have to pay mortgage insurance. If you're putting down 20% or more, you should be able to avoid that cost entirely. But if you're putting down less, ask the mortgage company to quote that separately.

Then, once you've accumulated 20% equity in the home, contact the mortgage company to get that insurance removed. The insurance protects the mortgage company, not you, and it's usually not required after you have 20% equity. You can save thousands of dollars in this way.

Divide and Conquer to Get a Better Deal on Cars

Just as you should negotiate financing and car prices separately (usually with separate parties), you should also treat your trade-in separately from the purchase of a new or used car.

If the dealer offers you $1,000 more for your used car than you think it's worth, he's probably offering you his car for $2,000 more than he thinks it's worth. And if he's offering you exactly what you think your car's worth and nothing more, that's still probably based on your paying him significantly more for his car than he would take at an absolute minimum.

Divide and conquer is the rule when buying a car. Do your homework on prices and values of the cars you may be interested in buying. Shop around and get financing rates. Know the value of your own car and its *potential* trade-in value by checking the asking prices in the newspaper and, more importantly, the N.A.D.A. book.

Then, when you see the car you want at the price you want — go and close the deal on the car. Leave the financing and the trade-in out of it.

If you need the trade-in for the down-payment, sell your car first. Cash is king. Because if you walk into a dealership with a trade-in that you'll need for a down-payment, you're telling the dealer you have to "liquidate" something in order to do the deal. And liquidate is another term for "sell at fire-sale prices."

But your goal is to buy at or below the market and even to buy at fire-sale prices when possible. But when it comes to selling, you want to sell at or near the market.

Do your homework and divide and conquer — car, financing, trade-in — and you'll be able to get a good deal on every car you buy.

The Moral of the Car Story

Get your children to use these techniques every time they purchase a car, and it can make a big difference in their financial future because a car is a major expense. And it's an area where a lot of young people begin to get into financial trouble. They buy a car that's too expensive and cuts into their ability to continue saving and investing, or they overpay for a car, or they buy a lemon.

What's more, since a car purchase is really the only non-investment we consider okay to buy on terms, it's important to make sure they're not borrowing money just to throw it away.

By keeping car payments within 5% to 8% of gross income limits, they can always can continue to save and invest along the *Seeds of Wealth* guidelines. Soon enough their net worth and passive income will continue to rise to the point that they'll be able to drive pretty much whatever car they like.

(Hopefully, however, even at the point where they have more than enough money for whatever car they want, they'll still do their homework before buying. After all, good habits are hard to break).

The Lowdown on Leasing: Don't Do It

Car leases seemed a good idea when they first came out in the 1980s. But, most of the time, what a lease really offers is convenience. And all you have to do is walk into a 7-11 store to see how expensive convenience can be.

Just about any car salesman will try to convince you that you're making out better with a lease. But when you add in all the fees and other costs, you'll usually find you'd be much better off owning.

For one thing, lease fees (costs in the beginning and at the end of the lease that are apart from the monthly payments) have a way of building up. For another, leases usually require you return the car in pristine condition.

That may mean buying a brand new set of very specific, expensive tires before you turn it in, as well as have the body touched up to make sure you're not charged dealership rates for fixing "pings."

And then there's the matter of insurance. Insuring a leased vehicle is usually hundreds of dollars more expensive per year than the insurance you'd pay for on the same car if you bought it. The reason is that the leasing company requires comprehensive bumper-to-bumper coverage on all leased cars.

In the course of a 3-year lease, for instance, this can easily add $1,500 or more to the cost of a car — a cost that is usually not taken into consideration when the lease is signed.

Even if you're acquiring a car for business purposes, purchasing will often be the better route to go. Granted lease payments and fees are 100% deductible for businesses, while only the interest on car loans is deductible, but you also get to depreciate cars you buy for business, and eventually you'll get some resale value — *and* you don't have to overpay for insurance and repairs at the end of the car's lease life.

Cars are not to be considered an investment. But they are a major expense and a necessary one for most people. Do full comparisons to thoroughly weigh the pros and cons when considering whether you should buy or lease. When you do, you're likely to see that owners continue to get far better value than renters.